INDEPENDENT FEATURE FILM PRODUCTION

INDEPENDENT FEATURE FILM PRODUCTION:

A Complete Guide from Concept Through Distribution

by

GREGORY GOODELL

St. Martin's Press   New York

Design by Kingsley Parker

Library of Congress Cataloging in Publication Data

Goodell, Gregory.
  Independent feature film production.

    1. Moving-pictures—Production and direction—Hand-books, manuals, etc. I. Title.
PN1995.9.P7G64   791.43'068   82–5746
ISBN 0–312–41307–6   AACR2

First Edition

10 9 8 7 6 5 4 3 2 1

For
Jennifer and Alexandra

TABLE OF CONTENTS

ACKNOWLEDGMENTS

In order to thank all of the people who contributed to this book I would have to list everyone in the film industry with whom I have had the pleasure of working. I have learned from each of them, and a part of each one can be found on these pages. I stand in particular debt to Graham Cottle for his technical assistance and moral support throughout the writing of this book. Others to whom I am indebted for specific contributions include John Brasher, Marc Bucci, João Fernandes, Jackie Frame, Wolfgang Glattes, Tony Masters, Eva Monley, John Muto, Martin Shapiro, Jack Sher, Deidre Simone-Hill, Roger Spottiswoode, Jose Villaverde, and Max Youngstein.

I am especially grateful to my parents, John and Bernadette, and to Mary Goodell, for their careful reading and insightful suggestions during early drafts of the manuscript. I am also indebted to David Kaufmann whose detailed notes and comments greatly expanded the scope and usefulness of this book.

I wish to express my sincere gratitude to Bob Miller at St. Martin's Press for his careful and meticulous handling of the manuscript and for his patient understanding of its author. Finally, my deepest gratitude goes to Jennifer and Alexandra, who watched the book stretch out in time, supported me every step of the way, and managed, somehow, to live through it all.

PREFACE

Alambrista!, Badlands, Benji, Best Boy, Billy Jack, Chariots of Fire, Dawn of the Dead, The Day After Trinity, Eraserhead, The Exterminator, Friday the 13th, Gal Young Un, Girl Friends, Halloween, Harlan County U.S.A., Heartland, Hester Street, The Legend of Boggy Creek, The Life and Times of Rosie the Riveter, Macon County Line, Mean Streets, My Dinner With André, Northern Lights, Polyester, Private Lessons, Return of the Secaucus Seven, Street Music, The Texas Chainsaw Massacre, Vice Squad, Walking Tall.

These films are as different from one another as night and day. Some are theatrical films, others are documentaries. Some are intense, personal statements; others are simply commercial products designed to turn a profit. Some have broken box office records and garnered fortunes for their makers; others have received widespread critical acclaim and have won numerous awards. A few have achieved both. But all of these films share a common bond. They are all independent features.

The term "feature" refers to the principal attraction playing in a movie theater, usually ninety minutes or more in length, as opposed to short subjects, cartoons and previews of coming attractions. When two features are playing on the same bill, the second film is called a second feature.

The term "independent" is not so easily defined. To some people, independent refers only to low-budget commercial pictures such as *Halloween* and *The Legend of Boggy Creek.* To others the term is reserved for filmmakers whose work exhibits a strong, personal, uncompromising statement about a subject to which they are deeply committed. For still others, the term "independent" conjures up images of The Ladd Company, Lorimar Productions, Orion Pictures, Polygram Pictures, and Rastar Films. Their films include such titles as *Annie, Arthur, Blade Runner, Body Heat, Excaliber, The Postman Always Rings Twice,* and *Sharky's Machine.*

In its broadest sense, the term "independent" refers to any feature production that is not made by one of the major studios such as Columbia, Disney, MGM, Paramount, Universal, or

Warner Bros. In that sense, 75 percent of all features produced are independent. However, since many independent production companies, including those mentioned above, rarely, if ever, enter production without a production-distribution tie to a major studio, they are not truly independent. Certainly not in the same sense as the people who make films like *Eraserhead, Gal Young Un, Heartland, Halloween, Northern Lights, Polyester, Private Lessons,* and *Return of the Secaucus Seven.*

In the purest sense, an independent filmmaker is one who has an idea for a film (or obtains the rights to an existing literary property), raises the funds with which to make the film, maintains substantial creative control throughout the making of the film, and ultimately arranges for marketing and distribution. The stories behind the making of every independent feature are as diverse as the films themselves.

After writing several produced screenplays, John Sayles tried unsuccessfully to get a job as a director in Hollywood. In 1980, he decided to make an independent feature as a showpiece for his directorial talent. He wrote and directed a 16mm, 110-minute film titled *Return of the Secaucus Seven.* The film was shot in twenty-five days for $60,000, two-thirds of which Sayles paid for with his screenwriting money and one-third of which he raised as he made the film. *Return of the Secaucus Seven* was voted one of the ten best films of the year by *The Los Angeles Times, Time* magazine, and *The Boston Globe.* It was the hit of the Filmex Festival and won The Los Angeles Film Critics Award for Best Screenplay of the Year and the Writers Guild of America nomination for Best Comedy Written for the Screen. In a review of the film, *Variety* magazine said, *"Return of the Secaucus Seven* should prove to filmmakers that extremely low-budgeted products can be just as entertaining as any multimillion dollar production turned out by the studios." After sixteen weeks, playing in only four theaters, John Sayles' $60,000 film took in close to $500,000. It broke the house record at the Outer Circle theater in Washington, D.C., earning $250,000 during its twenty-four-week continuous run. The total worldwide gross for *Return of the Secaucus Seven* is in excess of $2.5 million, the majority of which came from theatrical release in the United States and Canada. Mr. Sayles now has several writer-director deals with major studios in Hollywood.

John Carpenter directed and co-authored with producer Debra

Hill the now-famous independent feature *Halloween* for a budget of $320,000. Carpenter was twenty-nine-years old, Hill was twenty-eight, and the average age of the crew was twenty-six. The finished film was shown to, and turned down by, major studios for distribution. It was subsequently distributed by Compass International Pictures. In the first week, playing in 193 theaters, *Halloween* grossed $1.27 million. By the end of the sixteenth week it had grossed $9.5 million. The picture gained a tremendous word-of-mouth reputation, and when it was rereleased the following year, the box office literally *tripled* that of the first year. In the United States and Canada alone, *Halloween* grossed more than $67 million. Recent reports indicate a total worldwide gross in excess of $75 million, making it, dollar for dollar, the largest grossing independent film in history.

Producer David Puttnam, a veteran of nearly twenty films, wanted to make a picture that blended the spirit of athletic competition with the sensitivity and moral commitment of *A Man for All Seasons*. He came across an intriguing story that interlaced the lives of two runners in the 1924 Olympics, and hired Colin Welland to write the screenplay. Puttnam spent the next two years trying unsuccessfully to finance his $6 million project. Twentieth-Century Fox finally agreed to put up half the budget in exchange for foreign distribution rights (they, along with most others, felt that the picture would have minimal appeal in the United States and Canada). With the Fox deal in hand, Puttnam struggled for another six months trying to raise the balance of his budget. The money finally came from Dodi Fayed of United Star Shipping of Liberia. "Believe me," said Mr. Puttnam, "you've been fairly well around the track before you get to Egyptian shipping lines." Once the total budget was committed, Puttnam hired first-time feature director Hugh Hudson and cast his leading roles with virtually unknown actors. The film was shot in ten weeks and, upon completion, was picked up for domestic distribution by Warner Bros. through The Ladd Company. *Chariots of Fire* opened in New York at the 700-seat Guild theater and in the first week grossed over $70,000. The box office for the second week was even greater. The figures for the second Saturday rose 12 percent to $17,549 breaking the house box office record for a single day. This was *before* the film won four Academy Awards including Oscars for Best Original Screenplay and Best Picture of the Year. The day following the Academy Awards the grosses for *Chariots of Fire,* playing in 422 theaters, shot up an average of 97.5 percent per screen. *Chariots of Fire,* the film that nobody wanted to finance, became one of the most outstanding independent motion picture success stories in history.

Raphael Silver, a successful real estate man turned executive producer, raised $370,000 for his wife, Joan Micklin Silver, to write and direct her first feature film. She wrote *Hester Street,* an 1890's period piece based on Abraham Cahan's novel *Yekl.* She shot 120,000 feet of 35mm black and white film in thirty-four days. This was edited down to 8,200 feet (92 minutes). *Hester Street* was enthusiastically received at film festivals, especially at the Cannes Film Festival. As a result, the picture was sold to several foreign countries including Germany, Great Britain, France and Belgium. Distribution in the United States and Canada, however, posed a problem. *Hester Street* went the rounds of the major distributors *three* times and was rejected at every turn. The majors saw three elements in the film that minimized its potential for commercial success: black and white photography, a very low budget, and an ethnic orientation. The Silvers, however, believed that their film would become a big hit if it ever got the chance to play and, finally, decided to distribute it on their own. Nearly a year after its completion, *Hester Street* opened to rave reviews, breaking box office records in Philadelphia, Boston, St. Louis, and Beverly Hills. The film earned back its cost in the first five weeks of distribution and in some cities, including New York and Boston, played continuously for over four months. During its run the $370,000 film grossed over $4 million and received numerous awards including an Academy Award nomination for Best Actress of the Year for the film's leading lady, Carol Kane.

Baltimore-based filmmaker John Waters wrote, produced, directed, and photographed a 16mm 90-minute film titled *Pink Flamingos* for $12,000. The film, which was made over ten years ago, acquired a substantial following and continues to play in art houses and on cult circuits around the world. In the United States alone, *Pink Flamingos* has grossed in excess of $4.5 million. Waters followed his success with other 16mm features, then wrote, produced, and directed his first 35mm film, *Polyester.* The 86-minute feature was made for $300,000 and was filmed in "Odorama." This meant that each ticket-buyer received a numbered "scratch 'n sniff" card containing various aromas to be sniffed at appropriate times during the film. *Polyester* has been successfully distributed in virtually every important territory in the world. In the United States, the picture opened in multiple runs throughout the country, including twenty-two theaters in the Los Angeles area alone. In a single theater in Baltimore, the film grossed $18,484 in one week, more than double the previous house record. In the United States, *Polyester* has grossed over $2 million.

Beth Ferris and Annick Smith, both living in Montana, had an idea for a film about wilderness women. Beth Ferris wrote a story, called *Heartland,* set in 1910, and with it the two women ventured to New York. After interesting producer Michael Hausman and director Richard Pearce in their project, they applied for a grant from the National Endowment for the Humanities and were awarded $600,000 to make a feature film. They raised another $200,000 (Annick Smith mortgaged her ranch) and deferred $100,000 worth of payments to meet the total budget of $900,000. The 93-minute film was shot with a 25-member crew in twenty-five days. *Heartland* received rave reviews from the critics and won both the Golden Bear Award at the Berlin Film Festival and the top prize at the USA Film and Video Festival. During its first sixteen days at the Paris Theater in New York, *Heartland* grossed over $100,000. The total worldwide gross is currently in excess of $3 million and is expected to exceed $5 million over the life of the film. (Because of the costs involved in distribution and marketing, a picture generally must gross between two-and-a-half and three times its production cost to break even; therefore, a $3 million gross for *Heartland* is approximately the break-even point.)

Filmmaker Joe Camp established an advertising agency in Dallas, Texas called Mulberry Square Productions. After several years of making television commercials and sales-type films, he decided to make an independent feature. He set out to accomplish with live action what Disney had accomplished with animation: to tell a feature-length dramatic story totally from an animal's point of view. The title of his project was *Benji.* Based only on his concept and a nine-page description of the story, he raised $550,-000 from private investors, many of whom had never invested in films before. Camp wrote, produced and directed his 85-minute G-rated film using a crew that consisted largely of local film production people working on their first feature. When the film was completed, Camp screened it for major distributors, all of whom turned it down. They said that a G-rated picture, without Disney's name attached to it, spells death at the box office. Camp had a few cursory distribution offers but there was so little enthusiasm for the film's commercial potential that he established Mulberry Square Releasing, Inc. and distributed the film on his own. His gamble paid off. When Camp opened his film at the 450-seat Guild theater in New York (after warnings by a major theater chain that *Benji* would die in the big city) lines of kids and adults formed around the block outside the theater. *Benji* broke the house box office record and continued its New York run for ten straight weeks. The film broke several box office records, received tremendous critical acclaim, and won numerous awards. The domestic box office gross for *Benji* is currently in excess of $45 million. Camp followed *Benji* with a successful sequel, *For the Love of Benji,* which grossed over $25 million and produced, through Mulberry Square Productions, two Benji television specials for ABC. Additional spinoffs from the film include forty Benji products marketed in the United States by twenty different companies. These include Benji books, slides, greeting cards, calendars, T-shirts, coloring books, paint-by-numbers sets, games, puzzles, costumes, stuffed animals, banks, posters, and soundtrack albums.

Producer-director Barbara Kopple went to Kentucky in 1972 with $9,000 to make a short documentary film about coal miners. The following year she found herself in the midst of a strike at the Brookside mining camp in Harlan County. She lived with the miners for over a year while the strike lasted, recording the events on 16mm film with a rotating, mostly voluntary crew of between two and seven people. While making the film, Kopple went back and forth to New York to raise money, eventually some $350,000. Part of the money came from individuals, often in small amounts of between $1,000 and $2,000; some came from church and other groups and some from money Kopple earned along the way. She also received a grant from the National Endowment for the Humanities for $139,000 and a smaller one from the Ford Foundation. What emerged, after three and a half years of hard work, was Kopple's first feature, a 103-minute documentary titled *Harlan County U.S.A.* Despite the fact that most feature documentaries do not perform well in theaters, *Harlan County U.S.A.* opened to amazing business in fifty cities across the country, including Boston where it played against, and out-performed *Rocky, Black Sunday,* and *King Kong. Harlan County U.S.A.* received unanimous praise from the critics and won numerous awards including the Academy Award for Best Feature Documentary in 1977. In addition to its successful domestic distribution, the film has been adapted into six languages and sold throughout the world. To date, the $350,000 film has grossed nearly $1.5 million. Of this total, approximately $700,000 came from domestic theatrical distribution, $394,000 from foreign sales, $306,000 from non-theatrical distribution, $36,900 from a sale to PBS, and $5,950 from the sale of video cassettes.

Over a period of three years, John Hanson and Rob Nilsson wrote, produced, directed, and edited a 16mm, black and white, 90-minute independent feature titled *Northern Lights.* The film, a 1915 period piece, was shot entirely in North Dakota for a budget of $330,000, supplied in part by the North Dakota Committee for the Humanities and Public Issues. *Northern Lights* received excellent reviews and numerous awards including Best First Feature at the Cannes Film Festival in 1979. The film was initially distributed by its makers, drawing large crowds throughout the Midwest. Subsequently, Hanson and Nilsson founded New Front Films to distribute *Northern Lights,* and booked the film into theaters through First Run Features, a New York-based booking company which they helped to create. The film has been shown theatrically and on television networks in twenty countries, has grossed over $800,000, and is expected to continue its run for many more years to come.

Charles B. Pierce, a former advertising man from Texarkana, Arkansas, set out to make an independent, G-rated feature film about a legendary monster living in a nearby swamp. His previous film experience was limited to shooting 16mm television commercials for local clients. He raised $120,000, mostly through bank loans, gathered a crew of local high school students, assembled a cast of locals from the community, and borrowed a 35mm camera. He then produced, directed, photographed, and sang the theme song for his first feature—*The Legend of Boggy Creek.* When the film was completed, he rented (and personally cleaned) a 500-seat out-of-business theater in Texarkana, Arkansas for the opening. As Pierce recalls, "Me and my friend scrubbed all the seats in the theater and waxed the floor in the foyer. I called everybody I knew and said come on by or send flowers, we are fixin' to have a world premier!" In three weeks, in that one theater, *The Legend of Boggy Creek* grossed $55,000. Following his successful opening, Pierce peddled the film to individual theaters, carrying ten prints in the back of his pickup truck. His efforts paid off at the box office with impressive figures such as $45,000 in two weeks in Shreveport, Louisiana. Pierce subsequently arranged for distribution through Howco International Pictures, a small distribution company in New Orleans. To date, his $120,000 picture has grossed $22 million. Pierce followed his success with several other independent features including *Bootleggers, Winter Hawk, The Winds of Autumn,* and *The Town That Dreaded Sundown.*

Pittsburg filmmaker George A. Romero, working with a local semiprofessional cast and crew, directed, co-authored, photographed, and edited a 16mm, black and white, 94-minute feature called *Night of the Living Dead.* The budget was $60,000 ($114,-000 after deferred payments were met). The film acquired a substantial cult following, received remarkable critical acclaim, and grossed over $40 million dollars. Romero followed his success with a $700,000 feature, *Dawn of the Dead,* which, to date, has earned in excess of $55 million.

Florida filmmaker Victor Nunez wrote, produced, directed, and edited a 16mm, 105-minute, color film called *Gal Young Un* for $94,000. Thirty percent of the financing came from the National Endowment for the Arts, 25 percent from the Florida Fine Arts Council, and the balance from private investors. The film, a 1920's period piece based on a short story by Marjorie Kinnan Rawlings, was shot entirely in Florida. In addition to overwhelming critical acclaim, *Gal Young Un* received numerous awards including the Silver Hugo Award for Best First Feature at the Chicago Film Festival and the top prize at the USA Film and Video Festival. The film has been widely distributed in the United States, Canada, and Europe and has grossed in excess of $500,000.

Private Lessons, an independent feature about a woman who seduces a young boy, was made for $2.1 million. It was produced by R. Ben Efraim and financed entirely by Jack Barry and Dan

Enright of Barry & Enright Films, Inc. The film became a huge box office success, grossing nearly twenty times its cost, but at one point the 87-minute R-rated film was virtually written off as a total disaster. When the film was screened in June of 1980, most of the people involved, including Barry and Enright, considered it so bad as to be unreleasable. Efraim, however, was not convinced. He conceived a new approach for the picture and was given the go-ahead to re-edit. Everyone agreed that Efraim's new version was a vast improvement, but when screened for major distributors for distribution in the United States and Canada, all of them turned it down. Undaunted, Efraim sold the film to several foreign countries, recouping Barry and Enright's investment. But the idea was to make a profit, not merely to recoup the investment. In an effort to demonstrate the film's commercial potential, Efraim test-marketed *Private Lessons* in five U.S. cities. The results were so impressive that major distributors began calling *him*. Efraim, however, decided to go with an independent distributor, Jensen-Farley Pictures, headquartered in Salt Lake City, Utah. *Private Lessons* opened on a regional basis in the United States and Canada, and by the time it had played 24 percent of the territory it had grossed nearly $7 million. By the time it had played 47 percent of the territory the grosses had climbed to $13.6 million. *Private Lessons,* the $2.1 million picture that was almost put on a shelf and never shown, has earned over $30 million in the United States and Canada alone. The total worldwide gross is expected to exceed $60 million before the film is finally retired.

Connecticut filmmaker Sean Cunningham raised $650,000 from private investors to make his directorial debut and, hopefully, his passkey to Hollywood. He set out to make the scariest film ever made. It was titled *Friday the 13th.* Cunningham completed his film, brought it to Hollywood and, despite limited connections, had a distribution deal in four days. Before the film ever opened, Cunningham had distribution guarantees totalling $2.6 million. Paramount guaranteed $1.5 million in exchange for domestic (United States and Canada) distribution rights and Warner Bros. gauranteed $1.1 million in exchange for foreign distribution rights. The film grossed in excess of $41 million worldwide. This not only made Cunningham a wealthy man, it successfully opened the Hollywood doors for several of his future successfully opened the Hollywood doors for several of his future projects.

An entire book could be written about each of these films on its way to eventual success. The purpose of this book, however, is to guide others in the making of successful independent feature films. All too often a project begins as a terrific idea but never makes it to the screen or, if it does, falls considerably short of its potential, simply because the people making the film were not sufficiently trained in the process of independent feature production.

Each film travels essentially the same path from concept through distribution. This book examines, in depth, each step along the way. The information is organized to complement all areas of production and will prove useful for everyone from interested students to seasoned professionals. The contents have been divided into five sections:

1. Legal Structuring and Financing
2. The Preproduction Package
3. The Process of Production
4. Postproduction
5. Distribution and Marketing

Some portions address themselves specifically to the independent producer; other sections are written for the director. Certain technical aspects of filmmaking are examined from both points of view. These technical discussions are not intended as how-to-do-it sections; they are meant to explain what everyone on the production team does and how *they* do it. The more a person understands about the various parts of a project, the better he will understand the whole. A producer will be a better producer if he has an insight into the problems of directing; a director will function best if he has a knowledge of lighting techniques; a director of photography will find a knowledge of editing an aid to his photography; and so forth.

For the newcomer this book may, at first, appear complicated and difficult. I am not claiming to make the process easy; independent feature production requires tenacity, creativity, and just plain hard work on the part of everyone involved. However, the more you understand about the process, the less complicated and difficult it becomes. The real complexities come when you approach production without a thorough understanding of the process. Those of you more experienced in motion picture production may find portions of this book with which you are already familiar. There is the possibility that even in these areas you will find a useful new detail or a new slant that makes reading the entire book worthwhile.

I refer often in this book to modestly budgeted and low-budget features. By a modest budget I mean under $3 million; by a low budget I mean under $500,000. I have been cautious not to mention specific salaries and prices (except in sample production budgets) since these are subject to change. I have, however, included the information necessary to find current prices for such things as cast, crew, motion pictures services, facilities, and equipment.

Since there are women working in virtually every field of motion picture production, the use of "he" when referring to an individual seems limiting and unfair. However, I found it clumsy to keep repeating "he or she." The single "he" is the word I have used throughout the final version of this book. Please interpret this as an all-inclusive word for both men and women.

PART 1

Legal Structuring and Financing

Introduction

The manufacturing of any new product, including a motion picture, follows essentially the same pattern. It begins with an idea that is researched and developed to determine whether a prototype is warranted. Creating the prototype is usually the most expensive and risky phase of the operation. In the case of a motion picture, the prototype is the first trial composite answer print. If the prototype appears to have potential public appeal, the manufacturer develops an advertising campaign to promote the product, then test-markets the campaign, and finally sets up an operation to mass-produce and distribute the new product. Making a motion picture follows precisely this process from conception through production, marketing, and distribution.

The man-at-the-top in motion picture production is the *producer.* He is tantamount to a corporation's chairman of the board, establishing policy for the corporation. For the record, since definitions of the producer's role are as varied as snowflakes, I hereby offer my own: a producer is someone who views the process of motion picture production as a series of projects. A successful producer appoints the best people he can find to head each project, then supervises those people.

A motion picture director is similar to a corporate president, responsible for implementing whatever policy is set forth by the board.

It is in this light, paralleling the manufacturing of any new product with the making of a motion picture, that the reader should view the first part of this book.

CHAPTER 1

An Overview of Independent Financing

Financing is often the hardest part of making a film. Some say that once you've got the money, everything else is downhill. However, many independent feature films are successfully financed every year using a variety of financing and legal structures. One of the most common and successful approaches for an independent producer involves financing with private domestic investors using a limited partnership structure. This will be discussed at some length in Chapter 2, but for now I would like to present an overall picture of the various financing routes available to the independent producer.

The following discussion should not be construed as legal counsel or advice. Rather, it is a discussion about legal structuring and financing from the point of view of an independent producer. Prior to making a commitment to a particular structure for financing, it is important to obtain professional legal counsel.

One way to locate an appropriate attorney for your needs is through word-of-mouth reputation within the film community. Another way is through local bar associations, that have referral systems for various types of legal services. For example, if you are seeking an entertainment attorney in Los Angeles County, you can telephone the State Bar of California and they will guide you to the Los Angeles County Bar Association Referral Service. The referral service will locate an appropriate attorney in Los Angeles County and arrange an appointment for you. Attorneys who are listed with this referral service are those who meet certain bar association requirements and who pay a nominal fee for the listing.

Legal opinions vary enormously vis-à-vis the following and it is best to interview several potential attorneys before making a decision. When you have selected an experienced attorney that you trust and are comfortable with, stick closely to his advice.

The Studios

The principal source of motion picture financing comes from the major studios: Columbia, MGM, Paramount, Twentieth-Century Fox, United Artists, Universal, and Warner Bros. Consequently, the majority of critically and commercially important films are studio-affiliated projects. Major studios have the most clout in terms of financing, distribution, and availability of "name" talent. For these reasons, most producers ultimately seek studio affiliation. There are, however, a number of stumbling blocks that stand in the way.

First, it is rare for a studio to commit itself to production financing without a substantially developed package (i.e., script, stars, director, budget, etc.). It may agree to *develop* a property with an independent, and in such cases the studio will purchase a property such as a book, an idea, a story, or a script from an independent producer and finance its development and packaging. But many more pictures are developed than are produced, and in some cases the producer may have a difficult time regaining ownership of the original property. Generally, a development deal is a *step deal,* in which the studio pays the producer and other persons who are contributing to the property's development (such as a writer or director) a salary and sometimes expense money, in increments as the project is developed. Step one might be the outline for the screenplay. A first-draft script would follow as step two, and so forth into production. The studio will retain the right to back out at any step along the way.

A development deal is made official when the parties involved sign a letter (called a *deal memo*) outlining the basic terms of the agreement such as salary, time schedule, screen credit, and percentage participation in the film's profits. A formal contract containing the details of the agreement and the industry's standard legal boilerplate is negotiated and prepared by agents and attorneys while the project is in active development. The salary for which one negotiates in a development deal is the entire salary the individual will receive if and when the picture is actually produced. This may involve impressive sums of money, but the majority of that money is speculative. A development deal contract will usually allow for only a very small portion of that salary to be paid during development. The important money comes only if the picture is subsequently financed for production. A deal with a major studio is almost always a production/distribution (P/D) deal in which the studio ties up distribution rights from the beginning. Since the studio is financing the production, it will be in a powerful position to negotiate a distribution deal that weighs heavily in its favor. Given the sophisticated accounting techniques for which the major distributors have gained a formidable reputation, the independent producer is generaly advised to negotiate for a large up-front producer's fee, and not to expect much additional income from profit participation in the picture. A picture must be extremely successful for an independent producer's profit participation to become meaningful. This will be discussed further in Part V, "Distribution and Marketing."

Another disadvantage to the studio deal, at least for the beginning producer with a modest- or low-budget picture, is that the studios are not generally interested in small films. The average studio film costs close to $10 million dollars. Studios are contracted to the unions, which adds considerably to a film's budget. I know of one project for which the $8 million budget included $1 million for union drivers alone. There are also built-in overhead expenses involved in running a studio facility that boost production budgets by as much as 25 percent. Production and distribution costs for most studio films are so high that they must hedge their bets with expensive name stars, name producers, and name directors.

When a studio makes a commitment for production costs, it is not uncommon to require the producer to provide protection against overbudget costs by securing a completion bond. This bond is supplied by a third party called a *completion guarantor*. The bond guarantees to cover overbudget expenses, thereby guaranteeing that the film will not go unfinished for lack of funds. Most completion guarantors will provide overbudget protection up to $2 million per picture, but such a third-party guarantee is difficult to secure. On an independently financed picture, the gaurantor is in first position to recoup any money spent on overbudget, but on a P/D financed film, the guarantor is in second position—after the distributor. In other words, in a typical P/D deal, the distributor recoups all of the costs of production first; the guarantor then recoups any overbudget expenses. The guarantor's fee is usually budgeted into the cost of the picture and is almost always 5 percent of the budget plus a share in the film's profits, regardless of whether or not his money is actually used. Sometimes, if the film comes in on budget, the guarantor will offer a partial rebate.

In addition to, or in lieu of, a completion guarantee, some distributors will withhold a portion of the producer's fee until the picture is completed. This money will be the first used to cover overbudget expenses. In such a case the producer will receive the withheld portion of his fee only after the distributor has recouped all of its production costs.

There are also cases in which the producer is further induced to control the budget and schedule by means of a penalty formula. For example, if a production goes overbudget, the producer's profit participation is decreased by a predetermined formula. The standard formula for a large studio film is 1 point (or percent) of the producer's participation for every 1 percent that the picture goes overbudget.

A final consideration in studio financing is that the studio will insist on creative control over the picture, with power to override the producer whenever there is a difference of opinion. Overriding a producer isn't something a studio likes to do. A producer is hired to do a job, and the less the studio interferes, the better. However, in order to protect its investment, the studio invariably insists on artistic control, including final cut of the film. An experienced name producer with a good track record may negotiate for some of this power, but the majority of independents must relinquish creative control to the studios.

Independent Production Companies with Studio Deals

Independent producers often negotiate production deals with independent production companies such as Orion, Rastar, Polygram, and Lorimar. These companies finance independent producers but they are generally affiliated with a major studio for production and/or distribution. Consequently, their deals often have pros and cons similar to the direct studio deal. Other independent production companies without studio affiliation or distribution ties occasionally finance projects for outside producers, but the majority of their work is done in-house.

For the beginning producer, there are substantial roadblocks to direct or indirect affiliation with the studios, and often one must find an alternate source of financing.

The Specialists

Specialists in motion picture financing are usually tax attorneys or investment counselors. They have clients with high-risk capital who wish to invest in motion pictures. They will generally "pool" motion picture investment capital from a number of clients and invest in several films simultaneously, thereby cross-collateralizing the investment and minimizing the risks. The problems with the specialists, for the independent beginning producer, are similar to the problems with major studios. They are not generally interested in small films, but prefer substantially packaged major star properties.

Often, studio productions are cofinanced between the studios and the specialists. Columbia Pictures has a strong history of such cofinancing arrangements. Approximately a million dollars of the production money for *Chinatown* was put together by the specialists (a good example of a substantially packaged property: screenplay by Robert Towne, starring Jack Nicholson and Faye Dunaway, directed by Roman Polanski).

It is best to approach the specialists through an entertainment law firm or an experienced producer's representative. Their production financing, however, is generally unavailable to the beginning independent producer, especially in the absence of a substantially packaged property.

Bank Loans (Distribution Guarantees and Negative Pickups)

In order to obtain production financing from a bank or private lending institution, it is almost always necessary to obtain a *distribution guarantee* or a *negative pickup deal* from a reputable distributor.

A distribution guarantee means that a distributor will guarantee full or partial payment of the loan, usually within a two-year period following the film's initial release. The portion of the film's budget that a producer may borrow, and the interest rate on the loan, depend on the distributor's credit. If a major distributor guarantees the loan, the producer will probably be able to borrow the entire budget. If the guarantor is a small independent distributor whose credit rating is not sufficient to guarantee a loan for the entire budget, a pledge of assets such as stocks, bonds, and interest in other films may be required. In addition to the interest on the loan, lending institutions will sometimes request a participation in the film's profits.

An acceptable distribution guarantee, which is extremely difficult for an independent producer to secure, will not by itself ensure that the bank will loan the money. The bank will also require and carefully scrutinize a great deal of additional documentation and information. Among the documents that the bank will require are:

- proof of the producer's right to film the literary property under consideration.
- a copy of the distribution guarantee.
- a copy of the distribution agreement (see Chapter 22).
- a copy of the completion guarantee.
- a detailed budget.
- a complete financial statement of any other investors involved in the project.
- a security agreement that puts the bank in a first lien position with respect to the film, the literary property upon which the film will be based, and the producer's share of receipts from all sources (i.e., the bank has the first legal claim to these assets).
- an agreement between the bank and the distributor in which the distributor agrees to pay the producer's share of receipts directly to the bank until the loan plus interest is repaid, and in which the distributor agrees to pay any unpaid balance on the loan at the time of maturity or forfeit distribution rights. Should the finished film perform poorly at the box office, the distributor may be contractually required to make payments to the bank over and above the producer's share of receipts prior to maturity of the loan.

If the bank approves the loan, it will advance money during production, usually on a weekly basis, according to the budget schedule set forth in the documents listed above. Each advance must be preceded by a detailed cost report of monies spent to date. This procedure continues until the film is completed, at which time the bank will receive monthly distribution reports that will include release dates, prints, and advertising budgets, and an itemization of gross film rental, distribution fees, distribution expenses, and the producer's percentage participation.

Negative pickup is a very broad term that usually refers to a distribution agreement negotiated prior to a film's completion. It is an agreement whereby the distributor takes over ("picks up") the original negative from a finished film from which he will make release prints for distribution.

The principal difference between a distribution guarantee and a negative pickup deal is that in the latter the distributor does not guarantee the loan. Rather, the distributor agrees to distribute a producer's film contingent upon delivery of the completed picture. Quite often the distributor will also agree to pay the producer an advance against the film's profits, again upon delivery of the completed picture. Any overbudget costs in a negative pickup deal are solely the responsibility of the producer who must arrange for a completion bond that will guarantee delivery of a finished film. In this way there is little or no risk for the distributor if for any reason the film is not finished or if the finished film in any way fails to meet the requirements set forth in the negative pickup agreement.

A negative pickup deal may be used by a producer as collateral for a bank loan for production financing, especially if the agreement provides for a large distribution advance such as the entire cost of making the film (i.e., the negative cost). In some cases, the distributor will put the agreed-upon sum into an escrow account for release upon delivery of the film. Remember, however, that the larger the advance, the smaller will be the producer's percentage participation in the film's profits.

Like a distribution guarantee, a negative pickup deal is difficult to secure. One of the problems is defining the film that the producer will deliver. The script must be mutually agreed upon and adhered to during production. Deviations from the script during production may render the film unacceptable. An agreement must be drawn up that lists, and guarantees the involvement of, certain key people in the production such as the director and principal cast members. The agreement must also define acceptable standards of technical quality (any disputes regarding the technical quality of the finished film can usually be resolved by a competent laboratory). The distributor may request that the agreement include a copy of the film's budget in order to ensure that the producer will spend enough to produce a quality product.

The negative pickup agreement is subject to many complications and should include contingency plans for which the producer can negotiate. For example, what happens if a principal cast member becomes ill and the insurance company finds it more economical to replace that cast member rather than wait for his or her recovery? Ideally, a contingency plan in the negative pickup agreement will cover any such complications.

Upon completion of the film, assuming that all the terms of the contract have been adhered to by the producer, a laboratory or other mutually agreed-upon third party will issue a letter stating that the finished film is of acceptable commercial quality, that the script was substantially adhered to, that the agreed-upon cast members appeared in their proper roles, and so forth. Upon receipt of the film and the laboratory letter, the distribution advance, if any, will be released to the producer or lending institution to pay back the loan.

While some films are successfully financed in this way, the negative pickup deal is complex, time-consuming, and highly speculative. For a producer without a substantially packaged property, a distribution guarantee or a negative pickup deal is virtually impossible to obtain, and without either of these, a bank loan for production financing is usually out of the question.

Foreign Financing

One hears a great deal about the abundance of production money available in foreign countries such as Canada, Germany, Hungary, and Yugoslavia. The impression one gets is that a producer merely steps across the border and his financing worries are over. I personally know several producers who have crossed the border and failed; I also know a few who have succeeded.

The best route to foreign production money is through entertainment law firms that are knowledgeable in financing motion pictures in the country that best fits the producer's needs. For example, an entertainment law firm knowledgeable in Canadian production financing will have connections with Canadian specialists (i.e., Canadian law firms or Canadian investment counselors who represent Canadian film investors). However, the beginning independent producer must have something more to offer than just an idea, i.e., a package. Given a solid package, an experienced entertainment law firm will often succeed in financing productions with foreign money. An attorney experienced in financing motion pictures in this way may be found either through word-of-mouth reputation within the film community or through your local bar association, as described in the beginning of this chapter.

In several countries, the government has offered significant tax advantages for film investments; in some cases, the government itself will help subsidize productions. Their incentive for doing so is to stimulate their country's economy by offering production jobs to their people. Usually this means that the majority of the film must be shot in their country, using almost exclusively native technicians, facilities, and actors. A producer entering into such financing arrangements must become thoroughly familiar with the foreign regulations governing his project. This information is readily available through the country's embassy or through the law firm negotiating the deal.

Foreign tax advantages and foreign government subsidies for motion pictures are constantly changing. For example, it used to be in the United States that motion picture tax shelter leveraging was so great that even a totally unsuccessful film would generate a profit for the investor. The very nature of the investment guaranteed a profit. This was a very sophisticated process, and a similar situation exists today in Canada. The Canadian government now offers an investment tax shelter to Canadian film investors in the hope of stimulating their film production economy. However, what has been a Canadian production boom in recent years, as a direct result of the tax shelter laws, may soon become a slump. The Canadian tax shelter leverage is not as great as the leverage that was available a few years ago in the United States, and in order for the investments to pay off, the Canadian films need to generate a profit.

Canadian investors, anxious to get in on the tax shelter advantages, sometimes rushed into film investments without carefully analyzing the future marketability of the projects. These investors were unsophisticated in evaluating film properties and, as a result, several American producers were able to finance projects in Canada that had been turned down by more sophisticated sources for financing in the United States. Many of these pictures have performed poorly at the box office. These same investors will be far more hesitant the second time around. *Running,* a film starring Michael Douglas, is an example of one such Canadian picture that did not perform up to expectations at the box office. Fortunately for the investors, the producer was able to make enough money from distribution advances and television presales that the picture managed to achieve profitability, but all pictures aren't so lucky.

Grants for Independent Feature Production

Motion picture projects are commonly funded in part or in whole by grants from federal and local government agencies, private foundations, special interest groups, academic scholarships, educational research funds, and media organizations such as the Corporation for Public Broadcasting. Examples of independent features that have been successfully financed, either partially or completely, by such grants include *Gal Young Un, Harlan County U.S.A., Heartland, The Life and Times of Rosie the Riveter,* and *Northern Lights.*

There are thousands of organizations in the United States offering grant money for motion picture production, including over 25,000 in the private sector alone. There is no single reference book that lists them all, but a good place to start might be *Gadney's Guide to 1800 International Contests* listed in Appendix E.

Because grant programs are subject to continuous modification, it is important to conduct a thorough search in an effort to learn which organizations might be interested in funding a particular project, and to learn as much as possible about those organizations. Each funding source has unique requirements and restrictions regarding grants. Some will fund only individuals; some will offer grants only to non profit organizations (it is often possible for a filmmaker to obtain sponsorship from a non profit organization, thereby rendering his project eligible for such grants); some will restrict their funding to a limited field of interest; some will limit grants to persons living a particular region such as the state in which the funding organization is located; and virtually all of them have set limits on the amount of money they will award for any given project. This may range anywhere from $500 to $500,-000 or more depending on the nature of the project and the policy of the organization.

In addition to organizations that specifically award grants for motion picture production, it may be worthwhile to approach organizations that award grants in a particular field of interest. For example, if you are making a documentary feature that revolves around life in the sea, it may be worthwhile to approach organizations that fund oceanographic research projects. There are many reference books that list such funding sources, most of which can be found in the public library. Once you determine which organizations appear most likely to support your project, write to them requesting information about their organization and, specifically, about their grant program. Also request an application form. This information may help you to narrow down the list of potential funding sources. The next step is to send an inquiry letter briefly describing your proposed project. If the funding organization is interested, you will be asked to provide more information or, possibly, to submit a formal application.

An application for a motion picture grant usually requires a complete description of the proposed project, a detailed budget and timetable, biographical sketches of the principal people involved in the project, the specific objectives of the film, and the reasons that it is particularly significant and worthwhile. Preparing such an application requires a substantial amount of work. If you can narrow down the potential sources for funding with the inquiry letter, you will save an enormous amount of time and energy.

Prior to approaching organizations for grant money, it is usually helpful to obtain the support of a well-recognized specialist in your project's particular area of interest. For example, in the case of the project mentioned above, the support of a leading oceanographer, perhaps as a technical advisor, would go a long way toward strengthening the credibility of the project.

There is an overwhelming number of applications for motion picture grants submitted to funding organizations each year. Only a small fraction actually receive grants, so the chances for any one project to obtain such funding are slim. However, if one conducts a careful search to determine the most likely sources, and organizes the project information with care, the chances for acceptance are greatly improved. If a grant is denied, you may always write an appeal letter re-emphasizing the significance of the project and requesting specific information about why it was rejected. Based on the organization's response, you may wish to approach them a second time with a modified proposal.

Other Sources

There are many additional sources of financing for motion pictures. Members of the National Association of Theater Owners (NATO) such as General Cinema, United Artists Theaters, Plitt Theaters, and Mann Theaters, are beginning to sponsor productions; several independent distributors have allocated funds for production; wealthy entrepreneurs like Melvin Simon have financed several films independently; and the list goes on. But how does the independent producer tap into these sources? What's the key? The answer is that in every situation mentioned thus far, the financing entity (be it a major studio or an independent source) rarely, if ever, commits to production financing without a substantially developed package. At the very least, this means a completed screenplay, or the rights to an existing literary property, and at most it means commitments from stars, director, a detailed production budget and shooting schedule.

It is possible for an independent producer to make a development step deal with most of these sources. Bear in mind, however, that with the exception of the granting organizations, they will generally have little interest in developing a small-budget picture, and they are hesitant to develop a property with a new producer making his first feature. Further, of the pictures they do choose to develop, very few make it into production.

Where does this leave the beginning independent producer? Unless he has funds available to develop and package a property, the financing doors are pretty tough to open. The beginning independent producer must often turn to private domestic investors. He must convince them that his project has commercial potential, that it is a desirable investment, and that he is capable of delivering a quality picture on schedule and within budget.

When financing a picture entirely on your own, there are several legal structures to consider, such as a *public corporation,* a *subchapter "S" corporation,* and a *partnership.*

A public corporation allows one to solicit and receive investments from a large number of people. It also, however, requires registration with the Securities and Exchange Commission (SEC). This is difficult, costly, and time-consuming. A complete formal prospectus must be assembled, and an underwriter must be found to market the stock. There are instances in which going public has proven successful for financing independent films, but for many independent producers, the cost and difficulty far outweigh the advantages.

A subchapter "S" corporation is a variation on the corporate theme that does not require registration with the SEC. However, the financing restrictions are so severe as to render this structure impractical for most independent motion picture financing.

It is important to consult an attorney before determining which structure best fits your needs, but the most common and successful structure is the limited partnership. This structure may be used for financing an entire production or for financing the development and packaging of a production. The remainder of Part I is devoted to a detailed analysis of motion picture financing through private domestic investment, specifically in relation to modest- and low-budget pictures, using a limited partnership structure and a limited partnership investment memorandum.

CHAPTER 2

The Limited
Partnership

The details of any limited partnership agreement are delineated in the articles of limited partnership. A sample copy of such articles for a typical California limited partnership may be found in Appendix A. These articles are included as a reference guide, not as a do-it-yourself, fill-in-the-blanks document. Each project is different and requires modification of the basic agreement. Further, the laws governing limited partnerships vary from state to state and are subject to periodic change. It is advisable to obtain experienced legal counsel prior to preparing the articles of limited partnership for each project.

The principal advantage of a limited partnership over a corporation is that income from a limited partnership is filtered through the partnership directly to the investors and is taxed only once as income tax. In a corporation the income is taxed twice—first at the corporate level as corporate tax and, second, at the investor level as income tax. (A subchapter "S" corporation does not suffer the double tax but, as I mentioned before, the financing limitations are so severe that few motion pictures are successfully financed using this structure).

There are some financing restrictions in a limited partnership structure for both the producer and the investor that are detailed in the articles of limited partnership in Appendix A. Even within these limitations, however, independent producers often succeed in financing their films.

The Structure

A limited partnership is divided into two sections: the general partner(s), usually the producer, and the limited partners, the investors. Limited partners are so defined because their liability is limited to the extent of their capital contribution (i.e., their investment). This means that they are protected against any liability beyond their investment, such as overbudget costs, loans to the production, and law suits. This is extremely important to someone investing in a high-risk project, such as a motion picture. Any liability beyond the investor's capital contribution will be assumed by the general partner. The general partner may, in some cases, be a corporation in an effort to shield everyone from personal liability.

The investors are further limited in that they have no say in the running of the partnership. They invest their money. Beyond that, they have no involvement except, hopefully, to receive checks. This is a tremendous advantage to the independent producer who desires to maintain artistic control over his picture.

The general partner, assuming that he operates within the parameters of the partnership agreement, maintains total control over the running of the business and total artistic control over the making of the picture. This includes spending the money, maintaining the books, hiring personnel, scheduling production, negotiating contracts, and all other activities necessary for completion of the project.

Limitations and Gray Areas

The specific financing limitations for limited partnerships vary from state to state, but in all cases the law defines the legal number of potential investors that the general partner may *approach* for investment, and the legal number of investors allowed to *participate* in the limited partnership.

In California, the legal number of potential investors that the general partner may *approach* for investment is twenty-five. The legal number of investors allowed to *participate* in a limited partnership is restricted to ten. This means that if a picture is budgeted at $500,000, the general partner is allowed to solicit investment from no more than twenty-five individuals, and that of those twenty-five only ten may invest. Therefore, the average investment (assuming the maximum of ten investors) will be $50,000. If the general partner finances the entire picture with fewer than ten investors, the average investment goes up. For example, the average investment for five investors in a $500,000 property will be $100,000.

Limited partnerships are carefully structured private placement investments; they are *not* public offerings. At first glance, it may appear that this creates such an enormous roadblock that financing an independent picture becomes an impossible task. After all, how many doors will you have to knock on before you find ten investors, each willing to commit 10 percent of your budget?

A close friend was recently seeking film investors for a $350,000 horror film. During his years in film school he had accumulated friends and relatives who promised financial backing for his first feature project. Following graduation, he drew up his limited partnership papers and went calling on them. Twenty-five knocks later (no pun intended) he was exactly where he had started: point zero, except that he had used up his twenty-five solicitations allowed by California law.

Suppose he had knocked on twenty-five doors and come up with half his budget? Strict interpretation of the law dictates that he must return the money and start again. Anything beyond strict interpretation of the law falls into a gray area with respect to the Securities and Exchange Commission. A producer who finances his picture within the letter of the law is on solid ground, but the saving grace for many independents is that gray areas do exist. It's not all black and white. For example, how does one define solicitation? If you mention your newest film project to an acquaintance at a cocktail party, are you soliciting investments? That person may ultimately invest in your picture, but if he chooses not to, is it fair to include such a casual discussion as one of your twenty-five solicitations? This has never been clearly defined. Consequently, it is possible to bend, somewhat, the "approach twenty-five" restriction.

The principal thing to avoid is a public offering. If you are invited to speak to a convention of doctors in Las Vegas on the subject of motion picture investments, and at the end of the talk you say, "By the way, if any of you are interested in investing in films, come up and see me at the end of the day and I'll tell you about my latest project," you are clearly making a public offering that will probably get you in trouble with the SEC.

Investment Groups

The financing restrictions of a limited partnership require investors to make large minimum investments. As stated earlier, for a $500,000 picture the average investment, assuming ten investors, is $50,000. But suppose a producer has ten aunts and uncles who wish to invest $5,000 each? Since their total contribution will be only $50,000, strict interpretation of the law says they can't invest without the general partner's exceeding the maximum number of ten investment signatures on the limited partnership agreement. Here, too, there is a gray area. Suppose the aunts and uncles get together and form an investment group, pooling their money for the purpose of investing in their nephew's project? This requires nothing more than a letter of agreement among the ten aunts and uncles stating the purpose of the investment group and the individual selected as the group leader or captain.

The group leader will invest the group's $50,000 in the limited partnership under one signature, thereby fulfilling the minimum average investment per signature. Investment groups are common for almost any type of investment. In this instance, they may be formed by persons with small investment capital in order to participate in otherwise unavailable projects. However, in some states such an investment group is illegal with respect to limited partnerships.

CHAPTER 3

Selling
The Investment

The Investment Memorandum

The information contained herein is intended to guide the independent producer in forming an *investment memorandum* for financing a motion picture using a limited partnership structure. While professional legal counsel is essential in these matters, you may do a great deal of the work on your own. In doing so, you will save a substantial amount of money and learn something in the process.

The investment memorandum is the most important document for selling your motion picture to potential investors. The memorandum should contain all of the information necessary for an investor to make an intelligent decision about your project, and any information that the investor's legal and accounting counsel may need in order to evaluate the investment from their special points of view.

The general partner is required by law to present a complete picture of the investment, including negative as well as positive factors. It is therefore important to include in the memorandum a statement describing motion pictures as an inherently high-risk venture. Unless this is clearly stated, an investor who loses his money may subsequently sue the general partner for falsifying or, at the very least, giving an incomplete picture of the investment. It is customary to make a "risks" statement twice, presented first in general terms on the first page prior to the table of contents, usually in bold letters. It isn't necessary to go into the negative statistics of independent production such as "only one in three independent pictures ever gets distributed, and only one in ten pictures that get distributed ever achieve profitability." However, a clear statement of the nature of the investment is crucial. A sample opening page in a typical memorandum reads as follows:

> This memorandum describes the formation and operation of a limited partnership to engage in the business of motion picture production and exploitation.
>
> The contents of this memorandum are confidential and are disclosed pursuant to a confidential relationship and may not be reproduced or otherwise used except for the purpose intended herein.
>
> The partnership interests described in this memorandum will not be registered under the Securities and Exchange Act of 1933 or any local securities law and are described as for investment only and not with a view to resale or distribution.
>
> **The purchase of partnership interests described herein entails a high degree of risk and is suitable for purchase only by those who can afford a total loss of their investment. Further, risk factors as contained in this memorandum (which does not include all possible factors) should be carefully evaluated by each prospective purchaser of a limited partnership interest herein.**
>
> **The contents of this memorandum are not to be construed by any prospective purchaser of a limited partnership interest as business, legal, or tax advice and each such prospective purchaser will be required to demonstrate that he has the ability to evaluate the purchase of the limited partnership interests described herein or has retained the services of a representative who has such knowledge and expertise as may be necessary to evaluate said purchase.**
>
> This memorandum is neither an offer to sell nor a prospectus, but is informational in nature.

The second "risks" statement will fall within the body of the memorandum and will contain a more detailed description of the risks involved.

Following the opening statement will be a table of contents for the memorandum as follows:

the business of the partnership
distribution of revenues and allocation of profits and losses
sale of the partnership interests
sale of the film
tax consequences
investment tax credit
depreciation
the general partner
rights and obligations of the limited partners
rights and obligations of the general partner
conflict of interest
the motion picture
legal and accounting services
distribution
budget
timetable
risk factors
additional information

The information in the memorandum is a combination of legal and accounting boilerplate, and specific information about the motion picture in question. The following sections will describe the type of information customarily included under each title in the table of contents.

THE BUSINESS OF THE PARTNERSHIP

This section describes in brief the following elements.

The intention of the partnership to finance, produce, and cause the distribution of a feature-length, 35mm color motion picture tentatively titled, _____.

The anticipated rating for the motion picture from the Motion Picture Association of America. There are four MPAA ratings: G, PG, R, and X.

The anticipated date for completion of the picture.

The total capital required from the limited partners. For the sake of this discussion, we will assume a production budget of $500,000.

The stages of production through which the partnership investment will finance the film. In this case, we will say that the investment ($500,000) will finance the making of the motion picture through a first trial composite answer print. In other words, through the making of the film, but not the film's distribution. The costs of distribution will be borne later by the distributor.

The number of years for which the partnership will run.

The distribution of net profits. This may be divided in any way the general partner decides, but it is customary to divide profits 50 percent to the limited partners and 50 percent to the general partner. This will be discussed further in the next section, "Distribution of Revenues and Allocation of Profits and Losses."

A description of the partnership interests. Generally, 100 limited partnership interests will be offered. The cost for each interest will be 1 percent of the budget. In our case, each partnership interest will cost $5,000. In California, where the maximum number of signatures allowed on the limited partnership agreement is ten, it is customary to request a minimum purchase of ten limited partnership interests (or units) per limited partner. Remember that the *average minimum investment* must be 10 percent of the budget (in our case $50,000) in order to stay within the legal requirement of no more than ten signatures on the limited partnership agreement. If you sell half of your investment ($250,000) to your first limited partner, the average investment for the other $250,000, assuming you utilize the maximum of nine more investors, will be $250,000 divided by 9 = $27,777.78. It is unwise to start with less than a ten-unit investment in the hope of finding investors for more than ten units further down the road. If you sell only five units ($25,000) to your first investor, your average minimum investment for the remaining nine investors goes up to $475,000 divided by 9 = $52,777.78, and your job becomes all the more difficult. Wait until you've got the larger-than-ten unit investor committed, *then* lower your minimum—not before.

A description of what happens to the investor's money prior to production. Generally, it will be placed in a third-party escrow (holding) account for release to the general partner upon completion of financing. The general partner must establish a reasonable date by which financing will be completed or the escrow money returned to the investors. This date may be revised by mutual consent of the general partner and the limited partners. If, for example, the general partner has set eighteen months as the deadline for financing, and by that time he has raised only 90 percent of the budget, he may request an extention of the escrow closing date. There are variations to this procedure that are discussed in Chapter 6.

A recommendation that prospective limited partners carefully consider the risk factors described in the memorandum.

The mailing address for the general partner.

A statement that defines the investment memorandum as *informational in nature* and *not* as an offering to sell, or a solicitation. This is most important. This statement makes it possible for the general partner to circulate more memoranda than the maximum number of solicitations allowed by law. In California, as stated earlier, the maximum number of investors that the general partner may solicit is twenty-five. However, by defining the investment memorandum as *informational in nature* and not as a solicitation, the general partner moves into another gray area. Again, the principal thing to avoid is a gross violation of the law that may be interpreted as a public offering. In other words, don't print 500 memoranda and send them to the Fortune 500 mailing list.

DISTRIBUTION OF REVENUES AND ALLOCATION OF PROFITS AND LOSSES

Revenues from a motion picture will be derived from domestic and foreign theatrical distribution, sales to television, as well as any money-making ancillary and merchandising rights (see Chapter 23). Revenues received by the distributor are called *gross film rental* (or gross receipts). This section of the memorandum describes how gross film rental is filtered down from the distributor to the partnership and into the hands of the investors. The following is a typical course the distribution of revenues will run.

Gross film rental will be subject to distribution and merchandising costs (usually prints and advertising), as well as the distributor's percentage. After these deductions the film rental shall equal net film rental and shall be subject to production costs beyond the limited partnership investment capital, such as loans, extended credit, and deferred payments to talent and technical facilities; and partnership overhead expenses. After the foregoing deductions, the balance of net film rental shall equal partnership distributable cash and will be distributed 50 percent to the limited partners and 50 percent to the general partner.

The *order* in which these items appear is *crucial.* For example, if the distributor's percentage was listed first under gross film rental deductions, and distribution and merchandising costs were listed second, the distributor would be receiving a far greater share of the income. In such a case, distribution expenses would be borne solely by the partnership.

It is common to pay deferred salaries *after* the investors have recouped their investment but *before* they receive profits. In the previous example, deferred salaries are paid *before* the limited partners are paid.

It is also customary for the general partner to retain a certain number of percentage participation points (shares in the films potential profits) for major talent such as writer, director, stars, and composer. These are generally deducted off the top from net film rental, thereby being shared by both the general partner and the limited partners. Occasionally, they will be deducted solely from the general partner's share of partnership distributable cash. In the latter case, if the partnership distributable cash is divided 50/50 between the general partner and the limited partners, the percentage points for major talent will be worth exactly half as much as if they were deducted off the top from net film rental.

Everyone invests with an eye to profits, but of far greater importance to every investor is recoupment—getting his money back. Consequently, as an additional incentive for investors, the general partner may offer an accelerated rate of payback. From the investor's point of view, the ideal situation is a distribution of partnership distributable cash as follows: 100 percent to the limited partners until recoupment of their total capital contribution; 0 percent to the general partner during recoupment. Thereafter, partnership distributable cash will be distributed 50 percent to the limited partners and 50 percent to the general partner. In this way, money goes back to money first. However, if the general partner is unable to afford a zero income during recoupment, he may offer the limited partners an alternative rate of payback such as 90/10 in favor of the limited partners, or 80/20. An even greater incentive for investors is an accelerated rate of payment *beyond* recoupment. In other words, the general partner may offer the investors a 90/10 split until the investors receive 125 percent of their investment. At that point, the split becomes 50/50.

As you can see, the figures and their positioning may be adjusted in a variety of ways. Ultimately, the distribution of revenues should be structured in such a way as to make the investment as attractive as possible for the limited partners while maintaining a palatable and potentially lucrative position for the general partner.

Profits and Losses are generally allocated in the same relative percentage relationships as partnership distributable cash. They may, in some cases, differ. It is advisable to consult an experienced accountant before finalizing such allocation.

SALE OF THE PARTNERSHIP INTERESTS

This section describes a partnership interest as a capital asset and defines the manner in which gains and losses will be taxed. It is advisable to consult an experienced accountant for the specific wording of this section as it may vary from project to project.

SALE OF THE FILM

This section describes the film as a depreciable asset and defines the manner in which income or loss will be treated if the film is sold. Again, an experienced accountant should be consulted for the specific wording of this section for each project.

TAX CONSEQUENCES

This is a statement by the general partner saying that tax consequences of an investment in the partnership may vary depending on the investor's personal tax status, and that the general partner is not in a position to give tax advice or evaluate the tax consequence of this investment for any of the limited partners. This section recommends that all prospective limited partners consult their personal tax advisors regarding the projected tax consequences of the investment.

INVESTMENT TAX CREDIT

Motion picture negatives have been deemed to be depreciable, tangible personal property, and may therefore qualify for an investment tax credit. Since the death of motion picture tax shelters in the United States, motion picture investments have become far less attractive. However, they are still eligible for the investment tax credit. This doesn't amount to a great deal but it's an additional bonus that the general partner may offer to the investors.

The tax credit is available at the end of the taxable year in which the film is released, regardless of whether the partnership has a profit or loss during that year.

The investment tax credit amounts to 6⅔ percent of the invested capital. For a film budgeted at $500,000, the investment tax credit will be $500,000 × 6⅔ percent = $33,300. This amount may be deducted from the limited partner's taxes and will be allocated among the limited partners according to their percentage participation in the film's profits. A person who invests 50 percent of the budget ($250,000) will receive a tax deduction equal to 50 percent of the investment tax credit. In this instance, he will receive $33,300 × 50 percent = $16,650.

DEPRECIATION

This section describes the method that the partnership will use to determine depreciation of the film for federal income tax purposes. One such method that has been approved by the revenue rulings is the income forecast method. This provides for depreciation of the film over the period of time during which the film is expected to generate profits. The forecast is based on conditions known to exist when the forecast is made. At the end of each year, as more information becomes available regarding the remaining life of the film, the forecast may be revised upward or downward.

It is advisable for the general partner to consult an experienced accountant for the method of depreciation best suited for each project, and for the specific working for this section of the memorandum.

THE GENERAL PARTNER

This is a biographical sketch of the person(s) who will make up the general partner side of the limited partnership. Included should be background information substantiating the general partner's ability to deliver a professional motion picture within the parameters outlined in the memorandum. If the general partner has produced previous pictures, such credits should be included in this section.

RIGHTS AND OBLIGATIONS OF THE LIMITED PARTNERS

This section should contain a brief summary of the rights and obligations of the limited partners as described in Chapter 2. In addition, it is recommended that limited partners consult the limited partnership agreement for a complete understanding of their rights and obligations (see Appendix A).

This section should also describe any investment overcall provisions in the agreement. It is common for the general partner to require the limited partners to obligate themselves for additional contributions, such as 10 percent of their investment, if the partnership runs short of funds. The terms of this overcall should be clearly delineated both here and in the articles of limited partnership. If there is no overcall provision, it should be so stated.

RIGHTS AND OBLIGATIONS OF THE GENERAL PARTNER

Limited partners are advised to consult the limited partnership agreement for a complete understanding of the rights and obligations of the general partner. In addition, this section should briefly summarize these rights and obligations as described in Chapter 2. Also included should be:

- the fee, if any, that the general partner will take in addition to the general partner's share of partnership distributable cash.
- a statement describing the accounting and bookkeeping procedures that the general partner intends to use in running the partnership business.
- the availability of partnership records. It is customary to offer the limited partners access to partnership records upon request.
- the frequency with which statements of partnership operations will be sent to the limited partners.

CONFLICT OF INTEREST

This is a protective statement for the general partner that defines his services to the partnership as nonexclusive. The general partner retains the right to be involved with other projects, even similar projects that may be in competition with the activities of the partnership.

THE MOTION PICTURE

This is a description of the type of film that the partnership intends to produce. Often this takes the form of a brief, two- or three-page story synopsis describing the characters and principal events in the film. This is one of the most important sales tools in the memorandum. In addition to communicating basic information about the picture, the synopsis should be written in such a way as to capture the "feeling" of the film, whether it's comedy, action, suspense, or drama. This isn't easy to do in two or three pages but it's worth spending a little extra time on. It's better to capture the mood and feeling of the film than to outline the story points technically. The synopsis should whet the appetite of the investors.

The format for the synopsis depends on the subject matter. It may take the form of a short story or it may be presented more formally with an introductory paragraph, a paragraph on each of the principal characters, and a couple of pages describing the story.

At this stage in the development of your project, you may have nothing more than an idea on which to base your synopsis. If your project is based on an existing literary property or if you have a completed screenplay, indicate at the end of the synopsis that the completed screenplay or literary property is available upon request.

LEGAL AND ACCOUNTING SERVICES

This is a list of the legal and accounting firms that will represent and advise the partnership. Include their addresses and phone numbers.

DISTRIBUTION

If you have a prearranged distribution agreement, perhaps a cofinancing deal with a distributor, the details of such an agreement should be described in this section. Include a synopsis of pertinent information such as territories covered, advances, guarantees, definition of profits, and commitments to prints and advertising. It may be to your advantage to include a copy of the distribution agreement, but certainly this document should be made available to the limited partners upon request.

If you do not have a prearranged distribution agreement, this section may take the form of a "best efforts" clause stating that the gneral partner will use his best efforts to obtain a distribution deal for the film that, in the opinion of the general partner, will be in the best interests of the partnership. It is wise to include a description of the *minimum* distribution deal that the general partner will accept. Should the general partner be unable to negotiate a distribution deal for these minimum terms, he may always go back to the limited partners and request a modification of this section.

BUDGET

This should be a brief synopsis of how the money will be spent. You may utilize a standard budget summary forms as shown in Table 1.

Or you may simply wish to ballpark the budget as follows:

*Cost of financing (4%)	$ 20,000
Preproduction	30,000
Production	275,000
Postproduction	125,000
Subtotal	450,000
Contingency (11%)	50,000
Total	$500,000

*Note: The cost of financing covers direct costs incurred in raising money. This may include a finder's fee percentage, generally between 2 and 5 percent of money raised by outside parties as payment for their financing efforts.

Table 1   **Sample Budget Recap**

Title_____ Production company _____

Above-the-line

	100 Screenplay	$16,000	
	200 Producer	17,000	
	300 Director	12,500	
	400 Cast	55,000	$100,500

Below-the-line
Production

	500 Production staff	20,700	
	600 Extras	6,000	
	700 Set operations	34,800	
	800 Sets	17,000	
	900 Props	10,600	
	1000 Costumes	6,900	
	1100 Makeup and hairdressing	7,000	
	1200 Production equipment	21,000	
	1300 Locations/studio	12,800	
	1400 Laboratory and film	39,000	
	1500 Tests	500	
	1600 Production miscellaneous	16,500	192,800

Postproduction

	1700 Editing	46,000	
	1800 Sound	14,500	
	1900 Music	26,000	
	2000 Titles and opticals	5,000	
	2100 Laboratory	12,800	
	2200 Sound mix	11,800	116,100

Other costs

	2300 Insurance	$20,000	
	2400 Miscellaneous	25,100	45,100
		Total	454,500
	10%	Contingency	45,500
		Grand total	$500,000

If you have a detailed budget breakdown, it should be available to the investors upon request. Most investors will never ask for it. Detailed motion picture budgets are almost impossible for an inexperienced person to evaluate, and the budget summary usually includes all of the information an investor requires. It is often possible to determine a production budget based solely on an idea, prior to writing a screenplay and sometimes even prior to writing a story. This is discussed in Chapter 4, "Starting from Scratch."

TIMETABLE

As stated earlier, of paramount importance to every investor is the length of time his investment capital will be tied up. As this is directly related to the completion date of the film, the investor will be interested in the schedule for production. A timetable should include principal phases of the production process and should speak in terms of *anticipated* time periods rather than firm commitments. Further, since the financing of a film is the most unpredictable aspect of production (second only to the weather), it is a mistake to include dates—even approximate ones—in the timetable. Instead, speak in terms of *blocks of time* beginning with "completion of financing" as shown in Table 2.

RISK FACTORS

From the general partner's point of view, this section is a most unfortunate necessity. Motion picture investment is an extremely high-risk proposition and the general partner is legally bound to present a complete picture of this aspect of the investment.

This section should include a statement titled, "The General Unprofitability of Motion Pictures," that states that motion picture investment entails a high degree of risk even when the picture is substantially packaged prior to financing. Recoupment of the investment and additional profits are largely a function of the film's cost of production and distribution in relation to its public appeal. The extent to which the picture will appeal to the public is largely dependent upon unpredictable critical reviews and public taste. Unless otherwise stated, the investors in an unsuccessful

Table 2   **Timetable**

The following tentative schedule will begin upon completion of financing.

Financing completed	Begin writing period
6th week	Research and treatment completed
	Begin first draft screenplay
14th week	First draft screenplay completed
	Begin second draft screenplay
18th week	Second draft screenplay completed
	Begin polish
	Begin casting
	Begin crew allocation
	Begin location scouting
	Lock production schedule
	Allocate equipment, props, costumes
	Begin set construction
22nd week	Casting completed
	Crew allocation completed
	Locations secured
	Begin rehearsal
	Equipment, props, costumes secured
24th week	Begin production
	Begin editing
28th week	End production
29th week	First cut completed
37th week	Second cut completed
41st week	Fine cut completed
	Begin sound cutting
	Begin music composing
47th week	Score music
49th week	Sound editing completed
	Mix sound
50th week	Transfer to optical track
	Begin negative cutting
51st week	Negative cutting completed
	Begin first trial answer printing
52nd week	Screen first trial composite
	answer print

picture will have no opportunity to recoup their investment by investment in, or cross-collaboration with, any other picture. A substantial portion of motion pictures do not achieve profitability.

ADDITIONAL INFORMATION

Given the bleak nature of the "Risk Factors" section, it is helpful to shore up the memorandum with positive information about film investments. Include any information that will substantiate your project in the eyes of the investor. Copies of magazine articles that speak favorably about independent production, or about motion picture investments in general, are helpful. It's worth watching financial publications such as *Business Week* and *Forbes,* and the industry trade papers such as *Variety* and the *Hollywood Reporter,* for favorable articles about film investment.

If you have made arrangements with a writer for your screenplay, or with a director or actors, include a list of their credits. These credits will help solidify your project in the eyes of the investor.

It's also helpful to include art work. This may range from a simple home-art sketch or title treatment to a three-color printing of an original painting. The fact is that people don't like to read; they like to look at pictures. If you have a completed screenplay or a story outline, you might consider making a brief storyboard. Strive for a *visual representation of the mood of your film.* A mock newspaper ad might well serve this purpose and at the same time give the investor a feeling for how you intend to sell the finished picture.

These are just a few thoughts for how best to shore up your investment memorandum. Anything of this nature that you add to your presentation will be helpful in selling the investment.

CHAPTER 4

Starting
from Scratch

Step One: Defining the Concept

The conventional approach to producing a motion picture begins with a story, a book, a magazine article, or an idea that is developed into a screenplay. Based on the screenplay, a producer formulates a production budget and shooting schedule, assembles the necessary people and facilities, and guides the making of the film through production and postproduction. Based on the completed picture, an advertising campaign is developed. The picture and campaign are then marketed by a distributor.

There is an alternative approach that is well worth considering, especially for the producer with a modest- or low-budget picture. This approach *begins with the campaign*. It begins with a marketing concept that defines the specific audience for which the film will be made. When using this approach, it is helpful to stay within a commercially proven genre such as horror, sex, or action/adventure. Since producers with small-budget films cannot afford name stars or lavish special effects, it is important that their pictures contain some theatrically exploitable element that will draw audiences into the theater. The producer must think in terms of something that isn't available on television. This usually involves sex, violence, or some shock value that extends beyond the censorship limitations of television. This is not the only way, however, for a modestly budgeted picture to become successful. It may succeed without excessive exploitation elements simply because it has a compelling story with powerful characters who deal with issues that transcend the traditional television fare. But these pictures are rare; they often depend on standards of excellence that are extremely difficult to achieve within the limitations of a small budget and tight shooting schedule.

At this point, the important thing is to determine which elements in your film may be utilized to develop a powerful advertising campaign. How do you intend to sell your picture to the public? Why will people choose your picture over all the others? What you are after are concepts, or hooks, to draw people in. You don't need a finished newspaper ad, but mock-up ideas for title treatments, art work, and lead lines are important. A *lead line* is a descriptive phrase or sentence that elaborates on the title, e.g., "A haunting tale of ghostly terror." The campaign may change drastically before your picture is ready for distribution, but at least you know going in that you've got a marketable concept.

Once you have defined your genre and your approach to advertising, you may determine a budget for production. Obviously, without a screenplay it isn't possible to write a detailed budget. It is, however, possible to conduct a market research survey of your chosen genre, using available box office figures from such publications as *Variety* to determine a sensible total amount of money to spend on your project.

For example, consider a producer who wishes to make a modestly budgeted independent feature. He may choose the horror film genre. Within that genre there are subspecies such as monster films, supernatural films, and crazed killer films. Perhaps the producer develops a film idea about subterranean creatures who depend on oil for their survival, much as man depends on water. The creature's life source is rapidly vanishing as man pumps more and more oil out of the earth to run factories, homes, and automobiles. One night a group of "oil people" burrow out of the ground to seek revenge. They wreak havoc on a small town in oil-rich Texas. This is a variation on the standard monster theme. It has room for all of the terrifying, gruesome moments that horror film audiences enjoy. It also has some unique marketing hooks for the advertising campaign.

At this point, this is just an idea. But there is enough information to formulate a sales approach, including a title, artwork, and lead lines.

Step Two: Researching The Market

It is now possible for the producer to determine a sensible budget for production. By conducting a market research study of box office grosses for similar films over the past several years, a producer may get a pretty good idea of the grosses to expect from *his* film. These box office figures are routinely reported in *Weekly Variety* and are available in back issues either from the *Variety* office at 154 West 46th Street, New York, New York 10036, or from any film library such as the Margaret Herrick Library at the Academy of Motion Picture Arts and Sciences in Los Angeles, the American Film Institute Library, also in Los Angeles, or libraries at universities with strong cinema departments.

The producer must carefully select which films to include in his market research. It is easy to be deceived by grosses for pictures that happened to break out of a conventional run to become box office hits. Those films are the exception and it is foolish to begin a motion picture project expecting such a lucky break. The "hit" figures may be used to sell the investor on the notion that your picture has a *chance* to become a hit. This will be discussed further in the following section, but for now the producer must look to similar films that simply ran a standard circuit for low-budget horror films and never broke out, never became hits. This research will indicate a box office gross that is relatively safe for the producer to expect from his horror film.

A standard industry rule of thumb says that a picture must gross approximately three times its negative cost to break even. The multiple of three takes into account the theater's cut, the distributor's cut, the cost of promoting the film, etc. Once a producer determines his anticipated box office gross, determined by his market research, he divides by three to determine the maximum amount of money to spend on making his film. This will be the amount that he may reasonably expect his film to return. If the producer then budgets his film for less than this amount, the balance will be the expected profits.

The following is an example using fictitious horror films for the market research study:

Title	Worldwide Gross
Swamp Menace	$ 2,525,000
Attic Killers	2,800,000
Death by Design	1,625,000
The Closed Room	2,100,000
Vengeance Is Mine	1,850,000
Fear for Me	2,600,000
Total	$13,500,000

The average worldwide gross for the six films is $13,500,000 ÷ 6 = $2,250,000. Dividing this figure by the standard multiple of three, a producer will see that a sensible maximum budget for this genre will be $750,000. If he budgets the film for less, say $500,-000, the balance of $250,000 will be the expected profits. Obviously, if you can produce a quality picture for even less, say $200,000, your profit potential will be that much greater.

Even with this cautious approach to budgeting, there is no guarantee that a film will be successful. Success depends on the quality of the completed picture, on a reasonable distribution deal, and on the public's reaction to both the film and the advertising campaign. However, investors will be greatly comforted by this market research, knowing that you have hedged your bet, carefully weighing the downside, and budgeting the picture with maximum protection for the investors.

Step Three: Determining the Budget

After completing the foregoing research study to determine the maximum sensible budget for your chosen genre, you must list your potential investors to determine how much money you might realistically raise. This is difficult since you won't know how real your potential investors are until they've actually invested. However, it's a worthwhile exercise and may save you a great deal of trouble. There is nothing worse than going to all the effort of *partially* financing a picture and then giving the money back because you couldn't raise the balance of the budget. This list of investors will be combined with your market research to determine your final budget. Ultimately, you must settle on a figure that is both large enough to produce a competitive film within your chosen genre, and small enough to afford maximum protection for the investor. Above all, it must be an amount that you can realistically expect to raise.

Every aspect of production will be designed to fit within the parameters of the final budget. There is a further discussion of budgeting in Chapter 10, but for now all we need to understand is the process for arriving at this figure.

CHAPTER 5

Selling
the Investor

A producer who has followed the procedure outlined in the previous chapters has all of the information necessary to assemble an investment memorandum with which to approach potential investors. Before doing so, it is important to understand why people invest in motion pictures.

A few years ago, when the tax shelter laws provided tremendous leverage for motion picture investments, the answer to this question was obvious: Motion pictures were a good investment. Today, however, since tax shelters are no longer available for film investments, the statistical reality is that motion pictures are dangerously high-risk, "long shot" investments. Yet people still invest, and independently financed films do get made.

One reason for this apparent contradiction is similar to the reason people bet on a number straight up on a roulette wheel. The statistical odds are against them but there is a *chance* they'll hit a winner, and if they do, they'll win big. Motion pictures are a similar high-risk gamble. Nobody invests in films to beat bank interest; the risks are simply too great. But people do invest if they believe the film stands a chance of becoming a hit. A successful picture today is more successful than ever, and a winning film, like a lucky number on a roulette wheel, can return far greater profits to the investor than the so-called safe investments.

Most films don't make money, but that dismal statistical reality can be restated in a brighter light. Some pictures *do* make money, and of the ones that do, some make a hell of a lot. The history of the industry clearly demonstrates that everyone starting out to make a picture, from the established entrepreneur with the multimillion dollar studio spectacular to the first-time producer with a low-budget film, stands a chance of having a hit. A computer study that researched the success-to-failure ratio of producers and directors over the past twenty-five years, examining some 300 pictures, both majors and independents, arrived at the "absolutely inescapable conclusion that the ratio of success to failure is the same for any producer or director over a given span of time, regardless of reputation." No combination of producer, writer, director, stars, or story concept will guarantee a success. Alternately, it is *possible* for an unknown producer with a no-name, low-budget picture to produce a hit. Therein lies the key to selling any independent motion picture investment.

Another market research study of films in your genre will be helpful when communicating this concept to investors. This time, however, you must look to the pictures in your genre and your budget range that *did* break out to become box office hits. Such a survey might look like this (again, using fictitious titles and grosses):

Title	Worldwide Gross
The Blood Bank	$27,000,000
Kill Joy	$18,000,000
Mask of Doom	$12,000,000
The Open Tomb	$13,500,000

Such exceptional box office grosses are nothing to count on but they demonstrate that it's *possible* for your picture to generate similar grosses.

When talking with investors, talk about the hit. Talk about what's *possible*. A multimillion dollar return on a $500,000 investment is possible, as your market research will indicate. In addition, you've hedged your bet by establishing a budget that will be relatively safe to recoup. You can make no guarantees to your investors, but viewed in this light, you will be offering them an attractive business proposal in spite of the statistical odds against your film's eventual success.

Another reason that people invest in films today is a strictly human one. It has nothing to do with facts and figures. People invest in movies because it's exciting! It's fun! Nobody goes to a cocktail party talking about their commodity investments, but people love to talk about their movie investments. There is a certain glamour attached to it. Consider the people who invest in films. They are not generally film people, for whom the magic and glamour of the movies don't exist. Film people invest in safer things such as real estate. The people who invest in films are real estate people, or doctors or lawyers. They are generally professional people with high-risk gambling money—venture capital looking for an exciting investment. Offer them an opportunity to visit the set, to watch the filming and meet the actors. This is a daily routine for people in the film industry but to outside investors, it's something special. Even if they don't visit the set, the idea of an involvement in the entertainment world, especially movies, has a very special appeal.

You'll find, incidentally, that there is a downside to the glamour of the movies. As I said before, people love to talk about film investments. Consequently, you will find many people who will talk forever about the possibility of investing, but will never come through with a check. Don't let this discourage you. It's a reflection on the nature of the investment, not on your project or your ability to sell. The bottom line in seeking investment is getting the check. I've learned from bitter experience and from countless expectations and disappointments that nothing is real but the check. Don't count on the promises and verbal commitments of prospective investors until you've actually got the check and it has cleared through their bank.

CHAPTER 6

Variations on the Escrow Account

As stated earlier, the investor's money is placed in a third-party escrow account until a certain total is reached, generally the entire budget. Only then is the money released to the general partner. This is to prevent the general partner from spending any money until he has raised the entire budget. Should the general partner spend the first $50,000 that comes in, and then find himself unable to raise the balance of the budget, the picture will never be made and the first investors will have lost their money. The investors are risking their money on the film, not on the producer's ability to finance the film.

There are, however, variations on this basic theme. Assuming all of the limited partners agree, the escrow account may be released before the entire budget is raised. For example, if a budget of $500,000 is broken down as in the "Budget" section of the investment memorandum, as follows:

Cost of financing (4%)	$ 20,000
Preproduction	30,000
Production	275,000
Postproduction	125,000
Subtotal	450,000
Contingency (11%)	50,000
Total	$500,000

a producer might reasonably argue that the money should be released when the escrow account contains enough money to cover costs through principal photography—the production phase. This amount would be $30,000 for preproduction, plus $275,000 for production, plus $14,200 for the 4 percent cost of financing, plus $35,500 for the 11 percent contingency rounded off equals $320,000. The producer may argue that the most difficult money to raise is the preproduction and production money.

These first phases entail the highest degree of risk. What if the production is delayed due to unexpected weather, or what if the director is ill for two weeks during production? What if the film for an expensive day's shooting is damaged in the laboratory, or lost? These are potential risks, and often a modestly budgeted film cannot afford elaborate insurance policies and completion guarantees to cover these risks. Once the film is in the can, the risk for investors is greatly reduced. The balance of $180,000 will be relatively easy to raise once principal photography is completed, either from additional investors or perhaps from a distribution advance.

In a situation such as this, when the escrow account is released prior to completion of financing, the initial investors (class A investors) are taking a greater risk than the postproduction class B investors. It is therefore reasonable to offer class A investors a favored payback position to compensate for their additional risk. In other words, class A partners might be allowed to recoup their entire investment prior to class B partners receiving anything.

By structuring the escrow account in this way, a producer can begin making his picture with partial financing and raise the balance of the budget during production and postproduction. It is rarely easy to raise money, but the job becomes less difficult when you can invite potential investors to the set during production, or into the cutting room to view dailies.

At these stages, your project is no longer just words on paper. It's a concrete reality. It will be evident to the potential class B partners that you're going to make the film whether they invest or not. You're not depending on their investment to make your first move. This is an added plus for the producer since it's easiest to raise money when you're not desperate for money. As with finding a job, it's easy to find a job when you've got a job, but much more difficult when you're unemployed.

This approach can be broken down even further into class C partners, class D partners, and so forth. But it's best to keep the structure as simple as possible, ideally with one class of investor supplying the entire budget.

CHAPTER 7

The Development Company

After conducting a market research survey to determine the maximum sensible budget for your picture, and after listing all of your sources for investment to determine how much money you might realistically raise, you may find that you don't have enough contacts to raise enough money to produce a competitive film within your chosen genre.

Your project doesn't have to die simply because you don't have an obvious route to complete financing. You have the option of forming a development company to develop and package your project in such a way as to make production financing possible. In other words, if you don't have enough financing available through immediate sources, based solely on the material you have assembled (possibly just an idea at this point), you may use the limited partnership structure to form a development company for the purpose of assembling whatever elements, in your opinion, will make it possible to raise production financing.

Perhaps you'll need to raise the equivalent of your preproduction budget (in our previous example, the preproduction figure was $30,000) in order to assemble a complete production package of screenplay, cast, director, locations, detailed budget, shooting schedule, storyboard, etc. With this package under your belt, a whole new world of financing opportunities will open up to you. You're no longer limited to people who you know personally and who will invest simply because of an idea and your good word. You will have a substantially developed package that may be offered not only to private investors but to studios and distributors as well.

Development company investment is an extremely high-risk

proposition—far more so than production financing since many more pictures are developed than are produced. The consolation for the development company investor is that the partnership is usually structured so that development costs are built in to the production budget and are paid back to the development company investors upon completion of production financing. In other words, the development company investors are risking their investment capital not on the success of the picture but on the producer's ability to assemble a package of elements that will result in successful production financing.

In addition to recoupment of capital upon completion of production financing, the limited partners in a limited partnership development company will also have a profit participation in the film. This will generally be defined as a percentage of the general partner's share of profits. If the finished picture is successful, the development company investors will see profits along with everyone else. But even if the picture is a total failure, as long as it's financed, they will get their money back.

The limited partners in a limited partnership development company may require the general partner to guarantee a minimum participation in the production financing structure in order to ensure that they don't wind up with an insignificant percentage of the film's profits. As an example, a producer might offer the development company limited partners recoupment of their capital investment upon completion of production financing; 25 percent of all profits that the general partner receives from the film; and a guarantee that the general partner will offer no more than 50 percent profit participation in the film in return for production financing. In this way, the development company investors are assured a minimum 12.5 percent profit participation in the film, according to the following formula: 100 percent of the partnership distributable cash for the production financing limited partnership will be divided 50 percent to the general partner, 50 percent to the production financing limited partners. The general partner's 50 percent share equals 100 percent of the partnership distributable cash for the development company limited partnership and will be divided 75 percent to the general partner, 25 percent to the development company limited partners. The development company limited partners' 25 percent share of the development company's partnership distributable cash is equal to 12.5 percent of the total partnership distributable cash for the production financing limited partnership.

What the general partner offers the limited partners in a development company, and what restriction the limited partners place on the general partner's production financing negotiations, depend on the specifics of each project. Ultimately, throughout the process of financing, the producer must offer whatever is necessary in order to raise the money while at the same time maintaining a reasonable share of the film's profits for himself. He mustn't sacrifice so much that the project is no longer worth his while.

PART 2

The Preproduction Package

Introduction

The order in which preproduction elements are assembled varies from project to project. In some cases, complete production financing will be secured prior to beginning this phase. In other cases, a development company will assemble many of these elements such as script, budget, and cast. Perhaps a producer will borrow from a bank, or use savings, to begin the process. There are several permutations and the information contained in this part applies to all of them.

For the sake of simplicity, in the following discussion, I will assume two things: first, that the producer has completed production financing and is no longer concerned with legal structures but can devote full time to producing the picture; second, that the producer has raised the financing based only on an *idea* for a film, or perhaps a simple story line. Consequently, this section will examine the preproduction process, beginning with an idea for a film and following its development and packaging up to the first day of principal photography.

A general philosophy to apply during preproduction of a modest- or low-budget picture is "shoot for the moon, then compromise to fit the budget." Don't restrict yourself to actors, crew members, locations, and other elements that you're certain will be available within your budget. Try for more. In doing so, you'll get many rejections but you'll also get a few "yes's." In approaching preproduction in this way, you will know, when you've completed packaging your picture, that you have assembled the finest elements available within your budget; you will have set the highest standards possible for your picture. You will find that this attitude is contagious. It will spark the enthusiasm of everyone around you. People on all levels of production respond to a producer who is sincerely trying to make the best film possible within his budget.

CHAPTER 8

The Screenplay

If it were possible to overstate the importance of the story structure and screenplay for a film, I would do so. The screenplay is the foundation for a picture and it had better be good or everything else will crumble around it.

There is a saying in the business: "If it ain't on the page, it ain't on the stage." Rarely will a director make a good picture from a bad script. A director can cover flaws in the script, perhaps finding innovative ways to make tedious dialogue interesting to watch, but if he's working with a weak script, the finished picture will probably be just as weak.

Another reason to place strong emphasis on the screenplay is that given two scripts with essentially the same characters and production values, the better script *will cost less to produce.* There is an abundance of mediocre material floating around. Consequently, actors and even technicians will often take a sizable cut in salary for the opportunity to work with a sincere producer on a good script. This is especially true with a modest- or low-budget picture where financial considerations are paramount. If a producer settles for a routine story with shallow characters, depending solely on exploitation value to sell the picture, he'll find himself struggling with mediocre talent and little enthusiasm all the way down the line. But if he goes through the extra pain and effort necessary to generate a good script with a solid story structure and compelling characters, he will find a whole world of otherwise unavailable talent opening up to him.

In general, the process for writing a screenplay follows these stages:

1. *Treatment:* An essay style description of the story and characters. There is no specific length, but a treatment generally runs twenty-five to thirty pages.
2. *First Draft:* Complete screenplay in standard form. Usually longer than the final draft.
3. *Second draft:* A rewrite of the first draft.
4. *Polish:* Revisions of specific scenes. Not a complete rewrite.

A screenplay may undergo any number of treatments, drafts, and polishes before being either abandoned or completed. Generally, a producer will negotiate for a specific number of writing phases, paying a predetermined portion of the total writer's fee at the beginning of each phase.

If the project is in development (i.e., production financing has not yet been committed), the producer may negotiate for a substantial portion of the writer's fee to be paid only if the picture is financed. This is obviously an incentive for the writer to do his best since successful production financing will no doubt depend on the quality of the screenplay. However, in the long run it will cost the producer more. The writer will demand a larger total fee in return for deferring a portion of his fee contingent upon successful production financing. It is also common for a writer to receive a percentage of the film's profits. This, of course, is another incentive for him to do his best work.

Acquiring an Existing Literary Property

An existing literary property may be a completed screenplay or a published work such as a novel, short story, or magazine article.

A producer wishing to acquire the motion picture and television rights to a completed screenplay must first contact the author or the author's agent to determine the availability of the property. Contact information for the writer or the agent will probably be included on the title page of the screenplay. If not, the producer can usually find the information in the *Writers Guild Directory* or by contacting the Writers Guild of America at the address and phone number listed in the *Pacific Coast Studio Directory*. Both of these publications are listed in Appendix E.

If the property is available, the producer or his representative will negotiate for the appropriate rights including:

- all motion picture rights including sequel and remake rights
- all television rights including television series rights
- all merchandising rights associated with the above motion picture and television rights (see Chapter 23)
- publishing rights including novelization of the screenplay

A producer inexperienced in such negotiations should obtain the services of an appropriate attorney or literary agent. Such representatives may be found either through word-of-mouth reputation within the film community or, in the case of an attorney, by following the procedure outlined in Chapter 1. Most of the established literary agencies have agents within their organizations who are experienced in this type of negotiation. A list of literary agencies may be found in the *Pacific Coast Studio Directory.*

If a producer engages the services of an attorney to negotiate on his behalf, the attorney will most likely charge the producer on an hourly basis for his services. If a producer engages a literary agent to handle the negotiations, the agent will not charge the producer for his services nor will he take a percentage of whatever money changes hands. He will, however, insist that he retain the exclusive right to negotiate the producer's development and/or production deal for the property. If such a deal transpires, the agent will take the standard 10 percent commission on the producer's development and/or production fee.

Occasionally a producer will purchase a completed screenplay outright, in which case he will own it. More often, however, he will purchase an option for substantially less money, which gives him the exclusive right to purchase the property within a specified period of time. The purpose of the option is to allow the producer to tie up the rights to the property for a given period of time, during which he will seek development and/or production financing, secure in the knowledge that if he succeeds he has the exclusive right to purchase the property.

The price of an option is entirely negotiable and is paid against the eventual total purchase price of the property. For example, if the total purchase price is $75,000 and the option costs $3,000, the balance due the author, assuming the producer chooses to exercise his option and purchase the property, is $72,000. The time limit on an option is also negotiable. It can run anywhere from a few days to several years. Commonly, an option period runs between six and twelve months.

When the option period expires, the producer may either purchase the property, extend his option, or lose both the money he paid for the option and his rights to the property. Most option agreements provide for an extention of the option, usually under the same terms as in the original option.

An option agreement functions as an entire contract between a producer and an author, including provisions for the eventual success of the completed film. Such provisions include the total purchase price of the property, the author's percentage participation in the film's profits, the size and placement of the author's credit both on the picture and in paid advertising and promotional materials, and the author's rights in the event that a sequel, remake, television movie, and/or television series is produced.

A producer wishing to acquire the motion picture and television rights to a published work such as a novel, short story, or magazine article must first contact the publisher or magazine to determine the availability of the material and who controls the rights. Ownership of these rights is subject to negotiation between the author and the publisher. An established author with a substantial track record is more likely to retain these rights than an author publishing his first work. Sometimes these rights are shared between the publisher and the author, in which case the publishing contract will stipulate which party is empowered to negotiate the sale of these rights. If the author controls the rights, the publisher will refer the producer to the author or to the agent who negotiated the publication deal on behalf of the author.

Assuming the work is available, negotiations begin. Again, it is imperative that the producer either be skilled in this type of negotiation or that he obtain the services of an appropriate representative—either an attorney or an agent—to negotiate on his behalf. Negotiating for the rights to a published work is a specialized area so it is important that the producer take time to select carefully an experienced representative. If a producer fails to do so, certain rights to which he is entitled may be left out of the contract, thereby reducing the value of the option and, consequently, reducing the producer's negotiating strength with potential financiers.

In the case of a published work, the rights for which one must negotiate are similar to those for a completed screenplay. Publication rights are obviously excluded since those rights are already tied in to a publisher. However, the producer should obtain the right to publish a synopsis of the material (usually limited to between 7,500 and 10,000 words) to be used for noncommercial purposes in promotional materials such as pamphlets, brochures, and press releases.

In some cases, a producer will pay an outright purchase price for ownership of the motion picture and television rights to a published work. However, it is far more common to purchase an option on the material against an eventual purchase price. Optioning a published work serves the same purpose as optioning a completed screenplay—it allows the producer to tie up the rights to a property for a specified period of time, during which he will pursue development and/or production financing.

The amount of money paid for an option on a published work varies enormously depending on the material in question. A highly commercial short story by an established author appearing in a current issue of a major magazine will be considerably more difficult and more expensive to option than a short story that appeared twenty years ago in a lesser publication. The time limit on such an option also varies and is open to negotiation. As with a completed screenplay, an option period for a published work commonly runs between six and twelve months.

Once a producer has sealed his option, he may develop the property. This includes such things as hiring someone to write a screenplay based on the optioned material, seeking commitments from a director and principal cast members, and hiring a production manager to assemble a production budget and shooting schedule. In some cases the producer will finance this development himself. More often, however, he will seek a development deal with a financier based solely on the optioned material. If he succeeds, the financier will pick up the cost of the option and pay for the development of the property, including paying a fee to the producer for supervising such development.

Having secured the rights to a property, and having obtained development financing, the producer is now faced with the critical task of selecting an appropriate person to write the screenplay.

Selecting a Writer

If you have acquired the rights to a published work, or if you have an original idea for a film, it is safe to assume that you have in mind a *style* in which you would like to see your project executed. Look for a writer who exhibits a style and a sensitivity for the kind of picture you're making, be it action, comedy, suspense, whatever. To go with an untried writer in any given area is dangerous. Someone who has written several comedies may also be able to write suspense, but unless you see an example of it, you really can't be sure.

Even within a stylistic category, you must be highly selective. Each category covers a broad spectrum of styles. Someone who writes suspense may not write with a style that fits your image of how a particular suspense story should be treated. I am using terms such as style and sensitivity because there is no concrete formula or guideline for selecting a writer.

The best way to select the most appropriate writer for your film is to watch films. When you've selected a few pictures that exhibit the writing style you're after, *read the screenplays* for those films. You will learn a great deal more about the writer by reading his screenplay than by watching the finished film. Screenplays are available from film libraries, university cinema departments, or from the writer's agent.

The Writers Guild of America publishes a directory that lists member writers of both the West Coast and East Coast branches of the guild, along with many of their credits. The directory is updated every few years and is available for $5.00 (see Appendix E). A complete list of a particular member writer's credits may be obtained by phoning the Writers Guild in Los Angeles or New York, depending on whether the writer is a member of the West Coast or East Coat branch of the guild.

To contact the writer's agent, refer to the *Writers Guild Directory* or call the Writers Guild of America and tell them the name of the writer whose agent you wish to contact. They have this information on file and offer it as a service to producers. If the agents tell you that all of your chosen writers are unavailable, either because of prior commitments or because you can't afford them, the agents will undoubtedly recommend other writers within their agency. Having gone to the agent requesting a particular writer, you will have communicated to that agent in the most specific way possible the kind of writer you're after. You will also have set a standard of excellence for your project that will inevitably affect the attitude of the agent.

You can also contact literary agents without having a particular writer in mind. A reference guide for literary agents may be found in the *Pacific Coast Studio Directory* listed in Appendix E.

When discussing your project with the agent, tell him your budget limitations and the style of writing you're after. Be as specific as possible; use examples from well-known films to communicate what you're seeking. The agents will make recommendations and send you sample screenplays. Remember that it's the agent's job to find work for his clients. Remember also that if you're a producer with money to spend, every agency door is wide open. The only thing in your path will be a welcome mat.

Before making a final decision about the best writer for your project, ask the agent to send you at least two samples. It is important that the writer be consistently competent and the only way to judge this is to read several scripts.

If you are unable to afford the Writer's Guild of America minimum wage for your writer, you will have to go outside this standard system and locate an unrepresented, generally unpublished, unproduced writer. Good ones exist but are hard to find. The best way to find them is by word-of-mouth reputation. Talk to as many people as you can about what you're looking for and eventually it will come your way.

Working with the Writer (Script versus Budget)

If a producer establishes a fixed budget prior to starting the script (as described in Chapter 4) he must work very closely with the writer to ensure that the finished script is molded to fit the budget. The producer must carefully and completely budget each treatment, draft, and polish along the way, working with the writer to juggle the script so as to arrive at an optimum screenplay within the predetermined budget.

Many ideas with great merit will be discarded because of the budget. However, compromising in this way at the concept level, you don't run the risk of compromising during production and having an awkward scene in the finished film simply because you really couldn't afford to shoot it in the first place.

Any scene in your screenplay that you cannot afford to execute at the level of excellence that you set for your entire project must be discarded. This often means racking your brain to come up with an equally effective but less expensive scene. The time to make these compromises is during the writing. If you wait until you're on the set, you'll be trying to do the impossible and the compromises that you will be forced to make during production will stand out like sore thumbs in the finished film.

This constant juggling and rejuggling of script versus budget is not the ideal way to write the best possible screenplay, but if you're working within a small budget, it's probably the *only* way to produce a first-rate picture. This kind of careful, detailed planning will clearly evidence itself in a consistent standard of excellence throughout your finished film.

Script Timing

When you arrive at a draft of your screenplay that seems relatively close to what you're after, have it timed. The standard rule of thumb, one minute of screen time for each page written in standard screenplay form, is a useful guide, but its accuracy will vary depending on the style of the writer and the nature of the material. A more accurate timing may be obtained from a competent script supervisor. This will cost a few hundred dollars, but if it saves you from shooting more scenes than you need or from writing more material when you have enough, it's worth the expense. Actually, it's worth it just to *know* how long your film will run.

Script supervisors use a variety of methods to time scripts. Some will simply lock themselves in a room with the script and a stopwatch and act out every scene in the film. After many years of experience timing shots and sequences on the set (a routine responsibility for a script supervisor) and subsequently comparing notes with the running time of the finished film, script supervisors develop a remarkably accurate sense for timing scenes from a screenplay.

Table 3 offers an example of the kind of information to expect from a detailed script timing.

Table 3 **Sample Page from Script Timing**

Title ______________________ Page ________

Scene numbers	*Sets and action*	*Pages*	*Time*
104	*Interior Richard's Castle* Richard tells Alexis how he lost his kingdom.	3 4/8	3:05
105–106	*Interior Richard's Castle* Alexis follows Richard down stone steps.	3/8	0:27
107	*Interior Subterranean Chamber* Alexis is introduced to the knowledge of the kings.	6/8	1:06
108–110	*Montage: Interior Chamber* Alexis reads the scrolls as Richard looks on.	4/8	0:45
111	*Exterior Woodland Pool* Richard admonishes Alexis, calls for the test.	1 7/8	2:20
112–114	*Exterior Forest* Alexis rescues Jeremy and learns of the reward.	1 3/8	1:58
115	*Exterior Forest* Alexis sends Jeremy on his way.	1 2/8	1:24
116	*Exterior Richard's Castle* Alexis enters the castle.	1/8	0:12
117	*Interior Castle* Alexis sees herself in the mirror, slightly aged.	3/8	0:40
118	*Interior Castle* Alexis and Richard discuss the future.	1 1/8	1:04

Table 3 (cont.)

Title ————————————————— Page —————

Scene numbers	Sets and action	Pages	Time
119–124	*Exterior Forest* Richard hands Alexis a flower and she rides off.	1⅛	1:44
125,127,129, 131	*Exterior Encampment* Alexis says she has come to assist Jeremy.	3	4:05

The running time of a film will hopefully be determined by the length that most effectively tells the story. Feature films commonly run between 90 and 110 minutes. There are, however, films that run as short as 75 minutes and others that run in excess of 3 hours. From the theater owner's point of view, 100 minutes is ideal. This allows him to schedule showings every 2 hours with 20 minutes in between to sell tickets and popcorn and run previews of coming attractions.

CHAPTER 9

Selecting the Director, the Unit Production Manager, and the First Assistant Director

The Director

The screenplay is the foundation upon which a film is built, but it is the director who will translate the words on paper into the images and sounds of a film. It is best to bring a director into a project as early as possible. He will undoubtedly have contributions to make to the screenplay at one stage or another and if his thoughts can be incorporated during the early stages of writing, so much the better. If you can bring together a writer and director who work well together, the director will make contributions to the script right from the start. The director probably won't do the writing, but he and the writer will exchange concepts and ideas that will guide the development of the screenplay. The more a director understands about the structure of the story and the nature of the characters involved, the better will be his ability to translate the story onto film with a vision consistent with the writer's and the better equipped he will be to contribute to such things as casting.

When selecting a director, a producer must look for finished films that exhibit a style consistent with the producer's vision of his film. The producer must also consider the director's experience and reputation for working within the schedule and budget limitations anticipated for his project. It is generally safer to hire a director who has experience working on films smaller than yours rather than larger. When exploring a director's reputation it is often helpful to talk with the producers and/or production managers from his previous films. These individuals can usually be contacted through the production companies that made their films or through the distribution companies that released them.

If you are considering directors who are members of the Directors Guild of America (DGA) you can obtain a list of their credits and information about their agency representation by phoning the Directors Guild in Los Angeles, Chicago, or New York. You may also wish to refer to the *Directors Guild of America Membership Directory,* which is updated and published annually. This directory lists all member directors across the country along with agency information and many of their credits. This publication is available for $8.00 from the Directors Guild at the address listed in Appendix E.

If none of your selected directors is available for your project, their agents will undoubtedly recommend others. As with writers, you can also go directly to agents for recommendations without having a particular director in mind. Describe your picture and your budget limitations to the agent and if he has any appropriate people available he'll recommend them.

If you select a director who is not represented by an agent, but who is a member of the Director's Guild of America, you can write to that person, or leave a message for him, in care of the Director's Guild.

If you have a potential director in mind who is not a guild member, you can generally contact him through the production company or the distributor of the film upon which you based your selection.

If you select a director without seeing his work, chances are he's a personal friend and you could have skipped all of the above.

The Unit Production Manager and the First Assistant Director

One of the most important members of your team during pre-production and production will be the unit production manager. In essence, the production manager is responsible for the logistics of production through completion of principal photography. Together with the producer, he will finalize a detailed production budget.

Often, a production manager alone will write the entire budget for a film. He will also juggle all of the production elements into an economically efficient shooting schedule. He is usually empowered to negotiate deals for crew, equipment, locations, catering, etc., on behalf of the producer. This position requires a highly skilled, experienced individual with an in-depth nuts-and-bolts knowledge of motion picture production; it also requires a person with sensitivity, warmth, and understanding.

A production manager must walk the fine line between caring for the needs of the cast and crew (from supplying them with adequate film stock to ensuring that rest rooms are kept clean), letting each individual involved in the production know that his or her needs are being well looked after, while at the same time maintaining the producer's budget and schedule.

The production manager's work is interrelated with that of the first assistant director and both should be involved in preproduction as early as possible. The function of the first assistant director is discussed further in Chapter 17, but for now it is important to understand that he is responsible for running the production *on the set,* ensuring that everything remains on schedule. If a conflict arises between the planned shooting schedule and the director's wishes, it is up to the first assistant director to inform the director of the conflict. If the director wishes to proceed at the expense of the schedule, the first assistant director must then fight with the production manager on behalf of the director. If the production manager cannot find a way to accommodate the director within the budget and schedule, it is up to the production manager, not the first assistant director, to enforce the planned schedule.

On large-budget productions, the first assistant director is hired very early in the preproduction phase and is often responsible for organizing the shooting schedule. On smaller-budget pictures, this is rarely affordable and the schedule is initially assembled by the production manager.

Production managers and assistant directors are organized within the DGA. Consequently, if you sign a DGA contract in order to use a guild director, you must also use DGA support personnel. The *Directors Guild of America Membership Directory* lists all member production managers and assistant directors along with their phone numbers or agency representation and many of their credits. The most experienced production managers and assistant directors are members of the guild, but it is possible to find highly qualified nonguild people for these positions. Since there is no structured organization for nonguild people, one way to find them is by word-of-mouth reputation. Let your needs be known to as many people as possible within your film community and eventually the right people will come your way.

Another approach is to contact trade publications such as *Variety* and *The Hollywood Reporter* with information about your project. These papers routinely publish announcements about upcoming productions. Production personnel watch the trades for this information and often contact producers to offer their services. You can also take out paid advertisements in trade publications announcing your production plans.

It is important to hire a production manager and a first assistant director who believe in your project and are dedicated to its successful completion. Their attitudes will greatly influence the morale of everyone else involved.

Because of the profound influence the production manager and first assistant director will have on your picture, it is important that they be accustomed to working within the budget and schedule parameters of your film. A production manager or first assistant director who works regularly on multimillion dollar major studio productions may be ill-suited for a modestly budgeted independent project. Alternately, a production manager or first assistant director experienced only in low-budget films is usually a poor choice for an elaborate studio spectacular.

CHAPTER 10

The Budget

This chapter was preceded with discussions about the director, unit production manager, and first assistant director in order to stress the importance of selecting these people prior to finalizing the budget and schedule for your film. A truly accurate budget and schedule are almost impossible to assemble without their input.

One hears all the time about pictures going overbudget and overschedule. The studio blames the producer who passes the blame onto the director, or the star, or the cinematographer. Without question, there are cases in which these individuals contribute to the problem, but that doesn't come close to explaining why *most* pictures go overbudget and overschedule.

The truth is that most pictures are *under* budgeted and *under* scheduled to begin with. This is easily understood by anyone who has tried to get a picture off the ground. If you can convince investors or a studio that you can make a picture for less money in less time, it will be that much easier to finance. Consequently, producers often find themselves in the uncomfortable position of whittling their budgets unrealistically, or rationalizing that they can really do it for less, in order to make their project more appealing to potential sources of financing. But they suffer for it in the long run. Once production begins, a different attitude sets in. The producer who made those budget compromises on paper will do everything in his power to make the production as good as possible and he'll find himself torn. Either the project goes overbudget or the quality deteriorates below the level of excellence that he advertised to the investors. The difficulty of financing films is the principal cause of this painful dilemma. Remember that every single element in the production hinges on the budget. If you rationalize too optimistically when writing the final budget, the problems you create will haunt you throughout the making of your film. This is especially true on a modestly budgeted independent picture with little protection for overbudget costs.

If you have what should be a $500,000 project that you've managed to squeeze into a $450,000 budget and everyone involved does his utmost to stay within budget, even making some painful compromises, your project may still be $25,000 overbudget when you enter the post production phase.

If the production phase of the budget is any indication of how tightly postproduction is budgeted, you're in real trouble. Where does the money come from? Do you cut an already meager sound effects budget in half? Do you cut the music budget by a third? Do you eliminate dialogue looping? Do you go to a second-rate mixing facility? Or a third-rate optical house? You may do all of the above and still not fall within your $450,000 budget. Chances are that you will ultimately spend $500,000 on the picture and will have created an enormous headache for yourself by not facing that reality in the first place.

If you stick adamantly to an unrealistic budget, you will be forced to make severe compromises, and cutbacks in the quality of any portion of your film will drag down the quality of everything else in the film. You must strive for the highest level of quality attainable within your budget *throughout every aspect of production.* Everything in your film depends on everything else. You may go overbudget during principal photography in order to attain a certain level of quality, but if you get into postproduction and can't afford to maintain that level, your extra effort and expense during production will go right down the drain. You must strive for a consistent level of quality.

There are people in the industry who say that any film can be made for any amount of money. In theory, perhaps, it's true. I suppose they could have made *Gone with the Wind* in one location, using a backyard, a stucco house, and friends from the neighborhood, but chances are it wouldn't have been very successful. For any screenplay, there is a bottom-line budget, a minimum amount of money necessary to produce a film that meets the standards of quality *for that film's anticipated marketplace.* If your available financing is less than that minimum budget figure, change the script and rebudget until you've got a picture you can afford to make.

When assembling the budget, it is important to give equal emphasis to all stages of production. Production managers often make the mistake of carefully budgeting the principal photography stage, but only casually budgeting for postproduction. This is because, first, the principal photography stage is the most exciting aspect of production and, second, because production managers are not involved in postproduction and consequently they often know little about it. It is important for the production manager to consult with the director and the editor in order to budget postproduction accurately. If the principal photography stage turns out to be exceptional, there is usually room to expand the postproduction budget but this is not something to count on. All stages of production must be budgeted with equal care and accuracy right from the start.

It is important to bear in mind that even with a carefully planned budget, the producer and production manager must remain flexible enough to change the budget, if necessary, to accommodate unanticipated problems. Such changes should be made only if they improve the overall end result, not simply with an eye to solving an immediate problem.

The Ideal Budget

Feature motion picture budgets can range anywhere from a few thousand dollars to tens of millions. Two extremes are *Return of the Secaucus Seven,* made for $60,000, and *Annie,* made for $42 million. The average budget for a studio-affiliated feature is around $10 million; the average budget for a low-budget independent feature is $300,000.

The optimum figure, the budget for which producers strive, is that magic figure that will result in a maximum return on the invested dollar. This is not necessarily the minimum, bottom-line figure. For example, given three different production budgets for the same screenplay, the box office grosses might look like this:

Budget	$ 500,000	$ 1,200,000	$ 7,000,000
Box Office	3,000,000	17,900,000	22,000,000
Gross:			
Budget × 3 =			
breakeven point	− 1,500,000	− 3,600,000	− 21,000,000
Box office gross after			
breakeven:	=$1,500,000	=$14,300,000	=$1,000,000

The box office gross after the breakeven point is split between theater owners, subdistributors, national and international distributors, etc. In each of the three cases, there is a profit beyond the breakeven point for the investors. The $500,000 investors will realize a reasonable profit per dollar invested. The $7 million investors will realize very little profit, but the $1.2 million investors will realize an enormous return on their investment. The $500,000 project was sensible, the $7 million project was not, but the $1 million figure was the closest to an optimum budget.

When a producer has the flexibility to develop an ideal budget as opposed to a bottom-line budget, he is faced with the difficult task of determining what that figure should be. This approach to budgeting requires, first, writing an optimum screenplay without significant compromises for the budget and, second, basing the production budget on three things: the script; the potential market; the producer's ability to package elements with the script that will appeal to a maximum number of people within that market.

Costs for these elements must be balanced with the projected income they will generate. The important thing is that the costs of these added elements are not so great as to reduce the return on the invested dollar. For example, a series of elaborate special effects may increase the box office gross to such an extent that the investors realize an additional $1 million return. However, if the cost for these special effects exceeded $1 million, the additional expense will decrease the overall return per invested dollar.

The optimum, ideal budget is rarely achieved in motion picture production. It is an extremely difficult thing to gauge and it becomes increasingly difficult with the complexity of the project. A producer, in attempting to determine an optimum budget, must depend on the counsel of many specialists, from stunt coordinators to sound engineers, but eventually he must make the decisions, cross his fingers, and move on.

The Standard Budget

A motion picture budget is generally broken down into *above-the-line* costs and *below-the-line* costs. Above-the-line includes producer, director, writer, and principal talent. These are often fixed fees. Below-the-line is everything else, including atmosphere talent, technicians, equipment, location costs, and film stock.

The ratio between above-the-line and below-the-line costs varies from picture to picture. A reasonable balance for a big-budget film might be one-third of the budget above-the-line and two-thirds below-the-line. The breakdown of a standard budget, based on statistical averages from hundreds of film budgets, is 5 percent for the story and screenplay, 5 percent for the producer and director, 20 percent for the cast, 20 percent for studio overhead, 35 percent for crew, sets, costumes, equipment, film stock, etc., 5 percent for taxes, and 10 percent for contingencies. As a general rule, the lower the budget the greater will be the percentage of the budget spent below-the-line. In other words, the *relative* costs for producer, director, screenplay, and cast are less for small-budget pictures. A major superstar actor might receive $2 million or more for work on a single picture, whereas on a very low-budget film the entire cast might work for nothing more than free lunches and possibly a share in the film's profits. In the case of *Return of the Secaucus Seven,* the cost of film stock alone consumed one-third of the entire production budget.

The cost for below-the-line personnel is generally between 11 and 15 percent of the total budget regardless of the size of the budget. These costs may be as low as 8 percent or as high as 25 percent depending on the nature of the picture. The highest percentage of expenses for below-the-line personnel are incurred by films that involve elaborate special effects and exotic sets such as *Superman* and *Moonraker.*

A production manager writing a budget for a major studio film is faced with an enormously sophisticated task. He will base his cost estimates primarily on past experience with other films, but he will also rely on other production managers for counsel, often exchanging budgets and comparing figures, especially if the picture he's budgeting is to be shot in a location with which he is not fully familiar. Experienced production managers know whom to call for assistance when budgeting costs for specialty areas such as stunts and special effects. They will obtain input from specialists in these areas whose estimates for the costs in their particular departments will be incorporated into the final budget.

Because of the complexity of this task and the number of variables involved, production managers commonly request a production accountant to verify their figures, often using a portion of their fee to pay for this service. A production accountant is the person who sets up and maintains the books and payroll system throughout the making of a film and is therefore in a knowledgeable position to verify a production manager's cost estimates.

Reference sources for budgeting information that production managers find helpful are *Brooks' Standard Rate Book, Guide to Location Information,* the *Hollywood Production Manual,* and the *Pacific Coast Studio Directory.* Additional information regarding these publications may be found in Appendix E.

Table 4 is a sample "top sheet" for a $7 million studio budget. A detailed breakdown of this budget may be found in Appendix B.

Table 4   **Sample Budget Recap**

Title ———————————————— Producer ——————

Production company —————— Director ——————

Production manager —————— Script dated ————

Above-the-line costs

1100	Story rights and continuity	$ 48,695	
1200	Producer's unit	213,921	
1300	Direction	155,500	
1400	Cast	1,039,972	
1500	Traveling and living cost	52,204	
1600	Fringe benefits	100,618	
Total above-the-line			$1,610,910

Below-the-line-costs
    Production period

2000	Production staff	$ 169,525	
2100	Extra talent	92,708	
2200	Set design	122,150	
2300	Set construction	741,610	

Table 4 (cont.)

Below-the-line-costs
  Production period

2400	Set striking	20,000	
2500	Set operations	119,900	
2600	Special effects	103,700	
2700	Set dressing	121,300	
2800	Property	188,900	
2900	Men's wardrobe	102,000	
3000	Women's wardrobe	incl.	
3100	Makeup and hairdressing	73,850	
3200	Lighting	126,800	
3300	Camera	201,850	
3400	Production sound	50,961	
3500	Transportation	362,800	
3600	Locations	677,520	
3700	Film and laboratory	109,863	
3800	Process	20,000	
3900	Second unit	—	
4000	Tests	6,000	
4100	Miscellaneous expenses	—	
4200	Fringe Benefits	626,062	$4,037,499

  Editing period

4500	Film editing	$ 157,300	
4600	Music	85,000	
4700	Sound	40,000	
4800	Film and laboratory	47,500	
4900	Main and end titles	6,000	
5000	Fringe benefits	65,000	400,800

Other costs

6700	Insurance	140,000	
6800	General expense	60,464	
6900	Retroactive Salaries	—	200,464
Total below-the-line			4,638,763
Total direct costs			6,249,673
1.5% Legal			93,745
Add 10% contingency (below-the-line only)			461,376
Add 2% finder's fee			136,096

Total budget $6,940,890

The Low-Budget Budget

There are many systems for "ballparking" budgets, but the lower the budget, the more dangerous this becomes. This is largely because for low-budget films, any small change is a large percentage of the total, e.g., a small change in schedule can make a great difference in the budget. A multimillion dollar film can afford a few days' leeway, but that same few days for a low-budget film may have a disastrous effect. For many low-budget films there is little or no protection for overbudget costs.

The lower the budget, the more heavily weighted will be the below-the-line nonfixed fee costs. Extremely low-budget, non-guild, nonunion films in which the producer, writer, director, and actors work for nothing, other than (hopefully) a share in the film's profits, will have a zero above-the-line budget. Consequently, below-the-line costs for low-budget films must be examined with great care and in great detail.

Since the making of a film is dependent upon so many unpredictable variables, not the least of which is the weather, one solution to budgeting is to raise the contingency from a standard 10 percent to 20 percent. The latter is probably more realistic for most low-budget films. Begin by budgeting every aspect of your film down to the minutest detail, from the number of rolls of gaffer's tape to the number of razor blades the assistant editor will use six months down the road. A good production manager will be able to help estimate many of these costs quite accurately. Once you've listed every conceivable expense for your entire production, add 10 percent for the things you forgot. Then add another 10 percent for contingencies. Investors understand that a reasonable contingency figure is an essential part of budgeting. However, problems arise when an investor, unfamiliar with the nature of low-budget film production, sees a contingency as high as 20 percent and assumes that the producer doesn't have a tight rein on spending.

One solution for this is to budget each category of production with a built-in, hidden contingency of 10 percent, then add an additional overall 10 percent contingency to the top sheet of your budget. This will give you a 10 percent contingency on paper but an actual 20 percent contingency for the film. In order for this to work, you must realistically budget your picture for 80 percent of the total budget and do your utmost to stay within that figure. Don't fall into the trap of borrowing from the 20 percent. Consider it unavailable, spent money. It will invariably find a way of disappearing on its own with no help from you.

Table 5 is a sample top sheet for a $500,000 budget. A detailed breakdown of this budget may be found in Appendix C.

Motion Picture Insurance

In the course of his duties, a production manager may make many mistakes and still get the job done. One mistake that he *cannot* afford to make is not to be properly insured.

Insurance requirements vary from picture to picture. A film with many dangerous stunts will be more costly to insure than a drawing room mystery. For a big-budget film, insurance will generally cost 2 percent of the picture's budget plus the cost of worker's compensation, which is required by state law. A producer making a film for a million dollars or less should budget 2.5 percent plus the cost of worker's compensation. It is wise to obtain bids from several reputable insurance companies and negotiate among them for the lowest price.

The following information regarding various types of insurance coverages for motion picture and television productions is included as a courtesy of Truman Van Dyke Company, insurance brokers to the entertainment industry. For additional information, contact Truman Van Dyke Company at 6290 Sunset Boulevard, Suite 1800, Hollywood, California 90028, (213) 462–3300.

MOTION PICTURE AND TELEVISION INSURANCE COVERAGES
LIST

The following brief descriptions are general in nature and are not a complete explanation of the policy terms.

Cast Insurance: Reimburses the production company for any extra expense necessary to complete principal photography of an insured production due to the death, injury, or sickness of any insured performer or director. Insured performers (or director) must take a physical examination prior to being covered by this insurance. Physical examination cost to be paid by production company. Coverage begins two weeks prior to the beginning of principal photography.

Table 5   **Sample Budget Recap**

Title ———————————— Production company ————————

Above-the-line

100	Screenplay	$ 16,000	
200	Producer	17,000	
300	Director	12,500	
400	Cast	55,000	$ 100,500

Below-the-line
Production

500	Production staff	20,700	
600	Extras	6,000	
700	Set operations	34,800	
800	Sets	17,000	
900	Props	10,600	
1000	Costumes	6,900	
1100	Makeup and hairdressing	7,000	
1200	Production equipment	21,000	
1300	Locations/studio	12,800	
1400	Laboratory and film	39,000	
1500	Tests	500	
1600	Production Miscellaneous	16,500	192,800

Postproduction

1700	Editing	46,000	
1800	Sound	14,500	
1900	Music	26,000	
2000	Titles and opticals	5,000	
2100	Laboratory	12,800	
2200	Sound mix	11,800	116,100

Other costs

2300	Insurance	20,000	
2400	Miscellaneous	25,100	45,100
		Total	454 500
		10% Contingency	45,500
		Grand total	$ 500,000

Negative Film and Videotape: Covers against all risks of direct physical loss, damage, or destruction of raw film or tape stock, exposed film (developed or undeveloped), recorded videotape, sound tracks and tapes, up to the amount of insured production cost.

Coverage does not include loss caused by fogging; faulty camera or sound equipment; faulty developing, editing, processing, or manipulation by the cameraman; exposure to light, dampness, or temperature changes; or errors in judgment in exposure, lighting, or sound recording, or from the use of incorrect type of raw film stock or tape.

Faulty Stock, Camera, and Processing: Covers loss, damage, or destruction of raw film or tape stock, exposed film (developed or undeveloped), recorded videotape, sound tracks and tapes, caused by or resulting from fogging or the use of faulty developing; faulty editing or faulty processing; and accidental erasure of videotape recordings.

Coverage does not include loss caused by errors of judgment in exposure, lighting, or sound recording, from the use of incorrect type of raw stock, or faulty manipulation by the cameraman.

This coverage can only be purchased with negative film and videotape coverage.

Props, Sets, and Wardrobe: Provides coverage on props, sets, scenery, costumes, wardrobe, and similar theatrical property against all risks of direct physical loss, damage, or destruction, during the production.

Extra Expense: Reimburses the production company for any extra expense necessary to complete principal photography of an insured production due to the damage or destruction of property or facilities (props, sets, or equipment) used in connection with the production.

Miscellaneous Equipment: Covers against all risks of direct physical loss, damage, or destruction to cameras, camera equipment, sound, lighting and grip equipment, owned by or rented to the production company. Coverage can be extended to cover mobile equipment vans, studio location units, or similar units upon payment of an additional premium.

Property Damage Liability: Pay for damage or destruction of property of others (including loss of use of the property) while the property is in the care, custody, or control of the production company and is used or to be used in an insured production.

Coverage does not apply to liability for destruction of property caused by operation of any motor vehicle, aircraft, or watercraft, including damage to the foregoing; liability for damage to any property rented or leased that may be covered under props, sets, or wardrobe, or miscellaneous equipment insurance (*except* that loss of use of any such equipment is covered).

This insurance is not covered under a comprehensive liability policy. Property damage coverage written as part of a comprehensive liability policy excludes damage to any property in the production company's care, custody, or control.

Errors and Omissions: Covers legal liability and defense for the production company against lawsuits alleging unauthorized use of titles, format, ideas, characters, plots, plagiarism, unfair competition, or breach of contract. Also protects for alleged libel, slander, defamation of character or invasion of privacy. This coverage will usually be required by a distributor prior to release of any theatrical or television production.

Worker's Compensation: This coverage is required to be carried by state law and applies to all temporary or permanent cast or production crew members. Coverage provides medical, disability, or death benefits to any cast or crew member who becomes injured in the course of their employment. Coverage applies on a twenty-four-hour per diem basis whenever employees are on location away from their homes.

Individuals who call themselves "independent contractors" will usually be held to be employees as far as worker's compensation is concerned, and failure to carry this insurance can result in having to pay any benefits required under the law plus penalty awards.

Comprehensive Liability: Protects the production company against claims for bodily injury or property damage liability arising out of filming the picture. Coverage includes use of all non-owned vehicles (both on and off camera), including physical damage to such vehicles. This coverage will be required prior to filming on any city or state roadways, or any location sites requiring filming permits.

Coverage does not apply to use of any aircraft or watercraft, which must be separately insured before any coverage will apply.

Guild/Union Flight Accident: Provides motion picture/television (IATSE/NABET/SAG/DGA) guild or union contract requirements for aircraft accidental death insurance to all production company cast or crew members. Coverage is blanket and the limits of liability meet all signatory requirements.

Completion Guaranty Bond: Completion guaranty bonds are available for feature motion picture productions that meet certain minimum budget requirements. Completion guaranty will provide completion funds for up to 100 percent of total picture budget.

These brief descriptions provide a simplified explanation of the various types of insurance protection available to motion picture or television production companies. Most of these coverages will have deductibles of varying amounts depending upon the limits of insurance coverage required. Premiums for theatrical features are based upon the size of the picture budget and will vary between 2 to 3 percent of the total budget, depending upon location site, length of shooting time, and any special hazards or stunts.

Commercial and documentary production companies can obtain annual Producers Insurance Policies (PIPs) incorporating various combinations of film insurance coverages.

PRODUCER'S ERRORS AND OMISSIONS LIABILITY INSURANCE

The following information is provided to assist an applicant's attorney in making certain that all necessary clearance procedures have been taken before applying for an errors and omissions insurance policy. Issuance of this type of insurance is contingent upon approval by the insurance carrier of a completed application and a representation that all the following clearance procedures have been accomplished.

The script must be reviewed by applicant's attorney prior to commencement of any production to eliminate matter that may be defamatory, invades privacy, or is otherwise potentially actionable.

Unless the work is an unpublished original not based on any other work, a copyright report must be obtained and submitted with the application. Both domestic and foreign copyrights and renewal rights should be checked. If a completed film is being acquired, a similar review should be made on copyright and renewals on any copyrighted underlying property.

If the script or story is an unpublished original, the origins of the work should be determined—basic idea, sequence of events, and characters. It should be ascertained if submissions of any similar properties have been received by the applicant, and if so, the circumstances as to why the submitting party may not claim theft or infringement should be described in detail.

Prior to final title selection, a title clearance report should be obtained from one of the title clearance law firms. The title of any production is excluded from coverage until a satisfactory title report has been obtained. Either one of the two following title search firms can provide a title clearance report at a fee of approximately $85.00: Samuel W. Tannenbaum, Esq., Johnson and Tannenbaum, 250 West 57th Street, New York, New York 10019 (212) 265–4072; E. Fulton Brylawski, Esq., Brylawski and Cleary, 224 East Capitol Street, Washington, D.C. 20003 (202) 547–1331.

If music is used, the applicant must obtain all necessary synchronization and performance licenses.

Written agreements must exist between the applicant and all creators, authors, writers, performers, and any other persons providing material (including quotations from copyrighted works) or on-screen services.

If distinctive locations, buildings, businesses, personal property, or products are filmed, written releases should be secured. This is not necessary if nondistinctive background use is made of real property.

If the production involves actual events, it should be ascertained that the author's sources are independent and primary (contemporaneous newspaper reports, court transcripts, interviews with witnesses, etc.) and not secondary (another author's copyrighted work, autobiographies, copyrighted magazine articles, etc.).

If not previously submitted, a final shooting script must be submitted with the completed application. If the production is a documentary-type production, then the shooting outline or treatment should be submitted.

Coverage for errors and omissions insurance cannot be bound before the completed application has been approved by the insurance carrier's clearance attorney.

Whether the production is fictional (and locations are identifiable) or factual, it should be made certain that no names, faces, or likenesses of any recognizable living persons are used unless written releases have been obtained. Release is unnecessary if person is part of a crowd scene or shown in a fleeting background. The term "living persons" includes thinly disguised versions of living persons who are readily identifiable because of identity of other characters or because of the factual, historical, or geographic setting.

Releases are not required of persons who are members of Screen Actors Guild (SAG), American Federation of Television and Radio Artists (AFTRA), or Screen Extras Guild (SEG) as they were compensated for their performances/appearances as members of such guilds. Releases obtained from living persons referred to above, should conform to the sample personal release as shown in Table 6.

Table 6 **Sample Personal Release**

To:_____
          (Production company)
From: _____
          (Releasing party)
Re:_____
          (Title of production)

In consideration of your filming me, or otherwise recording me, my performance or voice in the above production, I hereby grant to you, which term shall include not only yourself, but your employees, agents, successors, licensees, and assigns, the irrevocable right and license to use, simulate, and impersonate forever my name, face, likeness, voice, appearance, actions, activities, career, and experiences either actually or fictionally, under my name as

Table 6 (cont.)

undersigned, or under any other name in, and/or in connection with, the production, distribution, exhibition, advertising, and other exploitation of the above production in perpetuity throughout the world.

The rights herein granted to you shall include the right to depict and/or portray me to such extent and in such manner as you in your discretion may determine, and to edit any of my statements or comments and/or to juxtapose my face, likeness, appearance, actions, activities, career, experiences, and/or statements or comments, or any simulation and/or impersonation thereof, with any film clips and/or other material. I acknowledge that any editing of my statements or comments and of all portions of the above production and/or juxtapositions of film clips and/or other material, shall be at your sole discretion.

Further, you shall have the right to distribute, exhibit, or otherwise exploit any such production, in whole or in part, by any method and in any medium, including theatrically, nontheatrically, and by means of television or otherwise in connection with the above production or separate and apart from the above production.

In granting this release, I understand you have relied hereon in making the above production and will incur substantial expense based upon such reliance. I warrant that I have not been induced to execute this release by any agreements or statements made by your representative as to the nature or extent of your proposed exercise of any of the rights hereby granted, and I understand that you are under no obligation to exercise any of your rights, licenses, and privileges herein granted to you.

I hereby release and discharge you from any and all liability arising out of any injury of any kind that may be sustained by me from participation in or in connection with the making or utilization of the above production or by reason of the exercise by you of any of the rights granted to you hereunder.

Name: _____
                                 (Sign)

Dated: _____   _____
                                 (Print)

                        Address: _____

                                 _____

Table 6 (cont.)

To be completed if participant is under twenty-one years of age:

I represent that I am the parent or guardian of the minor who has signed the above release, and I hereby agree that I and said minor will be bound thereby.

Name: _____
                              (Sign)

_____
                              (Print)

Address: _____

_____

Dated: _____

CHAPTER 11

The Shooting Schedule
and Continuity Breakdown

The Production Board

One of the primary responsibilities of the production manager, or in some cases the first assistant director, is to organize the shooting schedule for production. This is generally laid out on a multipanel production board, a portion of which is shown in Table 7.

The left-hand column lists and numbers each cast member, starting with the most significant player. The vertical strips across the remainder of the board represent all of the scenes in the film and contain the following information:

- the scene numbers that that particular strip represents
- the number of script pages these scenes cover
- whether the scenes are day or night, exterior or interior
- a brief description of the scenes represented by that strip
- which cast members are involved in the scenes; characters are listed by numbers opposite the character's name in the left-hand column of the production board

These strips are available in a variety of colors that the production manager may use to indicate information about the day's shooting. Blue strips might be used for exteriors, green for interiors, white for scenes requiring snow, and orange for rest days. How these colors are used depends on the requirements of the script and the preference of the production manager. In our sample production board section, the black strips are used to separate shooting days. Each vertical strip is removable so that the entire board can

Table 7   Sample Panel From Production Board

Date

			1	2	3	4	5	6	7	8	9	10	11	12	13
DAY OR NIGHT			D	D	D	D	D	D	N		D	D	D	D/N	N
PAGE COUNT			1½	1½	1½	1½	3	3½	1¼		1¾	¾	2		3
SCENE NUMBERS			8A	8B	178	87 88	104	105 106 107 108	110 116 308		2,3 61	62 63	219	218 287	62 85
Title THE WAND PRODUCER DIRECTOR PRODUCTION MANAGER ASSISTANT DIRECTOR **Script dated**			EXT. TELIMAN'S FORT	EXT. TELIMAN'S FORT	EXT. TELIMAN'S FORT	INT. TELIMAN'S FORT	INT. TELIMAN'S FORT	INT. TELIMAN'S FORT	INT. RICHARD'S CASTLE	REST DAY	INT. RICHARD'S CASTLE	INT. RICHARD'S CASTLE	INT. SUBTERRANEAN CHAMBER	COMPLETE ALL CASTLE INTS.	KING NELLIS'S ENCAMPMENT
Character	**Artist**	**No.**													
ALEXIS		1			1	1	1	1				1	1		
JEREMY		2					2	2	2		2	2			
MONROE		3						3							
JAGG		4													
TESSIE		5	5	5											5
LADIA		6	6												6
ILLANA		7	7												7
KING NELLIS		8													8
QUEEN JULIA		9													9
TELIMAN		10	10	10	10							10			
RICHARD		11				11	11	11	11			11			
AKNAR		12													
CYRIL		13													
LEYMAN		14													
HORSE THIEF		15													
SOLDIER #1		16													16
SOLDIER #2		17													17
LUTE PLAYER		18										18			
MAGICIAN		19	19											19	
FISHERMAN		20													
————		21													
————		22													
————		23													
————		24													
————		25													
————		26													
————		27													
————		28													
————		29													
————		30													
————		31													
————		32													
EXTRAS (#)		33	⑥	⑩	⑩			⑧	⑳		④				㉟
SPECIAL EFFECTS		34	X										X		
		35													

be readily rearranged to accommodate changes in the schedule.

Films are almost never shot in sequence, from beginning to end. From an economic standpoint, it would be extremely inefficient to do so. Consequently, the production manager juggles all of the production elements—cast, crew, locations, equipment, etc.—reordering scenes in the film for the most economically efficient shooting schedule. If there are several scenes in the film that take place in a single location, the production manager will arrange to shoot them back to back, regardless of when they will appear in the finished film.

In addition to location concerns, the production manager must consider the availability of cast members, allow adequate time for moving from location to location, allow time for set construction and set decorating, etc. He must weigh the cost of each element in the production before finalizing the shooting schedule. There will always be compromises and the production manager must decide where to make them.

A good production manager will always have a backup "What if . . . ?" plan. What if it rains? What if the lead actor gets sick? What if the equipment fails? For this reason, production managers will try to schedule exteriors early in the schedule. If it rains, they will have an alternate interior location at their fingertips. If they leave the exteriors until last, and it rains when the script calls for sunshine, the producer will either have to wait out the rain or rewrite the script to fit the weather.

The problems facing a production manager when scheduling a picture may be best understood by using a simple example. It will be a worthwhile exercise to cut up strips of paper and mock up a rough production board for the following scenario.

Consider a film with two characters—Amos and Nathan. The film will be shot in two locations—A and B—with a four-week shooting schedule, two weeks at each location. Amos will appear in all of the scenes at location A and will therefore work for both weeks at location A, but will be needed for only one week at location B. Nathan will work for only one week at location A, but for both weeks at location B. If Nathan begins work before the second week at location A, there will be some nonworking holding days for which, according to SAG regulations, he must be paid.

SAG requires payment for any holding time between work days if that holding time is less than fourteen consecutive days when shooting on distant locations, or ten consecutive days when shooting within the *studio zone* (an area in Los Angeles defined by a thirty-mile radius from the intersection of Beverly Boulevard and La Cienega Boulevard).

Likewise, if Amos's scenes aren't scheduled for the first week at location B, he will have nonworking holding days as well. It would appear best to schedule Amos alone for the first week at location A, with Amos and Nathan together for the second week at location A. However, the first scene in the script involves Amos and Nathan traveling in Amos's 1946 classic Rolls-Royce. They are in an accident. No one is hurt but the car is badly dented and Amos will be driving it that way throughout the film.

If the first week involves Amos alone, driving the damaged Rolls-Royce, the production manager will either have to repair the Rolls for the accident scene scheduled for the second week when Amos and Nathan will be together (which will require some down time to repair the car), or the production manager will have to buy a second 1946 classic Rolls for the accident sequence in the second week.

If Nathan is an extremely expensive actor, it may be less expensive for the production manager to buy the second Rolls-Royce than to hold Nathan over for an extra week at location A.

But suppose all of Nathan and Amos's scenes together at location A are exterior? Is it worth risking bad weather during the second week at location A with no interior backups? If bad weather sets in, it could cause a day or more of holding time, not just for Nathan but for the entire production.

Perhaps the production manager will swallow the added expense of holding Nathan for an extra week, saving the cost of the second Rolls and maintaining a flexibility to accommodate bad weather. In making this decision, the production manager must weigh not just the cost for each element but also the weather forecast and the area's reputation for predictable or unpredictable weather. There may not be an obvious decision, in which case the production manager will have to throw in a bit of educated guessing based on past experience.

Now, if you consider a picture with ten locations, fifteen cast members, production variables including set construction time, expensive special effects, an enlarged crew for particularly difficult sequences, makeup changes for aging or modifying the "look" of an actor partway through the story, unusual weather requirements such as snow, and continue to list all of the elements that a production manager must juggle in a typical screenplay, you will begin to get an understanding of the difficulties involved in scheduling a picture.

Having taken all of the above into consideration, developing the most economically efficient shooting schedule possible, with a maximum number of backup plans, the production manager is faced with still another problem. In scheduling a production, he must also take into account artistic considerations. It may be that the most economically efficient schedule dictates shooting a particular scene, say scene number 86, on the first day of production. But suppose the director refuses to shoot scene number 86 on the first day on the grounds that it's a difficult, intensely emotional scene for the actors, and he wants the cast to become familiar with one another and he wants the operation of the crew to become well oiled before attempting to shoot scene number 86. He suggests shooting it during the fourth or fifth week of production. This is a valid consideration and one that the production manager must respect. Moving scene number 86 to the fourth or fifth week, however, might throw off every other sequence in the schedule and the production manager may have to reconstruct the entire schedule from scratch.

I am not attempting in this section to teach the reader how to become a production manager. Rather, I am trying to convey a profound respect for the production manager's contribution to a film and to encourage every producer to weigh his decision carefully when hiring the individual who will manage his production.

Continuity Breakdown

A film is made up of several sequences, each consisting of one or more shots (camera setups and/or takes). Continuity refers to the consistency of the look and sound of each shot in the film. If an actor changes his action or dialogue from one take to another within a given sequence he fails to maintain continuity. For example, if he picks up a glass with his right hand in one take, then picks it up with his left hand in another take, the continuity between the two shots is broken and they will not cut together in the editing room. It is the responsibility of the script supervisor to bring continuity discrepancies in an actor's action and/or dialogue to the attention of the director.

Similarly, if a shot of a house seen early in a film reveals a "No Trespassing" sign on the front door, that same sign must be seen on the door in every subsequent shot of the house. A useful tool for maintaining continuity throughout a film are continuity breakdown sheets. These sheets contain all pertinent information regarding the visual and audio requirements of each scene in the film such as costumes, special effects, stunts, vehicles, props, and special sound equipment (e.g., wireless microphones). These breakdown sheets are an important reference for production personnel who are concerned with the continuity of the film such as the art director, property master, set dresser, and wardrobe supervisor. They are also useful for the production manager when constructing the production board since the scheduling of particular sequences may be dictated by information contained on the breakdown sheets.

A sample breakdown sheet is featured in Table 8.

Table 8   **Sample Page Continuity Breakdown**

Title _____ Producer _____ Breakdown
                                                    page _____
Set/location _____ Director_____ Script pages:___
Scene nos. 18, 18A, 37 Day or night D ____ 15, 34

Synopsis: POV shot from office building, down the street to
the warehouse.
Camera zooms in on warehouse as car stops in
front.
McGuff steps slowly from the car, passes "No
Trespassing" sign.
Yellow cab is parked in alley.
Montage: Coroner's stationwagon being loaded with
bodies of *McGuff's family.* VO of *prosecutor.*

Cast	Costume no.	Atmosphere	Props
McGuff	6	Coroner	"No Tres-passing" sign
		Attendants	Stretchers (4)
		Sheriff	Body bags
		Cab driver	

Bits	Special effects	Vehicles and animals
McGuff's family or shapes to match in body bags		McGuff's car Coroner's stationwagon Yellow cab Sheriff's car

Stunts	Sound	Special notes

CHAPTER 12

Casting

Once a detailed budget and board are completed, a producer knows how much money is available to spend on the actors and for how many days or weeks he'll need each one. By this time the script should be close to finished, with perhaps an additional polish or two left to go. This, along with a tentative date for the commencement of principal photography, is everything a producer needs to begin casting.

It is important that the film's director be intimately involved in the casting process. The director will guide the actors and their performances throughout the making of the film so it is crucial that the casting be consistent with his overall vision of the film. Many directors believe that their job is half over if the picture is well cast.

The Casting Director

The first thing most producers do when they cast a film is employ the services of a casting director. This is someone who specializes in finding and recommending the most appropriate actors for each speaking role in the film. His recommendations are subject to the approval of the producer and/or director. Casting directors commonly handle negotiations on behalf of the producer with agents regarding actors' contracts including salary and screen credit. Some casting directors will break down a total budget figure for an entire cast into detailed allotments for each character in the script.

Because of his experience and knowledge, a good casting director can save a producer both time and money. He has accumulated a vast file of actors and actresses, either in his head or in his office; he has devoted a tremendous amount of time to studying actors' abilities; he constantly has his feelers out for fresh new talent; he has a rough idea as to how much certain actors cost; he may have inside information about which types of roles certain actors are looking for; he may know about various actors' schedules and availability; he has a thorough working knowledge of SAG rules and regulations; he has a great deal of experience dealing with actors' agents and has established a working rapport with many of them. Furthermore, agents know they can't lie to an experienced casting director about an actor's price. The casting director probably has enough connections to find out what a particular actor received for his last picture.

Casting directors have no guild or union and consequently have no organization that establishes their qualifications, working standards, working conditions, or minimum wages. Depending on the budget of a film, the number of speaking parts, and the complexity of those parts, a casting director for a feature film will receive anywhere from $5,000 to $40,000.

Because there is no structured organization for casting directors, anyone can hang out a shingle announcing his qualifications to do the job. This makes it difficult for a producer to locate an appropriate person to cast his film. The most efficient way to locate a casting director is through Breakdown Services Ltd., 8111 Beverly Boulevard, Suite 308, Los Angeles, California 90048, (213) 658-8864. In addition to several casting services they offer, which will be discussed later in this chapter, they publish a directory called the *C/D Directory* that lists virtually all the casting directors, their associates and their assistants who cast for motion picture and television productions in the Los Angeles area (there are nearly 200). The directory lists the individual's name, title, address, and phone number. A new directory is published every three months and each new directory is updated every two weeks. This is because there is a 10 percent turnover of information in the directory per week (mostly address changes). The price for a year's subscription to the directory and updates is $31.80; a single issue sells for $5.30.

Breakdown Services Ltd. publishes a separate listing of New

York casting personnel that is updated less often and sold only on a single-copy basis for $3.00 per copy. This is because New York casting personnel move around much less frequently than those in Los Angeles.

In addition to their directories, Breakdown Services Ltd. maintains a file of resumes on virtually every casting director in Los Angeles and about 70 percent of the casting directors in New York. A producer seeking a casting director may call their Los Angeles number, discuss with them the budget and the type of picture he's making, and they will recommend casting directors they feel are most appropriate for the producer's picture and will make available to the producer the resumes of casting directors in whom the producer expresses interest. There is no charge for this service.

Other ways for a producer to determine an appropriate casting director for his film are through word-of-mouth reputation with other producers, watching films and noting the casting director on those films that seem particularily well cast, and seeking recommendations from actors' agents. These agents work closely with casting directors and will often recommend three or four that they feel are appropriate for the project.

Once a producer has selected a potential casting director he should arrange to meet with the film's director and the casting director to discuss the project, schedule, and budget. If all three feel comfortable with the prospect of working together, they may begin the next phase of the operation, which is casting the film.

In some cases a producer will decide to cast a film without the aid of a casting director. This is commonly done on low-budget films where the producer has more time and energy than money. For the following discussion on the casting process I will assume that a producer has decided to cast his film on his own. The process is the same whether a casting director is employed or not. The difference lies in who does the work—an experienced, knowledgeable casting director or a struggling producer whose budget simply cannot accommodate the luxury of a professional to do the job.

The Casting Process

One of the most valuable aids to casting a film, whether it's a student short or a major feature, is provided by Breakdown Services Ltd. This is a company that specializes in the dissemination of casting information to actors' agents and personal managers throughout the United States and in London. When a producer calls them with a project the first thing they will do is send a field representative out to discuss the project and pick up a copy of the script. They will then write a synopsis of the story and a descriptive breakdown of each character in the film along with any additional information the producer feels is pertinent to his project (e.g., he may request that the breakdown sheets not reveal any confidential story points in his script, or he may request that agents submit only name actors for certain roles). The breakdown sheets are sent to the producer for approval and then sent to actors' agents and personal managers throughout the country and in London (or to a limited area such as New York if the producer so requests).

The beauty of this system is that while agents and personal managers pay a subscription fee of $28.00 per week to receive this information, *the producer pays nothing.* Furthermore, Breakdown Services Ltd. carefully checks out agents and managers who wish to subscribe to their service and accepts subscriptions only from those who have established themselves as reputable representatives of actors. Consequently, producers will not be hounded by unprofessional or disreputable agents. They will, however, be inundated with mail-in submissions that will include a photograph and resume of each potential actor. There may be thousands of submissions for a single role and the only way to handle them is to sort through them, select the most likely candidates, and arrange to interview them.

This service is available to all producers and casting directors, whether they are making a 16mm non-SAG student film or a $40 million studio epic. The only requirements of the producer are, first, that he utilize sync sound in his film and, second, that he is willing to receive written submission for potential actors (photos and resumes) and is willing to make individual appointments with them (as opposed to "cattle calls," which will be discussed later in this chapter). Finally, a producer using this service must be prepared to have his project represented honestly on the breakdown sheets. If his project is non-SAG, the agents receiving the sheets must know this. If there is nudity, sex, violence, or excessive gore, this information must be included. The purpose of this system is to disseminate information quickly and accurately. If a project is misrepresented or incompletely described, the producer, agent, and actors will waste a great deal of time with useless submissions and interviews.

A producer who wishes to use this service should not send his script in cold. He should first phone and discuss his project with Breakdown Services Ltd. in Los Angeles at (213) 658-5684, in New York at (212) 666-0711, or in London at (01) 456-2781. If the producer is headquartered in one of these areas, a field representative will come out to meet with him, discuss the project, and pick up a copy of the script. If the producer is located outside of these areas, he will be asked to send his script by mail. All scripts are forwarded to the Los Angeles office for synopsis and breakdown. This office completes twenty to forty breakdowns per week. A feature film will usually be broken down within twenty-four hours of the time the script reaches the Los Angeles office.

This service is most effectively used when a producer is ready to begin casting, but it can also be valuable prior to that time. Breakdown Services Ltd. is concerned only that a producer have a serious intent to make his film. This does not necessarily mean that he is ready to begin casting or that he is even fully financed. In some cases Breakdown Services Ltd. will proceed with the breakdown but will not send copies out to agents and managers until the producer gives them the go-ahead. Since the subscribers to this service pay the same fee regardless of the number of script breakdowns they receive, the company is under no pressure to send out information. Consequently, in some cases a producer can obtain a copy of the breakdown to use as a quick-reference synopsis of his story and characters well before he is ready to begin casting.

Table 9 is an example of the kind of information commonly included on breakdown sheets. These sheets were prepared prior to casting *Arthur* and are included with permission from Breakdown Services, Ltd.

ROLLINS-JOFFE PRODUCTIONS
"ARTHUR"
FEATURE FILM
REVISED FIRST DRAFT

Producers: Rollins-Joffe
Director: Steve Gordon
Screenplay: Steve Gordon
Casting Director: Juliet Taylor—
Feuer & Ritzer
Start Date: Between 5/18 and 6/2, 1980

WRITTEN SUBMISSIONS ONLY
TO: Feuer & Ritzer
     1650 Broadway #1206
     New York, New York 10019

PLEASE SEND CARBON COPY OF WRITTEN
SUBMISSIONS TO: Juliet Taylor
              c/o Warner Brothers
              75 Rockefeller Plaza
              New York, New York 10019

ARTHUR . . . . CAST (DUDLEY MOORE)

LINDA DAVIDORF: She is a very beautiful, ethnic young girl whom Arthur rescues from being arrested for shoplifting. A brash, outspoken woman obviously from Queens, she has her own unique brand of sarcastic humor and moxie that Arthur finds so appealing. Wise-cracking and unconventional, she is attracted to Arthur, recognizing him as a kindred spirit. Linda is an aspiring actress working as a counter waitress in a sleazy coffee shop. She's very down-to-earth and, although obviously not of Arthur's class, she is able to fit in fairly well using a combination of wit, looks and off-beat charm. . . . LEAD (42)

HOBSON: He is Arthur's valet/surrogate father/best friend, a very stiff, formal man of about 60. A career servant—but a man of impeccable breeding and taste—he is possibly the driest, most sarcastic man ever. Every word Hobson utters is clipped, precise and possibly damaging and he appears to have great distaste for everything—especially the antics of his young master. Appearances to the contrary, Hobson is absolutely devoted to Arthur; the eccentric young man is his life's work, the son he never had. Hobson's realistic manner and earthy sarcasm absolutely delights Arthur and the old man is never shocked by his drunken behavior. If anything, Hobson understands Arthur's behavior even more than Arthur does and, having raised him from birth, commiserates with his problems without condoning his erratic actions. . . . LEAD (14)

MARTHA BACH: She is Arthur's grandmother, a tough old dowager who runs her wealthy family with a velvet-covered iron fist. Martha is very fond of her only grandson and, although she speaks in dulcet, high-pitched tones, can easily keep up with his zany non sequiturs. On the rationale that "love will come and go. Millions of dollars tend to stay forever," Martha threatens to cut Arthur off without a cent if he marries Linda Davidorf rather than the wealthy Susan Johnson; she's a shrewd, realistic old lady. Martha is genuinely sorry that she missed the sexual revolution and her earthy—but genteel—humor belies her sweet demeanor . . . . 38 speeches & 33 lines, 4 scenes (57)

STANFORD BACH: He is Arthur's successful, wealthy father, a trim, good-looking man of about 55. Tough, smart and not the nicest of men, Stanford Bach's sole failure in life has been his son —and he doesn't like it. Arthur is his cross to bear and, confronted with his son's irrepressible irresponsibility, Bach can totally lose his characteristic cool and be sent into a frustrated rage . . . . 22 speeches & 26 lines, 5 scenes (27)

BURT JOHNSON: He is Arthur's father-in-law to be, a wealthy, impeccably dressed man whose manner can't hide the fact that he is a time-bomb ready to go off. While Stanford and Arthur Bach were both born into money, Burt Johnson is a self-made man who matter-of-factly boasts that he killed his first man at age 11. Usually menacing, the soft spot in Johnson's personality is his beloved daughter—he'd rather see Arthur dead than Susan hurt. Hobson disdains him as a "vulgarian" but Johnson has the clout and money to travel in the best of circles. He's a menacing, volatile man . . . . 14 speeches & 16 lines, 4 scenes (71)

SUSAN JOHNSON: She is Burt Johnson's daughter, a pretty, bright and serious girl who knows what she wants—she wants Arthur, much to everyone's amazement. A self-effacing woman, Susan suspects that a "real woman" could stop his drinking and she is content to wait for his occasional phone calls and attentions. She is nice and un-assuming . . . . 6 speeches & 20 lines, 3 scenes (75)

BITTERMAN: He is a black man in his 40's, Arthur's chauffeur and good friend. A tight-lipped, discreet fellow, Bitterman accompanies Arthur on his revels and does his best to keep him out of trouble. He is frequently the focus of many of Arthur's puns and spends a great deal of time trying not to be a straight man. It's clear that Bitterman, like Hobson, is very fond of Arthur and feels as much pity as love for him. . . . 12 speeches & 35 lines, 9 scenes (2)

RALPH: He is Linda's father, a man who spends most of his time in Queens playing solitaire in front of the TV. When he learns that his daughter's new suitor is a millionaire, Ralph tries to interest him in a chain of fast food restaurants. He is on very good terms with Linda and it is obvious that she is a chip of the old block. . . . 7 speeches & 10 lines, 3 scenes (51)

GLORIA: She is a very attractive hooker whom Arthur picks up on a street corner and takes to "21". Out of place in the exclusive restaurant, Gloria gamely sticks with Arthur and gives him the companionship and affection that he needs. . . . 2 speeches & 29 lines, 3 scenes (2)

OWNER: He is the older owner of a plant store who speaks with a Jewish accent and amiably compares notes with Arthur on being in love. Dry-humored and a real character, the Owner is surprised by Arthur's outgoing manner and finds himself telling the stranger about his sex life. . . . 8 speeches & 11 lines, 1 scene (54)

JANE BACH: She is Arthur's mother, a frail, nervous woman in her early 50's. Chattering on and on with inconsequential small talk, Jane bores Burt Johnson at a pool party. She's just a little dittsy. . . . 6 speeches, 1 scene (88)

PRESTON LANGLY: A rich, nice looking young lawyer, he is a socialite who tries to pick up Linda at a party. He makes small talk with Linda and uses a smooth but not glib line on her. . . . 4 speeches & 7 lines, 1 scene (101)

MAN: He is a large, menacing man, one of Burt Johnson's goons. After trailing Arthur to Linda's apartment, the Man threatens him and warns him to stay faithful to Susan Johnson. . . . 4 speeches & 3 lines, 1 scene (119A)

SALESLADY: She's is the rather stiff, snobby lady clerk in a jewelry store who tries to throw the drunken Arthur out until she realizes who he is. . . . 3 speeches & 5 lines, 1 scene (38)

SECURITY GUARD: He is an alert department store security guard who tries to arrest Linda Davidorf after seeing her shoplift a tie. Polite but firm, he is surprised when Arthur intervenes. . . . 3 speeches & 4 lines, 2 scenes (43)

YOUNG WOMAN (HEATHER):   She is a beautifully dressed young woman at Arthur and Susan's engagement party who was "simply shattered!" when she learned that Arthur was no longer available. A flirtatious, harmless sort. . . . 4 speeches & 1 line, 1 scene (97)

ARTHUR AS A BOY: Arthur as a precocious 7-year-old is a hard-drinking, sad little boy on his way to boarding school. . . . 4 speeches & 1 line, 1 scene (1)

MAID: She is young Arthur's maid, a compassionate woman who tries to cheer the sad little boy up. . . . 3 speeches & 2 lines, 1 scene (1)

PETER BACH: a white-haired, prosperous-looking gentleman and PEARL BACH: a rather portly, bejeweled dowager, are

Arthur's aunt and uncle whom he runs into at "21". Distressed
to see him rip-roaring drunk, Aunt Pearl is even more uncomfortable when Arthur insists on breathing Scotch right into her face.
Uncle Peter, a disapproving but concerned man, advises him to
"grow up, You'd make a fine adult.". . . . 3 speeches & 3 lines,
1 scene; 2 speeches & 2 lines, 1 scene (8) respectively.

DOCTOR: He is Hobson's young doctor, a calm, matter-of-fact
man who carefully tells Arthur that the old man's condition is
terminal. . . . 3 speeches & 3 lines, 2 scenes (125)

OLD WOMAN: She is a sweet-faced old woman laden with
packages whom Arthur strikes up a conversation with. He leaves
her happy and chuckling. . . . 2 speeches & 8 lines, 1 scene (35)

LADY: A fat, loud-mouthed dragon LADY and her calm,
PERRY: huge husband, PERRY, are the Davidorf's neighbors.
The lady insists on screaming at Arthur and Perry is terribly
hen-pecked. . . . 2 speeches & 2 lines, 1 scene (79); 1 speech & 2
lines, 1 scene (80) respectively.

BUTLER: He is a rather stiff older butler who admits Arthur
to the Johnson's mansion. . . . 1 speech & 7 lines, 1 scene (69)

MRS. STREET: She is Stanford Bach's secretary, a severe
woman in her 50's who welcomes Arthur and asks him if it isn't
a little early to be drinking. . . . 1 speech & 5 lines, 1 scene (25)

ALFIE: He is a black poet who shows up in a sweatshirt at
Arthur and Susan's black tie engagement party. A good-natured,
cynical man. . . . 1 speech & 4 lines, 1 scene (97)

ELEVATOR OPERATOR: He is a poker-faced elevator operator in Arthur's building who discreetly doesn't notice that Arthur
and Linda are having a fight in the hallway. . . . 1 speech & 4 lines,
2 scenes (108)

GIRL: She is an attractive hooker working the street with
Gloria who is puzzled and curious about Arthur. . . . 1 speech &
2 lines, 1 scene (2)

DOORMAN: He is a uniformed doorman at Arthur's building who is well used to seeing Arthur stumbling home drunk. A polite, friendly man. . . . 4 lines, 2 scenes (24)

KID: They are two boys playing football in the road who are
OTHER KID: impressed with Arthur's car. They are good-natured 12-year-olds. . . . 3 lines, 1 scene; 2 lines, 1 scene (68) respectively.

OLD MAN: They are two of Linda's customers at the sleazy
TEENAGER: coffee shop. An OLD MAN gets hostile when she forgets to serve his roll while the TEENAGER in a leather jacket eyes her hungrily and tries to pick her up. . . . 4 lines, 1 scene; 1 speech, 1 scene (95) respectively.

CAPTAIN: He is the regular captain at "21" who effusively greets Arthur. . . . 2 lines, 1 scene (7)

WAITER: He is the friendly waiter at "21" who serves Arthur and Gloria. The waiter is obviously used to Arthur and can't help but chuckle at his puns. . . . 2 lines, 1 scene (10)

EXECUTIVE: He is a bemused executive at Stanford Bach's office who is disgusted by Arthur's drunken behavior. . . . 1 speech, 1 scene (27)

SALESLADY: She is a sales clerk at Bloomingdale's who waits on Arthur. . . . 1 line, 1 scene (42)

HARRIET: She is Martha Bach's black maid. . . . 1 line, 1 scene (59)

COUNTER MAN: He is Linda's co-worker at the sleazy coffee shop who asks her to work overtime. . . . 1 speech, 1 scene (96)

WAITER: He is an understanding waiter at a French restaurant. . . . 1 line, 1 scene (76)

LADY: She is a guest at Arthur and Susan's engagement party. . . . 1 line, 1 scene (108)

STORY-LINE: ARTHUR BACH, the notorious millionaire playboy/lush, is ordered by his father—STANFORD BACH—to marry SUSAN JOHNSON, the daughter of wealthy BURT JOHNSON. Arthur, unfortunately, is a whimsical type who just can't bring himself to marry a woman he isn't in love with—even though he has been threatened by grandmother MARTHA BACH with being disowned. Matters are complicated when Arthur meets LINDA DAVIDORF, an off-beat girl from Queens whom he falls in love with. When his best friend and valet HOBSON becomes terminally ill and dies, Arthur is forced to mature a little. This is a big break-through for the eccentric young man and he finally garners enough courage to break off his engagement to Susan and propose to Linda. As luck would have it, Martha is so proud of her grandson's newfound courage that she decides to keep him—and Linda—in the will. . . .

Another important tool for anyone casting a film is a two-volume publication put out by the Academy of Motion Picture Arts and Sciences titled the *Academy Players Directory*. Each of the two volumes is the size of a large telephone book and together they contain a photographic listing of virtually every actor and actress in the business. In addition to the actor's name and photograph there is information about his agency representation and guild affiliation. This book is particularly useful when you are looking for recognizable faces and names for certain roles in your film. When thumbing through the photographs you will inevitably find a number of potential actors for your film whom you might have overlooked if you had relied solely on your memory.

The *Academy Players Directory* can be found in most film libraries, or you can purchase a set directly from the academy at the address listed in Appendix E.

Casting for most films can be broken down into three categories: principal players (major speaking parts), secondary players (nonmajor speaking parts), and extras (nonspeaking atmosphere talent).

Principal Players

The only way you will ever know how someone will appear on film is to see him on film. Videotape will tell you a great deal, but nothing will tell you as much as the big screen. Usually, when casting principals, you will base your choices on actors you've seen in other films. If you are considering someone who's never been in a film, by all means shoot a screen test.

The difference between a screen test and an audition is that in a screen test the actor performs a scene from the producer's script *on film,* usually in full costume and makeup. This is probably the most effective way to determine an actor's suitability for a particular role. Prior to shooting the test, the actor's entire deal with respect to the picture will be negotiated as though he were set to perform in the film. The deal is then contingent upon satisfactory completion of the test. Actors are not generally paid for a screen test but they will usually receive a copy of the completed test to use as a sample of their work. If you can't afford to shoot a test on film, borrow a home video unit. The principal players can make or break your picture, so it's well worth the effort to test their talent thoroughly before hiring them.

Assuming you select actors for your principal roles based on their performances in other films, your first step will be to contact their agents. Agency information can be found either in the *Academy Players Directory* or by contacting the Screen Actors Guild. The function of the agents is to counsel their clients, to negotiate on their behalf, and to protect their interests.

The agent will ask to read the script, and if he finds the material of interest he'll send it to his client. This is assuming that he feels you can afford to pay his client's fee, and that the client has no prior commitment that conflicts with your schedule. Remember that it is the agent's job to negotiate on behalf of his client for the best deal he can get. This is often based on the last deal he negotiated for that client, each deal setting something of a precedent for the future. However, a good agent will also look to the long-range implications in a project. If he sees a role that could launch the actor into a whole new area of opportunity, he'll take that into consideration in negotiating the deal and will perhaps bend a bit to accommodate the producer. Don't hesitate to stress the strength of the role you have to offer. This is worth a great deal and is often a more powerful inducement than money. The worst that can happen is that the agent turns you down and recommends another client better suited, in his opinion, to your project.

In discussing the screenplay, I said that the most important consideration for an *actor* is the screenplay. Every actor is on the lookout for a vehicle that will best serve his talents or expand his horizons. This is true for the top-paid superstar as well as the struggling newcomer. An actor who has become well known for his portrayals of dramatic heroes may wish to expand his horizons, perhaps into comedy. He will almost certainly be willing to take a cut in salary for the opportunity to play a comic role. But since he's known only for his dramatic work, who's going to offer him a comedy? A comedy screenplay will first go to the actors who have proven themselves in that field, and if all of them turn it down it might be sent to a dramatic actor. Rarely will he get first crack.

If you can find the right person at the right time, with the right script, you'll not only negotiate a reasonable price, you'll have an energetic, enthusiastic performer. An actor who takes on a role because of moderate, routine interest in the script, or purely for the money, will be limited to a competent, professional performance. He will not, however, give you that added magical energy that's sparked by a genuine enthusiasm for the project.

Finding an actor whose enthusiasm will be sparked by a role in your film isn't easy. Occasionally, word-of-mouth will advertise what sort of role a particular actor is seeking, but this is often third-hand rumor information. The answer to this dilemma is to expose your project to whichever actors you consider right for your project. Don't limit yourself to the ones you *know* for certain you can afford—the ones who'll take the part simply because you can pay their fee. As with seeking your writer and director, always go for the best, at least a cut above what is safe. Don't be afraid to shoot for the moon.

Approaching your casting in this way, you will suffer many rejections, but expecting the rejections will make them easier to take. And, occasionally, you'll get a "yes." With some roles, you will have to compromise, falling back on actors that fit more easily within your budget. Following this pattern, shooting for the moon, then compromising to fit your budget, you will be setting the highest possible standards for your picture and you will know that you have assembled the best possible cast within your budget.

This is not to say that an actor's ability is measured in terms of the money he costs. A film may be exceptionally well cast with actors who work for SAG minimum or with non-SAG actors who are happy to work for nothing more than a screen credit. However, if you are seeking actors with substantial experience performing for the camera and several screen credits to back them up, they will undoubtedly be members of SAG and will almost certainly expect overscale salaries.

A producer who wishes to hire SAG actors must sign a guild agreement, thereby giving SAG jurisdiction over all speaking parts in the film. The agreement provides for minimum contract requirements such as minimum salaries, the number of working hours in a day, meal penalties, and overtime provisions. An actor's agent is not permitted to take his commission, usually 10 percent, from the SAG minimum scale wage. Consequently, you must budget SAG scale plus 10 percent as a minimum wage for any actor you hire through an agent.

You can obtain a copy of the standard SAG/producer's agreement from the Screen Actors Guild, 7750 Sunset Boulevard, Los Angeles, California 90046. If you have a personal connection to a potential actor for your film, it's often best to bypass the agent. The worst the actor will say is, "Call my agent."

Supporting Players

Your principal players will be utilized to their fullest potential only if they are surrounded by strong support people. For this reason, the philosophy for hiring principal players applies to supporting players as well—go for the best, most experienced actors, then compromise to fit your budget.

The *Academy Players Directory* will be a useful aid when casting supporting players, but if you are working with a modest budget you may have to utilize actors who have never appeared in films and, consequently, you won't recognize them in the directory. If you use the service offered by Breakdown Services Ltd., as described earlier in this chapter, you will receive a multitude of submissions from which to choose your supporting players. Also, any agent who reads your script for a particular client will invariably recommend clients for a half-dozen other roles in your film as well.

Another way to find actors is through a casting newspaper called *Drama-Logue*. This publication is available at newsstands throughout California, in New York, and in Las Vegas. It is also read by subscribers throughout the United States and in Europe. *Drama-Logue* routinely publishes announcements that describe producers' casting requirements and information about how actors may apply for those roles. Producers interested in placing such announcements should contact John Kirby at the *Drama-Logue* office, (213) 464-5079, or write him at P.O. Box 38771, Los Angeles, California 90038.

Producers can also place casting announcements in trade papers such as *Variety* and the *Hollywood Reporter* or in local publications such as newspapers. Even without public announcements it's astonishing how fast news travels when a producer is actively casting his film.

Since you will probably be dealing with less experienced players for your supporting roles, it is important to spend extra time carefully weighing your choices. Again, the ideal way to judge their talent is by viewing film or videotape. If that isn't available, perhaps because the actors have had only stage experience, and if it isn't practical to shoot screen tests on each of them, you must judge them based on readings from the script. This is not an entirely adequate way to judge a performer's ability.

An actor who comes in to read a portion of the script for the producer, director, and perhaps the screenwriter, is at something of a disadvantage. The pressures in a reading situation are quite different from those on a working set, or when performing for a screen test. The audience in a reading is not the objective eye of the camera but the collective eyes of people who will decide whether or not to give the actor a job. Often the actor is required to read material he has never seen before. This is called a "cold" reading. Many top name stars will readily admit that they are worthless at cold readings. Likewise, many inadequate actors who have trained specifically for interview situations are terrific at cold readings. There is such emphasis placed on this approach to casting that there are entire acting courses devoted to nothing but cold readings and interview techniques. Have you ever heard of an actor being required to read lines he's never seen before in an actual performance on the set? This situation is carried to its worst extreme in casting call sessions (often called "cattle calls"). A producer will have several people, often as many as fifty, appear at the same time to read for the same part. The actors sit together in the lobby or waiting room. They are all there for the same job and the atmosphere of hostile competition that pervades the room is enough to make an actor go back to waiting on tables. It's terribly destructive to their feelings of self-worth. The problem is compounded further when they are called in to read. They enter a room and are asked to read something they've never seen before in front of a group of strange faces who've been hearing the same lines all morning. When the actor finishes reading, he is ushered out with little or no feedback on his performance.

Consider readings, especially cold readings, a second-best approach to determining the ability of an actor. Often there is no alternative, but at least consider the problems it creates for the actors and judge them accordingly.

Extras

Nonspeaking atmosphere talent is not covered under SAG but under SEG (Screen Extras Guild). Signing a SAG agreement does not automatically require you to use SEG talent unless portions of your picture are filmed within a 300-mile radius of Columbus Circle in New York City, in which case you must use SEG talent for all scenes requiring extras that are filmed within that area. For the rest of the country, you may or may not choose to sign the SEG agreement. The advantage of signing with SEG is that you will have available any number of extras at a moment's notice, either through the guild or through an extras casting service. With the casting services you can even specify the attire. One hundred people are yours with a phone call and a check. The drawback, however, is that SEG talent is expensive. You can obtain a copy of the SEG/producer's agreement, which lists fees and contract requirements, from the Screen Extras Guild, 3629 Cahuenga Boulevard, Los Angeles, California 90068.

If your extras requirements are small, and if you are filming outside of the New York City area, you might be better off using your friends. You can always get a handful of people who will work for a free lunch and a chance to appear in a film. Be aware, however, that they will probably be inexperienced in front of the camera and will need a bit of extra guidance.

What's in a Name?

There is a small handful of actors and actresses who are considered "bankable" stars. This means that simply attaching their name to a project will guarantee financing. This may increase a picture's chances of becoming a hit, but it's no guarantee. Many name-star pictures have gone the way of the Edsel, while no-name pictures sometimes rise to the top of the charts. What the bankable star *will* guarantee is a bottom-line return. Even if the picture is a flop, there is a guaranteed audience who will go simply because of the star.

Who these bankable stars are depends on what part of the world you're in. There are American actors with a tremendous following in Europe but with little appeal in America. Such actors would be of value if you're financing a picture with European money. There are also actors with a large television following. Attaching their name to your picture may not increase sales at the box office, but it will make an eventual sale to television far more lucrative.

There are a few actors who have both box office drawing power *and* a high television rating. These "crossover" actors aren't powerful enough to be considered bankable but they can add a great deal to a film's worth.

Most actors whose names or faces you recognize are not bankable, either domestically or in Europe, and aren't particularly strong names on television. But that doesn't mean that they are without special value. The truth is that *any* recognizable name will add to your film's profits but in a less obvious way than the bankable stars and television personalities. The following thoughts on the value of names are of particular importance for the producer packaging a modestly budgeted picture.

The very first thing anyone will ask about your film, from the casual acquaintance at a cocktail party to the marketing chief of your potential distribution company, is "Who's in it?" The difference between a recognizable name and no name at all is like night and day. If you answer, "No one you've ever heard of," you're a maverick producer and immediately behind the eight ball. If you can name any actor they've heard of, your picture will instantly be raised to a level of acceptable respectability.

The involvement of such an actor will also make a difference in the attitude of the rest of your cast and even in the attitude of your crew. Everyone likes to feel that his work is a part of something important and everyone likes to talk about it. Nothing will contribute an air of legitimacy and importance to your project more readily than a cast name that people recognize. It costs very little to add such an actor to your cast, perhaps just for a one-day cameo appearance, but that single element will pay off many times over in the morale and status of your production.

CHAPTER 13

The Production Crew

Members of the Team

In addition to the director, production manager, and first assistant director, the key people on most crews are director of photography; sound mixer; gaffer; key grip; production designer; property master; wardrobe master; key makeup artist; special effects expert; stunt coordinator; location manager; still photographer; set construction foreman. A typical crew for a modest-budget film will consist of these key people and whatever portion of their support staffs is appropriate to the project.

The following are brief descriptions of the functions of key members of the production team and members of their support staffs.

THE DIRECTOR

The director is responsible to the producer for translating the screenplay into the images and sounds of a motion picture. He directs the activities of the cast and crew during preproduction, production, and postproduction.

First Assistant Director: The first assistant director works closely with the production manager to organize an optimum shooting schedule, is responsible to the director for the efficient execution of that schedule on the set, and assists the director, when required, in the direction of extras, crowd scenes, and special effects. The assistant director is also responsible for production paperwork including overtime authorizations, model releases, and call sheets.

Second Assistant Director: The second assistant director assists the first assistant director. This position involves mostly production paperwork and legwork.

Dialogue Director: The dialogue director is responsible for reviewing lines with actors prior to a take. One of the reasons for this is to ensure proper memorization of the lines by the actors. Often, when a part requires a particular accent or dialect, a dialogue director who specializes in that accent or dialect will coach the actor in the delivery of his or her lines.

Script Supervisor: The script supervisor is responsible for taking detailed notes during production, recording such information on the shooting script as scene and take number, camera position, performance continuity, dialogue changes, and the running time of each shot. These notes will be an aid to the director during production and to the editor during postproduction.

PRODUCTION MANAGER

The production manager is responsible to the producer for assembling the budget, organizing the shooting schedule, expediting all aspects of the production, and authorizing all expenditures.

Assistant Production Manager: The assistant production manager is responsible to the production manager and aids him in the performance of his duties.

Associate Producer: An associate producer is generally involved in preproduction, production, and postproduction as a supporting producer. In some cases, particularly in Europe, the associate producer may fulfill virtually all of the standard producer functions. This credit is sometimes given to a production manager or a first assistant director for contributions that greatly exceed his routine duties. For example, a production manager who supervises a project from preproduction planning through postproduction editing may receive an associate producer credit. In addition to acting as a sort of 'thank you' from the producer, there are several advantages to this. First, the associate producer credit usually appears with the credits at the head of the film (production manager and assistant director credits are generally listed at the end of the film). Second, an associate producer credit may be included with the principal credits in paid advertising such as posters and newspaper ads. Third, since the credit reflects a substantial contribution to a film, a person who commands such a credit can generally command more money.

DIRECTOR OF PHOTOGRAPHY

The director of photography is responsible to the director for achieving optimum photographic images for the film. His primary duties include selecting the camera and lighting equipment, supervising the camera and lighting crews, and determining the lighting pattern and exposure for each scene.

Camera Operator: The camera operator is responsible for operating the camera at all times and maintaining the composition established by the director or, in some cases, by the director of photography.

First Assistant Cameraman: The first assistant cameraman is responsible for maintaining and cleaning all elements in the camera package, setting up the camera with the appropriate lens and filters for each shot, and setting the lens stop and focus for each shot.

Second Assistant Cameraman (also referred to as the "loader"): The second assistant cameraman is responsible for loading and unloading film, maintaining all camera department paperwork such as camera reports and shipping labels, preparing the slate for each take, and aiding the first assistant cameraman in whatever way is required.

GAFFER

The gaffer is the chief electrician and is responsible to the director of photography for the safe and efficient execution of the lighting patterns outlined by the director of photography.

Gaffer's Best Boy: The gaffer's best boy is the first assistant electrician. He is responsible for assisting the gaffer in the performance of his duties and for supervising the operation of the lighting and electrical equipment.

Electricians: Electricians are responsible to the gaffer and the gaffer's best boy for rigging and operating lighting and electrical equipment.

Generator Operator: The generator operator is responsible to the gaffer for the operation and maintenance of electrical generators.

KEY GRIP

The key grip is responsible to the director of photography for supervising all grip crews. The principal responsibilities of the grip crews are to assist the gaffer during lighting procedures and to maneuver the camera unit during moving shots. Additional grip responsibilities include aiding various production departments such as sound, electrical, wardrobe, and property in the moving and handling of their equipment.

Dolly/Crane Grip: The dolly/crane grip is responsible to the key grip and the director of photography for the operation and maintenance of all dolly and crane equipment. When a dolly grip is not employed, the key grip usually fulfills this function.

Hammer Grips: Hammer grips are responsible for performing the various functions that fall under the jurisdiction of the key grip.

SOUND MIXER

The sound mixer is responsible for selecting and operating all sound equipment. He is called a mixer because one of his most important responsibilities, during takes that require the use of more than one microphone, is the *mixing* (balancing level and equalization) between microphones (level refers to volume; equalization refers to the relative intensity of various frequencies, e.g., treble, midrange, and bass). The sound mixer is also responsible for monitoring each recording and keeping accurate records on the sound reports.

Boom Operator: The boom operator is responsible to the sound mixer for operating the microphone boom, ensuring that the microphone is properly positioned at all times during a take and that the movement of the boom does not interfere with the lighting equipment, camera equipment, or the actors' movements. He is also responsible for voice-slating wild sound takes (see Chapter 17, under "Production Sound").

Cableman: The cableman's primary responsibilities include stringing and connecting all cables related to the sound recording equipment and handling such cables, if required, during moving shots.

PRODUCTION DESIGNER

The production designer works closely with the director to establish a "look" for the picture, and is responsible for conceiving, planning, and supervising the overall visual design of the film.

Art Director: The art director works closely with the production designer and is responsible to him for planning and executing the design of the sets. This requires both an artistic design sense and a thorough knowledge of architecture.

Costume Designer: The costume designer is responsible for purchasing and/or designing and supervising the making of all costumes for the production in accordance with the production design established by the director and the production designer.

Draftsman: The draftsman is responsible to the art director for executing sketches and drawings that will facilitate the work of the various art department functions including the design sketches for sets, props, and costumes.

Model Builder: The model builder is responsible for designing, building, and operating all miniature models required for the production in accordance with the production design established by the director and the production designer.

Prop Maker: The prop maker is responsible for designing, building, and operating any special props required for the production in accordance with the production design established by the director and the production designer.

Set Decorator: The set decorator is responsible for selecting and placing all props and set dressings in accordance with the production design established by the director and the production designer.

PROPERTY MASTER

The property master is responsible for the inventory and maintenance of all props associated with the production.

Set Dresser: The set dresser assists the property master and the set decorator in the performance of their duties.

Greensman: The greensman is responsible to the property master for selecting and maintaining all greenery such as plants and flowers necessary for the production.

WARDROBE MASTER

The wardrobe master supervises the operation of the wardrobe department including the inventory and maintenance of all wardrobe necessary for the production.

KEY MAKEUP ARTIST

In addition to applying makeup to the actors, the key makeup artist organizes and supervises the operation of all personnel in the makeup department including hairdressers, body makeup artists, and makeup assistants.

Assistant Makeup Artists: Assistant makeup artists assist the key makeup artist in applying and touching up actors' makeup.

Hairdresser: The hairdresser is responsible to the key makeup artist for the styling of actors' hair, wigs, toupees, etc.

Body Makeup Person: The body makeup person is responsible to the key makeup artist sor applying any makeup required on an actor from the neck down.

SPECIAL EFFECTS TECHNICIAN

The special effects technician is responsible to the director for safely and effectively planning and executing all special effects required for the production.

STUNT COORDINATOR

The stunt coordinator is responsible to the director for safely and effectively planning and executing all stunts required for the production.

LOCATION MANAGER

The location manager is responsible for scouting locations and recommending suitable sites for production. He is also responsible for securing any permits and/or related paperwork necessary for the use of selected locations.

STILL PHOTOGRAPHER

The still photographer is responsible to the producer and/or publicist for any still photography associated with the production.

SET CONSTRUCTION FOREMAN

The set construction foreman is the key carpenter and is responsible for supervising all construction associated with the production including sets, set dressings, and scaffolding.

Carpenters: Carpenters are responsible to the set construction foreman for constructing, delivering, setting up, and maintaining all construction pieces for the production.

Painters: Painters are responsible to the art director and/or set construction foreman for any painting necessary for the production.

Drapery Man: The drapery man is responsible to the art director for making (or purchasing) and installing any drapery and/or upholstery material required for the production.

Paperhanger: The paperhanger is responsible to the art director and/or set construction foreman for applying wallpaper, tile, and other related materials to the walls, floors, and ceilings of sets.

Plasterer: The plasterer is responsible to the art director and/or set construction foreman for any plastering required for the production.

Welder: The welder is responsible to the art director and/or set construction foreman for any metalwork or welding required for the production.

ADDITIONAL PRODUCTION PERSONNEL

Animal Specialists: Animal specialists are responsible to the director for caring for, handling, transporting, and directing animals and wildlife such as birds, dogs, snakes, and lions.

Wranglers: Wranglers are responsible to the director for caring for, handling, transporting, and directing livestock such as horses and cattle.

Publicist: The publicist is responsible to the producer for preparing, arranging for, and disseminating promotional information about the production such as newspaper stories and interviews.

Drivers: Under the supervision of a driver captain, drivers are responsible for maintaining and operating production vehicles.

Production Assistants: Production assistants are responsible to the producer, director, production manager, or assistant director. Their responsibilities include assisting in whatever manner best aids the production, such as running errands, typing production notes, carrying equipment, and making coffee.

First-aid Person: The first-aid person is responsible for the first-aid care of any person on the cast or crew requiring such attention.

Craft Serviceman: The craft serviceman is responsible for unskilled manual labor such as running errands, guarding sets and equipment, and keeping sets clean during shooting.

Selecting the Crew

The director is crucial to a film's success, but his talents will only be fully realized if he is surrounded by a strong, talented support staff. It has often been said that film is a director's medium. The truth is that film is a cooperative medium and really belongs to everyone who participates in making the film. The importance of a director's contribution increases if he is also the producer or the screenwriter or the star. But will he also light the sets and record the sound and apply the makeup? A director can take on additional responsibilities successfully only up to a point. The point of diminishing returns varies with the individual, but nobody goes it alone. It is therefore crucial to a director's success that his support personnel be selected with great care.

The producer, director, and production manager will select the key members of the crew. These decisions will be based on technical requirements, budget, and personal preference. The director may have a preference for certain key people such as the director of photography and script supervisor. The producer and production manager will suggest additional key people such as the makeup artist and stunt coordinator.

Once you have determined the key people, the job of crewing is over. Each of these key people will bring his own support staff. The director of photography will have a favorite camera operator and camera assistants. The sound mixer will pick the boom operator, and so forth.

If you have special production problems such as stunts, special effects, or animals, *hire a specialist.* There are highly skilled people in virtually every specialty area and what they can save in time, money, and anxiety is usually well worth their fee. A professional in any field will not only ensure that the scene plays well in the finished film but will also ensure that it's executed with a maximum emphasis on safety. If you can't afford to hire a professional, consider omitting the scene.

At least as important as the technical expertise of the crew is their spirit of dedication to the production. A technically qualified key grip who is accustomed to big-budget studio conditions with unlimited supplies, a leisurely shooting schedule, and lots of assistants, may be a poor choice for a low-budget film. He has paid his dues and has earned the right to work in comfort. The working conditions simply can't meet his expectations and he may become dissatisfied and disillusioned with your project. This isn't always the case but it's a danger worth considering.

The ideal situation for a low-budget film is to assemble key crew members who are technically brilliant in their fields but who haven't yet broken through to major league status. For these people, on the way up, each project is desperately important. If they believe in your picture they will go well beyond the call of duty to ensure that their work fully reflects their talents.

Union versus Nonunion

The terms union and nonunion, when applied to motion picture production, refer to whether or not a producer has signed a labor agreement governing his below-the-line personnel. A producer setting out to make a feature film must make this decision very early in the game. The principal purpose of the union is to protect its members. There are, however, advantages to a producer signing a union contract. First, he has access to any members of the union who are available within the framework of his schedule and budget. Second, the producer knows that union members have met certain qualifications for membership. A technician's title isn't based on his own subjective opinion of his talents. Furthermore, pictures that are made under the jurisdiction of a union often run more smoothly than nonunion pictures because the labor agreement defines an organized structure within which everyone must work.

The disadvantages to a producer who signs a labor agreement are that he must abide by the rules and regulations set forth in the agreement; he must abide by state and federal laws governing labor contracts; he must pay his employees no less than the union's minimum wages and he must pay whatever overtime is provided for in the agreement; he must pay fringe benefits for health, pension, and welfare.

The largest, most powerful union governing motion picture production is the International Alliance of Theatrical Stage Employees and Moving Picture Machine Operators of the United States and Canada (IATSE and MPMO). This organization is affiliated with the AFL-CIO and is generally referred to as the IA. In addition to all below-the-line job categories, the IA encompasses such positions as laboratory technicians, film distributors, projectionists, motion picture mechanics, and film salesmen.

All of the major studios and many independent producers have signed a long-term contract with the IA and consequently the majority of feature films are made with their crews. They have approximately 18,000 members on the West Coast alone and have been known to put out over a hundred complete production crews in a single day. A producer who signs an IA contract has available to him practically all of the top below-the-line talent in the industry. Each job category local will supply a signatory producer with a roster of available technicians from which he may choose his crew. Locals will not recommend any one individual over another; such recommendations are generally made by an experienced production manager.

Members of the IA are generally highly qualified individuals with substantial track records. Many of their key crew members have come up through the ranks of apprentice and assistant positions for six years or longer. Most of those who have bypassed this traditional route are individuals who established a significant reputation in their particular job category prior to joining the IA. There are, of course, a few unqualified members but they are uncommon and they almost never work.

An individual must work for thirty consecutive days in a particular job category on an IA production before he is permitted to join the union in that category. For many individuals this presents a catch-22 situation. They can't work on an IA picture without being a member of the union and they can't become a member of the union without working for thirty days on a union picture. The break for many individuals comes during peak production seasons when all available technicians in a given category are working. Producers may then hire nonunion personnel in those categories and, provided they work for thirty consecutive days, they may join the union. There are exceptions, but this situation commonly provides individuals with entrées into the IA.

A producer who signs with the IA is required by the union to employ a minimum number of union production personnel, usually no less than twenty-five for a feature film. Job categories for IA members are rigidly defined by the various locals, and rarely will members deviate from their specific functions. For example, a sound technician is not permitted to carry grip equipment; a camera assistant cannot touch a light. On large pictures this structure is useful and effective; on smaller pictures it is inefficient. Smaller films demand a family spirit, a team effort where everyone is willing to lend a hand to everyone else.

Each job category within the IA has local offices throughout the country, each of which has jurisdiction over a specific geographic area. If a producer signs an agreement with the IA in Los Angeles but wishes to shoot part of his production in New York, he must hire a New York crew for that portion of his production or hire New York "standby" crew members for each IA person he brings with him from Los Angeles. For example, if a producer wishes to maintain a consistency in the lighting style of his film, he may bring his Los Angeles director of photography with him to shoot the New York portions of his film, provided he hires a New York director of photography to stand by on the set throughout the filming period in New York.

Members of the IA are not permitted to work for producers who have not signed an IA contract, nor are producers who have signed an IA contract permitted to hire non-IA personnel in job categories over which the IA has jurisdiction. As far as the union is concerned, a picture is either 100 percent IA or it's not IA.

IA members occasionally work on nonunion films, but if the union discovers them doing so, the locals for those particular job categories will come to the set and request that their members leave the project. Union members will generally comply with this request. Those who don't comply face a possible fine, membership suspension, or expulsion from the union. This puts the producer of a mixed-crew film in a tough spot. If he has completed 80 percent of his film using IA members in a few crucial categories, such as director of photography, gaffer, and key makeup artist, he will have to stop production until he replaces those individuals. This will be costly for the producer and possibly damaging to the quality of the finished film. Finding replacement crew members may take several days. Such a break in production usually has a negative effect on the morale of the crew. Furthermore, since everyone has a unique working style, the work of the new crew members may be inconsistent with that of their predecessors and the look of the finished film may suffer.

It is not uncommon for producers to proceed with a mixed crew in spite of these dangers. The risk of discovery by the union is minimized if a producer maintains a low profile, perhaps going off to some remote location for his production. The risk is increased if he takes out large announcements in trade papers and shoots on public streets in the heart of Hollywood. In any case, the potential danger of being shut down partway through production is worth carefully considering before proceeding with a mixed crew.

A producer interested in more information regarding the minimum contract requirements of an IA production may contact the IA office at the address and phone number listed in the *Pacific Coast Studio Directory*. Information regarding minimum wages for the various IA job categories may be found in *Brooks' Standard Rate Book* and in the *Hollywood Production Manual*. These publications are listed in Appendix E.

A common misconception in the industry is that a producer who signs an IA contract must use teamster drivers for his production. The teamsters are a separate union from the IA and require a separate contract. The reason most IA signatory producers also sign with the teamsters is because most of the facilities that supply dressing rooms, honeywagons (portable toilets), camera cars and cranes, catering services and buses for transporting the cast and crew are signatories to the teamster contract. Consequently, it is often difficult for a producer to obtain these services without signing a teamster contract. Should an IA signatory producer decide against a teamster contract, the teamsters have no recourse except possibly to throw up a picket line at the production site. Since the IA must honor their separate contract, they will not, except in very unusual circumstances, honor such a picket line.

The advantage for a producer signing a teamster contract is that he has available to him a virtually unlimited number of professional drivers under the supervision of a driver captain and cocaptain. This is particularly useful on large-budget pictures. On smaller pictures the expense of professional drivers who contribute nothing more than moving vehicles from one place to another may be prohibitive.

Another motion picture union that has been authorized by the AFL-CIO to represent below-the-line personnel is the National Association of Broadcast Employees and Technicians (NABET). The film section of NABET was started by broadcast organizations, primarily ABC and NBC, in the early fifties. For the first ten years work for NABET crews was slow. Then, in the early sixties, a NABET crew was hired to make one of the biggest independent films of all time—*Easy Rider.* The success of that picture gave impetus to the independent movement and put NABET on the map. Since then many successful features have been made with NABET crews including *Executive Action, Vice Squad, Hester Street, Born Losers, Joe, A Boy and His Dog, Steel Arena,* and *The Exterminator.*

Since a producer cannot be a signatory to both NABET and the IA, NABET is specifically interested in attracting independent producers and has streamlined its contract to meet their needs. For example, there are no minimum crewing requirements for a NABET picture. The producer, director, and production manager determine the key crew members and, in consultation with those key crew members, determine how much support staff will be required. The complexities of the production dictate the minimum size of the crew.

Unlike members of the IA, NABET members are not bound by geographic restrictions. If a producer is making a NABET picture in Los Angeles but wishes to film portions of that picture in New York, he may bring whichever members of his Los Angeles crew he wishes to New York without having to hire New York standby crew members.

NABET is open to new members who meet certain qualifications including passing a test for each job category. There are no apprenticeship requirements for membership in a particular category. This is an advantage to a producer who wishes to use a nonunion person such as a director of photography in conjunction with a NABET crew. Assuming the director of photography meets NABET qualifications he may join the union and the producer can include him as part of the crew.

Because NABET is more accessible to nonunion technicians

than the IA, many qualified individuals get their start with this union. However, by the time a NABET member achieves a significant reputation he is usually in demand by IA signatory producers and often leaves NABET to join the IA. An individual may not be a member of NABET and the IA simultaneously. Directors of photography such as Haskell Wexler, Vilmos Zsigmond, Laszlo Kovacs, and, more recently, Caleb Deschanel, began with NABET and have since joined the IA.

NABET permits their members to work on nonunion productions provided they are not working for less than NABET's minimum terms. If NABET discovers a member working on a nonunion picture for NABET minimums or better, the union will request that the producer sign a labor agreement but they will not request that their member leave the production. If that member is working for less than NABET minimums they will request that he leave the production or subject himself to a possible fine, membership suspension, or expulsion from the union.

NABET has specific guidelines and definitions for various job functions, as does the IA, but NABET crews are generally less rigid about this than IA crews. For example, a NABET camera assistant might lend a hand to the lighting crew, a sound technician might help move some props, etc. This is partly because all NABET members are represented by a single office and, consequently, have a closer tie to one another than members of the IA (the IA has a separate local for each job category). From a producer's point of view, it is simpler to deal with one office than with several locals.

Because NABET has its own driver category, NABET signatory producers do not generally become involved with the teamsters. Since producers cannot be signatories to the IA and NABET simultaneously, IA signatory producers do not have access to NABET drivers; they will usually have to sign with the teamsters in order to make their pictures.

The regulations governing NABET drivers are less stringent than those governing the teamsters. For example, NABET will permit a crew member such as a gaffer or sound mixer to drive his own equipment truck. The teamsters require that each and every vehicle in the production be moved solely by professional teamster drivers.

Since independent producers generally don't produce several

pictures in a row, a NABET contract is usually signed only for the duration of a particular project. A producer wishing to sign with this union will negotiate the basic labor agreement with a NABET business representative. He will then obtain a roster listing union members and their phone numbers. NABET membership is considerably smaller than IA membership so the number of technicians available for a NABET production will be more limited than for an IA production.

When a producer has selected his potential key crew members from the roster (usually in consultation with his director and production manager) he may obtain a list of their credits and sample reels of their work by contacting the individuals directly. The union does not provide lists of credits or sample reels. If a producer wishes to hire a member of NABET who is accustomed to working for above-minimum terms (most experienced members generally receive above scale) such terms must be negotiated directly with the individual or his agent. All such negotiations will be incorporated into the labor agreement.

Although a producer may hire NABET members on a nonunion project, he is more likely to negotiate for minimum terms if he signs a labor agreement with the union. The reason for this is that members feel protected and, consequently, more secure on the job if the producer has signed a labor agreement. If the producer does not sign a labor agreement, they are less protected and will often ask for more money to compensate for the risk of working without the protection of a labor agreement. Another reason is that members often feel that if they are willing to offer their talents at scale, the producer should respect their union and sign a labor agreement.

NABET will, at the request of a producer, contact crew members directly and assemble the crew. The advantage of having the union make the contacts is that they deal with their members on a regular basis; they know their temperaments, what they're used to getting, and what they will accept. Consequently, they may be more successful than the producer in assembling an optimum crew within the producer's budget.

As an example, the producer for *The Exterminator* signed a NABET contract in New York but wished to film portions of his film in Los Angeles. His budget was limited to NABET minimum wages for his below-the-line personnel. He contacted NABET in

Los Angeles and asked them to assemble a crew of technicians to support the key crew members that he brought with him from New York. In four days the Los Angeles office assembled a crew of forty people, most of whom generally work for above scale, all of whom worked for minimum scale on *The Exterminator.* The union contacted their members on behalf of the producer, explained the producer's situation, and assembled a crew to meet his needs.

In addition to members of the IA and NABET there are many qualified nonunion individuals available for each below-the-line job category. They are harder to locate and their talent is often more difficult to judge. They are not backed up by an organization that has established criteria for qualifications in each category and, in most cases, they are less experienced than their union counterparts. The best way to locate such individuals is through production managers who have had experience working on nonunion pictures. Other ways include advertising in trade papers such as *Variety* and the *Hollywood Reporter,* advertising in film schools, and inquiring at motion picture equipment rental houses. Equipment houses are often aware of which nonunion people work most often.

The most important thing to avoid is hiring unskilled or unqualified labor. There are many such people who would gladly die for an opportunity to work on a motion picture production but virtually every below-the-line position including second camera assistant, hammer grip, best boy, electrician, makeup artist, and boom operator demands a competent, experienced, highly trained individual. A producer who naively hires unqualified below-the-line technicians in an effort to save money probably will spend more money in wasted time during production and will ultimately produce an inferior film.

The question of whether to use an IA, NABET, nonunion, or mixed crew is one that independent producers face with each new project. The information contained herein is intended to give an overview of the pros and cons of each approach. The best way to determine which is most suitable for a particular project is to visit the union offices to discuss the project, then consult with other producers and production managers who have made similar pictures in the past. Ultimately, the decision will be dictated by the unique problems of each production.

Selecting a Director of Photography

A cinematographer's work is often judged on the basis of a sample reel. This is especially true of cinematographers seeking work on low-budget features. Producers often believe that a sample reel is a condensation of the very best work of which the cinematographer is capable. This is a naive attitude that I would like to dispel. In reality, especially with beginning cinematographers, a sample reel is a compilation of the best work he could get his hands on. Often his reel consists of scenes shot under limiting, low-budget conditions and represents the best the cinematographer could do under the circumstances—not the best of which he is capable.

Getting any scene from a film for a sample reel is difficult. Printing small sections of a film is hard on the negative and in order to get a two-minute scene the cinematographer may have to buy an entire reel. The cost of this is often prohibitive. The cinematographer often turns to the distributor and purchases used material, either an entire print or one reel at a time. When a distributor sells an old print, chances are it will be scratched or torn, perhaps in the best scenes. The cinematographer might be stuck showing second-best scenes, perhaps ones that were shot under extreme time pressure with little lighting equipment. This clearly is not representative of work of which the cinematographer is *capable*. In order to best judge a sample reel, be sure to do the following.

Divorce yourself from the *content*. The material may be distasteful to you, or the acting may be awful. But that's not what you're judging, so don't let it interfere with your judgment of the cinematography.

Look for a style of lighting that is consistent with your vision of what your picture should look like. Watch especially for interior lighting, which is usually more difficult than exterior lighting.

Don't confuse the cinematographer's talent with the placement of the camera. This will generally not be the cinematographer's responsibility. The principal function of the director of photography is to light the scene, not place the camera. A good cinematographer will usually make contributions to placement, but this responsibility is ultimately the director's.

If you are working within a budget that requires hiring one

person to work as both director of photography and camera operator, watch for smooth, steady moves. If you see a problem such
as an awkward jerk or bump, look for the consistency of that
problem. Every operator has awkward moves on occasion and in
low-budget films there often isn't time to correct them with a
second take. If you don't see a repetitive problem, it may not be
a problem.

Be wary of flashy, tricky reels that utilize a series of fast-paced
action sequences, such as car crashes or promotional trailers with
lots of sound effects and bombastic music. These sequences may
evoke an emotional response, but is it because of the cinematography? Or is it the editing, or the music, or the sound effects? Poor
cinematography can often be masked with these tricks of the
trade. Further, it is difficult to judge lighting when each scene is
on the screen for less than a second. When you encounter an
action reel of this kind, try viewing it a second time without the
sound. Watching it silent will tell you a great deal more about its
visual impact.

Production Design

Designing a production refers to the task of creating an overall
"look" for the film including sets, costumes, special makeup, special effects, and all other visual elements in the picture. The execution of the production designer's plan is up to the specialists in
their respective departments. The art directors must plan the construction of the sets; the costume designers must select fabrics and
supervise the making of the costumes; the special effects team
must decide how to execute the special effects created by the
production designer; the makeup artist must determine the best
way to create the proposed makeup designs; and so forth.

An art director is generally responsible for designing sets, not
for the overall design of the picture. A production designer is
usually employed only when a picture requires more than one art
director. On *Lawrence of Arabia* there were four art directors,
each working in a different country, under the supervision of one
production designer. On *The Deep* there were two art directors
working under the production designer—one for the underwater
sequences, and one for the above-water sequences. On *2001: A
Space Odyssey* there were forty designers working on costumes,

sets, special effects, special makeup, etc., under the supervision of one production designer.

The work of a production designer on a big-budget picture is often less taxing than the work of an art director on a smaller film. On a large picture, most of the work beyond the original design is delegated; on a small picture the art director must not only design the sets, he must also draw the renderings and architectural plans for his designs.

The credit for a production designer is given only on special films. In order to receive the credit on an IA union film, the Society of Motion Picture and Television Art Directors must evaluate the work on the film in question to determine whether or not the credit is warranted. Without such approval the credit cannot appear on the film.

CHAPTER 14

Equipment, Facilities, and Services

Equipment

The equipment package will be determined by the requirements of the director and the director of photography. The producer and production manager will negotiate with equipment rental houses for the best price for that particular package. A list of rental houses around the country is included in Appendix D.

Generally, equipment houses will offer a four for seven rental price, where you pay for four days but keep the equipment for seven. This is most helpful when shooting six-day weeks. Prices are negotiable depending on the package, how long you need it, and the season of the year. You will be able to negotiate for better gear at a lower price during slow production seasons. Prices will vary from house to house, depending on your particular needs. One house may have less expensive lighting gear but more expensive grip equipment. Shop around for the best price for your particular package.

In addition to price, consider the house's reputation for maintaining, servicing, and replacing gear quickly if something breaks down. Find a house that offers adequate backup gear and replacement parts. There is nothing more frustrating than a delay in production caused by equipment failure. The rental house must be able to solve any such problems quickly. An experienced director of photography will either know or be able to find out about a particular house's reputation in these areas.

A director of photography or gaffer will commonly own his own gear and will offer it to the production with his services for a very reasonable package price. This can be a terrific deal but there are two drawbacks to consider before making a decision. First, the owner of the gear may be unreasonably cautious or conservative in its use. This could cost you time during production. A gaffer who would normally support a lightstand with a couple of sandbags might, if he owns the light, also nail it to the floor! Another consideration is that it becomes very difficult to fire someone if it also means replacing his equipment and renegotiating for a replacement package with a rental house halfway through production. I suggest these downside considerations in order that producers entering into such arrangements do so with a full understanding of the potential problems and not simply with an eye to price.

Unlike most technicians, sound men almost always bring their own gear but this, too, is available from rental houses.

Laboratories and Sound Facilities

Motion picture laboratories offer a variety of services, most of which are discussed in Part V, "Distribution and Marketing." In brief these services are:

- processing (developing) the camera negative
- making a positive work print from the negative
- making black and white dupes from the work print
- making interpositive prints from the original negative and internegative prints from the interpositive (these are used for the majority of optical effects work and, in some cases, for making release prints)
- making a color reversal internegative (CRI) from which release prints are made
- developing the optical sound track
- making color and density corrections from scene to scene within the film (called "timing")
- making release prints for distribution

In addition to the above, most laboratories have negative cutting departments on their premises for conforming the original negative to the edited work print.

Laboratories that have reputations for handling feature films can generally be relied upon to produce quality work. There are also many smaller laboratories with less substantial reputations that are capable of handling feature films. If you are considering such a facility it is important to scrutinize it carefully. If their experience has been limited to industrial and educational films, they may be an inappropriate choice for a feature production. One way to find out is to ask for references. Ask if they have handled projects in the past that are similar to yours. If not, you may request that such a facility run a test. This involves giving the laboratory a sample piece of film to process and print. There is usually no charge for this. A producer can often make a satisfactory judgment about a laboratory's capabilities based on such a test.

The prices for laboratory services are competitive and negotiable. Pick the laboratory you feel is best suited for your picture, then shop around at various laboratories for the best price. Your first-choice lab will make a sincere effort to match the best price and will probably succeed.

Sound facilities offer a variety of services including transferring, syncing, looping, recording, and mixing. These services will be discussed later in this book. The prices for various services at sound facilities vary enormously and are less negotiable than the prices for laboratory services. A major sound facility might charge $135 per hour for recording wild lines or narration, while a smaller facility with comparable equipment and engineers might charge as little as $30 per hour. The differences are literally that great. Your decision must be based on both price and reputation. A competent sound mixer will be able to offer guidance in this area.

Full-service sound houses will often offer a deal for an entire package of services including transfer, syncing, sound effects, mixing, and optical transfer. Like the gaffer's equipment package, this may be an extremely good price. But, again, there are downside considerations. If you get halfway through your production and the sound facility's services deteriorate (perhaps they become overloaded with additional, unexpected work), you may have a difficult time taking your film elsewhere. You will have committed yourself with a deposit and a guarantee. There are enough problems in producing a film without fighting an uphill battle for quality work at an overextended sound house. It's comforting to maintain the freedom to walk away. You may pay for the freedom, but sometimes it's worth it.

Again, this is not intended to rule out the possibility of a package deal but simply to caution producers about considerations beyond the immediate dollar.

When selecting an equipment house, a sound facility, or a laboratory, lean on your specialists for guidance. Consult your director of photography and sound mixer. They will undoubtedly have preferences and will have established strong connections with certain houses. This can be a great asset if you run into problems or require special services during production.

Sound Stages versus Practical Locations

In most scripts there are choices to be made between shooting certain scenes on location versus building sets on a sound stage. In most large cities, there are stages or similar facilities available for rent. The advantages of a sound stage are that it offers flexibility and speed. Rigging for lights and cable, as well as a generous supply of power, are at your fingertips. They are sound-proofed, which eliminates waiting for traffic noise or airplane noise to die down before shooting a scene. The floor surface is smooth for dolly moves. Since most sets are built with wild (movable) walls, they offer a flexibility in camera placement and movement that would not be possible on location.

The drawbacks to sound stages are that you must pay for the construction of sets, you must pay for the facility during construction, you must pay for any holding time between construction and shooting, and you must pay for the time you're shooting. These prices are often negotiable, especially during a slow season.

A practical location such as a working restaurant or private home, is generally rigged and shot at the same time so you will rarely pay for holding time. Further, a practical location may offer something useful that is difficult to duplicate on a stage, such as a large window overlooking a busy street. Locations will usually have to be rigged with power and lights, and the space must be large enough to accommodate the scene in question *and* the production crew.

Most pictures utilize a combination of sound stages and practical locations but the smaller the budget, the more you'll be leaning toward shooting in practical locations. The decision must be based on economics, feasibility, and artistic considerations—not necessarily in that order.

Many states have established motion picture location coordinators to encourage producers to shoot in their state. Since film production stimulates their economy, they will go out of their way to aid producers, sometimes paying the expenses for a location scouting trip. A complete listing of motion picture coordinators for each state may be found in the *Guide to Location Information* listed in Appendix E.

Film Stock

Most feature films are shot with 35mm negative film, using an aspect ratio of 1.85 : 1. The aspect ratio refers to the relative size of the width and height of the projected image on the screen. A 1.85 : 1 aspect ratio means that the projected image is 1.85 times wider than it is high. Other 35mm formats include 1.33 : 1, 1.66 : 1, and 2.35 : 1. A 2.35 : 1 aspect ratio produces a very wide image and is most appropriate for pictures requiring many outdoor panoramic scenes. The format for a film is generally selected by the producer, director, and director of photography.

Virtually all motion picture theaters throughout the world are equipped to project 35mm prints. Some of the larger theaters are also equipped to handle 70mm prints. 70mm prints are made either from 70mm original negative or "blown up" from 35mm original negative. The latter has become more common since, in recent years, the price of film stock has risen dramatically. If a film is shot using 70mm original negative, the image must be reduced to make 35mm prints for distribution to theaters that are not equipped to handle 70mm prints. These are called "reduction prints."

Some films, such as John Sayles's *Return of the Secaucus Seven,* are shot using 16mm original negative, then blown up to 35mm for distribution. This is generally done when a producer has very limited funds for production and cannot afford to shoot in 35mm. In addition to the cost savings, some other advantages of shooting in 16mm are that the equipment is lighter and more maneuverable and the running time for a given length of film is considerably longer than in 35mm. Both 16mm and 35mm film travels at the rate of twenty-four frames per second (called "sound speed"), but since a 16mm frame is smaller than a 35mm frame, the number of feet passing through the camera in a given span of time is less in 16mm. 16mm film travels at thirty-six feet per minute; 35mm film travels at ninety feet per minute. Shooting in 16mm is especially advantageous to documentary filmmakers who must move very quickly, often filming events on the spur of the moment.

There is a 16mm format called Super-16 that was developed over ten years ago in Sweden specifically for the purpose of blowing up to 35mm. This technique utilizes standard 16mm film but exposes, in addition to the standard 16mm picture area, the optical soundtrack area on the edge of the film. Since this format closely approximates a 1.85 : 1 aspect ratio, there is effectively 40 percent more information area on a Super-16 frame than on a standard 16mm frame. When shooting in Super-16 the lens selection is somewhat limited and one needs more light to assure a successful blow-up, but the end result is significantly better than with the standard 16mm format.

The principal disadvantage of shooting in either 16mm or Super-16 is that the quality of prints made from a blow-up negative suffers, primarily from increased contrast and grain. Rarely will such a print look as good as a print made from a 35mm original negative. Also, when the blow-up is made, the original 16mm negative is subjected to an optical printing process during which the danger of scratches and tears in the negative is increased.

Another consideration regarding film size has to do with the attitude of the cast and crew. Since most films are released in 35mm, many people expect them to be *shot* in 35mm. Such people may be less enthusiastic about working on a 16mm production than on a 35mm production. The size of the film may have little or no effect on the impact of the finished film but the attitude still prevails.

This attitude extends into the world of distribution. A producer who screens a 16mm print for distributors is at something of a disadvantage because distributors have a built-in bias that favors 35mm films. If a film is made in 16mm and the producer cannot afford the cost of the blow-up, it may be wise for him to show potential distributors a video cassette of the finished film. In this way, unless the distributor knows that the picture was shot in 16mm, he will not be biased unfavorably by the size of the film.

Although it is less expensive to make a film in 16mm, the cost of the blow-up to 35mm is considerable and sometimes outweighs the savings. If a producer has enough in his budget to pay for the blow-up he might have enough to shoot in 35mm.

In cases where the budget limitations are such that the producer has no alternative but to shoot in 16mm, and cannot afford the cost of a blow-up, he will complete his film, negotiate his distribution deal, and then make the blow-up. In such cases the cost of the blow-up becomes a distribution expense and the distributor will put up the money.

Additional information regarding film formats and film sizes may be found in the *American Cinematographer's Manual* listed in Appendix E.

Most film stock is purchased direct from the manufacturer, usually Eastman Kodak. However, if your budget is very tight, there is an option available for the purchase of raw stock. Major studios purchase all of their film stock at the beginning of each production. If, when they finish the film, they have leftover, unopened cans of raw stock, they sell them at reduced prices to one of several film exchanges. The film exchanges, in turn, sell to producers for less than the manufacturer charges.

It is not advisable to purchase bits and pieces from several productions with a variety of emulsion numbers but often you can find 100,000 feet or more of unopened 35mm negative with one consistent emulsion number that was left over from one picture. It's wise to buy one can first and run a test to see if it's okay, before committing yourself to the entire purchase. There is no getting around the risks involved, even with a test roll. Perhaps half of the stock was left sitting in the heat of direct sunlight for a week but your test can happened to be one of the rolls that was kept refrigerated. Chances are, however, that if your test roll looks good, the rest is okay. Studios are pretty good about storing and handling raw stock.

CHAPTER 15

The Final Step

By this time, your script should be polished to a spit shine. You have completed casting, you have a full crew, a full complement of equipment, location and studio arrangements have been made, and your laboratory and sound houses are standing by to receive dailies. Any additional elements needed for production, such as props, special makeup, and animals, will be handled by the appropriate key people on your crew.

But you're still not quite ready to begin production. If you intend to work efficiently, produce a quality picture, and stay on schedule, the director must take time to prepare the entire cast and crew thoroughly, reviewing with them his plan of attack for production.

Every member of the cast and crew is responsible for a special part of the picture. Consequently, each of them views the project from a somewhat narrow perspective. It is the director who must maintain a vision of the entire film. He must have a sense for the interworking of all of the individual parts, and direct each part toward a consistent goal.

Prepping the Cast

In negotiating contracts with principal actors, it is to everyone's advantage to include time for rehearsals. This time may be used not only to boost the actor's performance but also to iron out awkward scenes in the script *before* beginning principal photography. Such scenes reveal themselves much more clearly when acted out than they do as written words in the script.

Rehearsal generally begins with discussions about the story, characters, relationships, and motivations. It's often helpful to assemble the entire cast in one room, seat them in a circle, and have them read through the script from start to finish. The director can fill in the connective tissue with descriptions of non-dialogue scenes, such as car chases. In this way, the actors will get a feel for the continuity of the story and the director will get a sense for the interplay among characters. Remember that this is just a reading, not a performance.

The second phase of rehearsal involves work on individual scenes. This may be done in any quiet room. The principal reason for doing this is to block the action (also known as "staging"). It is often a mistake to work on fine-tuning a performance this early in the game. Many actors feel that it is easy to overrehearse for a film. Their performances may become stale, losing their spontaneity and life. On the other hand, some actors believe that no amount of rehearsal is too much. It is important for the director to remain sensitive to his actors' preferences.

Director George Roy Hill once said that getting the right script and the right cast is 75 percent of directing. When asked what the other 25 percent is, he said "Staging it." If you stage a scene properly and have good, well-cast actors, the scene will often fall into place with no additional help.

The blocking of a scene should appear natural and comfortable. It should also contribute visually to the scene's purpose or statement. There is a marvelous example in *Butch Cassidy and the Sundance Kid,* which was directed by George Roy Hill. The scene involved Butch (Paul Newman), Sundance (Robert Redford), and Etta (Katherine Ross) in a three-way dialogue scene on the front porch of Etta's house. Etta, if you remember, was their mutual friend, but she was also Sundance's lover.

Etta and Sundance were seated on the porch but the director placed Butch inside the house, leaning out a window overlooking the porch for his part of the dialogue. With this simple blocking, the director created a visual image of the relationships among these characters. This was a far more interesting approach than seating all three on the porch and hoping that the words alone would carry the message. This is a simple example of good blocking. The problems become far more involved when there is movement or activity in the scene.

The importance of blocking the action during rehearsal is to give the actor an opportunity to practice his moves, incorporating them into his overall performance. Further, if you block a scene during rehearsal and find that it's not flowing the way you had intended, you will have time to rethink the moves and correct the problem. Knowing what you're after in a scene and knowing how to communicate it is a large part of directing; knowing when you've got it is the rest.

In addition to blocking, the rehearsal time is an opportunity for the director and actors to arrive at a mutually understood direction for each scene. It's an opportunity to play around with the script, to try a variety of approaches and blocking patterns. Once you feel certain that what you're after in a scene is within reach, stop. Don't wait until you've actually got it or you may never get it again. Do not overrehearse. Block out the overall action and search for a mutual understanding of each scene with the actors, but don't press for a polished performance. If you've cast the film carefully and have properly blocked the scene, the polished performance will come when it's supposed to—in front of the cameras.

Prepping the Crew

This is one of the most important, yet often minimized responsibilities of the director. Prepping the crew reduces production problems, contributes to an efficient work force, and boosts morale. A well-informed crew, involved in the preproduction planning process, will work harder to contribute their talents than a crew that is expected simply to arrive on time and do a job. This attitude of treating the crew with respect and consideration should prevail throughout the making of the film.

In-depth discussions with the cinematographer, art director, costume designer, property master, etc., will establish a direction for the look of the film. Intercourse of this kind, guided by the director, contributes to consistency and coordination. This process should begin with general discussions about style, mood, and approach, and evolve into concrete discussions concerning color, fabric, texture, props, sets, wardrobe, makeup, and lighting.

For example, consider a scene in an intimate French restaurant. An attractive woman, dining alone, catches the eye of the maitre d'. The director is looking for a warm, romantic, somewhat lonesome mood, perhaps the stylized feeling of the forties. He intends to approach the scene from the point of view of the maitre d', so we will first see the woman in long shot from across the restaurant where the maitre d' is standing. Each of the specialists involved in the look of this scene will contribute to the director's goal. But in order to do so properly, they must coordinate their efforts. They must communicate closely with each other and proceed with a total understanding of how each of them will contribute to the scene. In this way, if the actress wears a red dress, the art director will not paint the walls red, and the set decorator won't use a red tablecloth.

Prior to beginning principal photography, it is of great value for the director to walk through the sets and locations with all of the key crew members. Ideally, this includes the director of photography, gaffer, key grip, production designer, sound mixer, assistant director, special effects, and stunt people. All of these people may not be available at the same time, in which case it may be necessary to do it a couple of times to accommodate them all. The information gained from a preliminary walk-through will make a tremendous difference in the efficiency of your production.

The director and director of photography will have an opportunity to discuss the look and lighting style for each location. The director may be looking for a particular quality, perhaps a glowing, bounced light effect. But what if the room is small with a low ceiling and there is no practical way to hide the lights for a bounced effect? The director of photography can communicate these difficulties and discuss alternatives. Perhaps he'll suggest using an imaginary off-camera light source, such as a window or table lamp to accomplish a similar effect.

A sound man will pay close attention to extraneous noise such as traffic, air conditioners, and airplanes. He will either plan for a way to work around the problems (e.g., locating the main air conditioning on-off switch) or he will inform the director of the potential difficulties.

A gaffer will immediately seek out the power source to determine how much power is available, how much cable will be required, and whether or not he'll need a supplementary generator.

The key grip will consider problems of rigging in each location. He will also pay close attention to the floor surface. Is it smooth and level for dolly moves or will he need to lay dolly tracks?

In this way, each key crew member will have an opportunity to make constructive suggestions for improving each scene. Each will also have an opportunity to express any problems they foresee in achieving the director's goals. This information is invaluable to the director. He will be able to plan scenes more thoroughly, making any necessary alterations or compromises *before* beginning production. Further, should the director decide to go ahead with a plan in spite of certain problems it creates for the crew, he'll know ahead of time what he's getting into and what compromises he'll have to live with. In short, there will be no surprises.

Involving the crew in walk-throughs of this kind will not only help the technical quality of their work but will also increase their involvement and enthusiasm for your project.

Storyboarding

One of the best ways for a director to organize his thoughts and to communicate them to his crew is by means of a storyboard. This is a multiple-panel pictorial representation of the film, similar to a comic book. A detailed storyboard will have a separate panel for each camera setup and possibly several panels to indicate camera movements. For example, if the camera dollies in from a long shot to a close-up in a single take, the storyboard may indicate this with two panels—one for the long-shot starting position and another for the close-up ending position. A detailed storyboard may also include color coordination and styles for costumes, sets, and props.

A less elaborate but often adequate way for a director to organize his camera setups is by means of a floor plan. The director can draw onto the floor plan the position and movements of the cast and any important props. He can then draw in a series of camera positions, noting any camera moves and then number these positions in the order in which he intends to shoot them. It will also be useful to list and describe the camera setups on a separate page. This page is referred to as a "shot list." The order in which these shots are listed is extremely important and are discussed further in Part 3, "The Process of Production."

PART 3

The Process of Production

CHAPTER 16

Directing

Interpretation and Style

During production, the principal artistic force behind a film is the director. Part of the process of any art form is change. If you ask an artist which of his works is the greatest, he is likely to tell you the most recent is the greatest. To say anything else indicates a lack of growth in the artist. This concept holds true for all directors who approach their work as an expression or extension of themselves, whether they are making student films, art films, documentaries, low-budget features, or major studio productions.

Just as every director's life experience is unique, so every director's work is unique. What, then, makes certain directors consistently stand out in the crowd? The answer encompasses two parts: *interpretation* and *style*.

The former is a result of the unique life experience and genetic makeup of the individual. Interpretation comes alive in the director's mind when he reads a script. The more he reads and studies each scene, the more his interpretation develops into an overall vision of the film. It is important to remember that since every director's interpretation is based on a unique life experience, every director's interpretation is valid. There is, however, an invalid use of style, but this will be discussed later.

If a picture is worth a thousand words, a moving picture with sound must be worth a million. It is impossible to write a screenplay so completely that it leaves no room for interpretation. This, then, becomes the director's first responsibility. He must know what he's after in each scene. He may not know immediately how to get it; that's another problem. But he must have a sense for what the scene should "feel" like. He must have a personal interpretation that works—for him. If, after studying a screenplay, a sensible cinematic interpretation doesn't develop in his mind, he's probably got the wrong screenplay.

Style is the way in which a director translates his interpretation onto film. In other words, it is the learned application and manipulation of the tools, or elements, that turn words on paper into the images and sounds of a movie. How a director applies his technical knowledge will depend on his interpretation, but the more a director understands about the elements that make up a film, the more stylistic choices will be available to him. Some of these elements are actors, words, movement, locations, color, makeup, sound effects, music, camera, lenses, film stock, editing, opticals, stunts, and light.

Sidney Pollack, who has been called an actor's director, once said, "It's very enjoyable for me to get into the technical end of it all. I like to understand everything about how the teeth and claws work inside the camera, about the operation of the sound equipment, and I have the same curiosity concerning sets and wardrobe. I like to get into the details."

The style a director chooses will be dictated by his interpretation. For example, consider this scene: "A boy on a horse silhouetted against an ominous sky." What does this scene feel like? Does it feel nervous, uncomfortable? If so, the director may choose a staccato style, handling the scene in quick cuts back and forth between the boy and the sky, each cut moving closer to the boy's face. The director may add the neighing of the horse, a howling wind, and a background percussion track that sounds like a quickened heart. This will result in a nervous sequence—an effective translation of the director's interpretation.

For another director the scene may feel tumultuous, chaotic. An appropriate style would be a hand-held camera circling the boy and the horse as the horse frets and bolts. The director may add a fully orchestrated score with strings and horns that build to a crescendo as the horse suddenly bolts and lightning cracks the sky.

Another interpretation might be a strange sense of calm. The sky could be a metaphor for an intense power building in the boy.

The director may choose a more lyrical style, perhaps a floating camera that gently drifts closer to the boy, settling on his fixed gaze at the darkened sky. As the first drops of rain strike the boy's face, he smiles, drops back his head, and opens his mouth to taste the rain.

It could be that a director has a "feel" for the scene but isn't certain how to get it. He may try a number of approaches, playing with the scene, working with the boy, perhaps improvising, until the feeling begins to gel. The point is simply that interpretation and style *depend* on each other. They are inextricably intermingled.

The more a director understands about his craft and about the elements and tools at his disposal, the better able he will be to translate his interpretation of the screenplay onto film.

No scene in a film is identical to any other scene in any other film. Two scenes might be very similar but they are never identical. Consequently, a director must evaluate each scene as a new experience. This requires the director to think for himself and to act on his convictions. This takes courage. One must never fall back on a formula approach simply because it's safe. A conventional approach is valid only when it effectively communicates your interpretation.

Likewise, one must never use technique simply to advertise one's knowledge. An *original* approach is also valid only if it effectively communicates your interpretation. It is often a temptation to use a new technique, simply because it's new, even if it doesn't quite fit the material. Approach each and every scene with a single-minded determination to arrive at a style that best communicates your interpretation of the story.

I believe that anyone interested in directing can learn to become a good director. Everyone can interpret the words of a screenplay in terms of his life experience and certainly can learn all of the techniques involved in filmmaking. But the questions still remain —what makes some directors consistently stand out; what makes someone a great director? Miles Davis answered these questions with an excellent analogy to music, "The difference between a fair musician and a good musician is that a good musician can play anything he thinks. The difference between a good musician and a *great* musician is what he thinks."

Organization and Communication

The efficiency of the cast and crew during production is more closely coupled to the operation of the director than anyone else. A director must not only conceive an artistically effective approach to each scene in the film; he must also organize and clearly communicate his concepts to the cast and crew. If they don't receive this information, if they don't have an understanding of what the director is after in a scene, they flounder, groping around for some direction for their work.

All too often a director will have a brilliant concept but will lack the ability to communicate it clearly. Eventually, with enough tenacity, he may get what he's after, but not without a good deal of frustration and wasted time along the way. This section describes an efficient way for a director to approach *any* scene in *any* location and to communicate this approach to his cast and crew. The following is intended only as a guideline from which a director will often deviate. However, such a guideline, as a jumping-off point, can be of tremendous value to every director when planning and organizing his approach to production. For directors working within tight budget limitations, it is absolutely essential.

Prior to beginning production, the director has spent time with the cast, ironing out any difficulties in the script and blocking the action. The actors, in turn, have incorporated the blocking into their preparation for each scene. The director will also have spent time with the crew, discussing the suitability of locations and a general approach to handling each one.

When the director arrives on the set, ready to begin principal photography, he must have a specific, detailed plan for how each scene for that day will be shot. A detailed pictorial storyboard is often the best way to organize each scene. In addition to his plan, it is essential that the director maintain a sense of improvisation, or flexibility, for the following reasons: first, because of the collaborative nature of film nothing will end up exactly as it appears in the director's mind. He must be able to guide the flow of creative energy, but he must also be prepared to flow *with* it. Second, a better plan may emerge at the last minute; a cast or crew member might suggest an improvement in the dialogue or in the placement of the camera. It's important to be flexible enough to take advantage of spontaneous ideas. Third, if the director falls behind schedule, he must be flexible enough to alter his plans in order to compensate for the loss in time.

The director's first responsibility for each scene is to take the crew members onto the fully dressed set to explain his plan. This usually takes the form of a shot list and the *order* of these shots is extremely important. The most efficient ordering of shots is from largest to smallest. The reasons for starting with the largest shot are as follows: first, the largest shot establishes an overall look, or lighting pattern for each scene. As you move in for closer shots, the basic look will already be established and the director of photography and gaffer won't have to worry about maintaining a sense of continuity to the lighting. If you begin with the close-ups and get progressively larger, the crew will have to relight for each shot, adding light after light. When you finally get to the longest shot, you'll be lucky if anyone remembers exactly what the close-ups looked like. The *continuity* of the lighting will therefore suffer. Second, the largest shot is usually the biggest, most time-consuming lighting job. If you get it out of the way at the start, the lighting crew has only to make small adjustments for closer shots. In this way they can work with maximum efficiency as you progress from shot to shot.

Starting with the largest shot is also an advantage for the actors. The largest shot is usually the master shot and contains a complete performance. By starting with the master shot, the actors go through the entire scene prior to doing any close-ups or inserts, which are often just parts of the whole scene. In this way, when shooting closer shots, they have an immediate recollection of the *context* of each part of the scene. Consequently, their performance in each of their close-ups will be more in keeping with their performance in the master shot. In this way they are better able to maintain a sense of continuity throughout their performances.

Once the crew understands exactly how the director plans to shoot the scene, the next step is to bring on the cast. This is *before* they go into makeup and wardrobe. The director walks through the scene with the actors, not attempting to polish the performance but rather to walk through the blocking on the dressed set with the real props. This will familiarize the actors with the environment of the fully dressed set. As they review the scene in their minds during makeup and wardrobe, they will be thinking of the scene in the context of the specific environment in which they will be performing.

An equally important reason for the preliminary walk-through with the actors is to demonstrate to the key crew members the specific action that will take place on the set—where the actors will stand in relation to one another and how they will move.

Following this walk-through, the actors are sent in to makeup and wardrobe. The crew then goes to work with a clear understanding of how the scene will be blocked and photographed. This will enable them to approximate closely a finished setup before the actors arrive from makeup and wardrobe. They will have discussed the order of shots with the director (beginning with the largest) and they will have witnessed the specific action that will take place on the set during the scene.

The director of photography and gaffer will arrange the lighting specifically for the action. No one will walk into darkness unexpectedly and no one will wash out because they're too close to a light.

The camera operator and assistant cameramen will know where to place the camera and approximately what focus changes will be required.

The key grip will know which part of the floor will need to be smoothed and leveled for a dolly move.

The boom operator will determine the ideal place to stand in order to reach the action without causing microphone shadows.

The sound mixer will know in advance if the actors will be walking out of range of the boom operator and he will place additional microphones to accommodate such moves.

In short, there will be no surprises. Without this preliminary information, the crew would only roughly approximate the setup. There would be a good deal of guesswork and, when the actors arrived on the set, the crew would take a considerable amount of time adjusting their work to accommodate the action.

In situations where this approach can be directly applied, it will prove efficient and economical. There are a multitude of considerations beyond this, however, and each scene must be approached in the manner most appropriate for that scene. The method described herein is not intended as an absolute rule. It is meant as a useful guide, a springboard, for thinking about any scene, at any time, in any location.

CHAPTER 17

Production

Priorities: Taking Care of Your People

The very first thing that happens on every day of every production I've ever encountered is the serving of coffee and donuts to the cast and crew. I've never been on a set where this was overlooked but I have seen a production assistant arrive late with coffee and donuts. Two things happened: first, the crew began work feeling disappointed. Second, when the coffee and donuts finally arrived, the crew took a break from work. I'm making a big point of this in order to stress the importance of treating the cast and crew well. It is a primary responsibility of the producer to ensure that his people are well looked after. The details of executing this responsibility often fall on the production manager or production assistants, but in the eyes of the cast and crew, it is the producer who is ultimately responsible for their well-being.

Taking care of your people involves such things as clean rest rooms and comfortable changing facilities for the cast, but the most obvious way to express concern for everyone's well-being is through the quality of the food. I have heard more crew members relating their experiences on various pictures in terms of the food than any other aspect of the production. One key grip, when asked if he recalled a production he had worked on in Montana, replied, "Yeah, we called it the peanut butter sandwich shoot." He said it without smiling.

Francis Ford Coppola, well aware of the importance of food as a way to communicate respect for the cast and crew, carried this idea to the other extreme when he made *The Conversation*. He allotted enough money in the budget to have rich, gourmet meals catered daily to the cast and crew with all the champagne they could drink. That's not the most effective way to keep the cast and crew working efficiently throughout the day. In fact, the crew was noticeably sluggish in the afternoon. Serving champagne lunches went beyond the point of diminishing returns.

Neither extreme—peanut butter sandwiches nor champagne lunches—will result in an efficient work force. Lunches should be wholesome, hot meals with a variety of beverages. They should be served with silverware, not plastic forks. There should be a comfortable place for people to sit during the meal. Don't expect anyone to sit on the floor. Grass, maybe, but not the floor. There should be plenty of food for second and third helpings. There should always be a dessert—something special to top off the meal. Use a catering service that appreciates the importance of appearance. Half the battle is over if your caterer makes the meal attractive and serves it with style.

Any special diet requests such as vegetarian or salt-free meals should be respected. The needs of such individuals should be as well served as those of the rest of the cast and crew. Occasionally, such a person may prefer to fend for himself. If so, he should be given a cash allotment equivalent to the catered meal allotment.

The Assistant Director

In the same sense that the production manager runs the logistics of the production from the front office, the first assistant director runs the production on the set. Once the director has reviewed his plan of attack with the key crew members for a particular location, and once the crew has witnessed the blocking of the action for that location, it is up to the first assistant director to keep the crew informed and working efficiently throughout the day, preparing them for each setup in the scene. The first assistant director is the conduit for information from the director to the crew and is responsible for the crew's efficient execution of the director's plan. He is also responsible for every member of the cast and crew being in the right place at the right time. He will coordinate the activities of cast and crew so that everyone will be prepared for each shot at approximately the same time. He must therefore schedule makeup and wardrobe to ensure that the cast is fully costumed and out of makeup in time for the first shot. This is not always a popular position. When the whip needs to be cracked, it's the first assistant director who does the cracking.

Although it may cost more to hire a top-notch first assistant director, a producer usually saves money by doing so. In a sense, the producer is buying insurance that his production will run smoothly, that all of the actors and crew members will arrive on schedule, that the correct props will be at the right place at the right time, that the various production teams will be properly informed about all aspects of the production, and that the activities on the set will proceed quickly and efficiently. If an assistant director fails in any of these areas he will cost the producer a great deal of money in delayed production time.

For a studio picture, a top-notch first assistant director may cost $500 more than the going rate per week. During a ten-week shooting schedule the extra cost will be $5,000. Studio pictures commonly cost $50,000 per day during production, so the extra $5,000 is equal to one hour of production time. A top assistant director will save considerably more than an hour of production time over a ten-week schedule. During expensive days on big-budget pictures, the production will cost considerably more. There were periods during the filming of *All That Jazz* when the production cost as much as $130,000 for a single day, and the value of the first assistant director's contribution increased accordingly.

On low-budget independent films the role of the first assistant director is no less significant. The day by day expenses may be less than on a studio picture, but the margin for error is less as well. Low-budget films, perhaps even more than major features, demand clockwork-like precision. Without an experienced first assistant director, such precision is virtually impossible to achieve.

Occasionally, on very low budget films, a producer will hire one person to function as both production manager and first assistant director. It is virtually impossible for any one person to function effectively in both capacities simultaneously. The producer may save a small amount of money by hiring one person instead of two, but neither position will receive the attention it deserves and the overall production will suffer accordingly.

The first assistant director is aided in the performance of his duties by the second assistant director. It is usually the second assistant director who does the paperwork and legwork. Since both the first and second assistant directors are intimately involved with the daily scheduling and operation of the cast and crew, both must have a thorough knowledge of the regulations of all guilds and unions governing the production.

Another function of the first assistant director, and sometimes the second assistant director, is the directing of extras and/or crowds if the director so requests.

The Call Sheet

These sheets are made up for each day of the production, usually by the second assistant director, and are handed out to each member of the cast and crew. They contain the following information: the locations for the day's shooting; which cast members will be required for the day; the time each member of the cast and crew is expected to arrive (call time); any special requirements for the day such as stunt coordinators or special effects equipment. The call sheets are usually prepared and distributed each evening for the following day's work.

A sample call sheet is shown in Table 10.

The Actors in Makeup

The makeup artist can have a tremendous influence on an actor's performance. Makeup is the actor's last stop prior to going before the cameras. The better an actor feels about himself, the more relaxed and confident he is, the better will be his performance. A good makeup artist understands this. In addition to a competent makeup job, he will contribute to the actor's morale and self-esteem. In order for a makeup artist to do this, however, he must feel appreciated and well cared for. The makeup artist will generate positive feelings to the actors only to the extent that the producer generates positive feelings to the makeup artist. Give him a comfortable environment in which to work. Ideally, a quiet room with a sink, a large mirror, and plenty of light. Allow him adequate time to do a careful job. Your efforts will evince themselves in the quality of the makeup and in the attitude of your actors on the set.

Table 10

Sample Call Sheet

CALL SHEET

Date _____		Director _____	
Company _____		First AD _____	
Title _____		Second AD _____	
Producer _____		PM _____	

Scene #	Set/Location

CAST

Name	Character	Makeup Call	Wardrobe Call	Set Call

CREW

Job Title	Call Time	Job Title	Call Time

Special Equipment	Props	Special Effects

The First Take

When the actors come out of makeup, the crew will have completed preparations for the first shot. Now is the time for the director and the actors to polish the performance. While they are doing this, the crew will fine-tune their work as well. There is usually a noticeable difference in the actors when they are in full costume and makeup. The scene becomes real for the first time. It may be that only one or two walk-throughs are necessary before shooting the first take. While the actors are walking through their final rehearsals, the director of photography is fine-tuning the lights, double-checking exposure, and making last-minute adjustments. The sound mixer is adjusting levels on the recorder. The camera operator, assistant cameraman, and dolly grip are practicing their moves as the actors walk through the scene. The beauty of this system is that everyone works together, fine-tuning their special areas of responsibility, targeting on a mutual goal.

When the director feels that the actors are on the verge of a polished performance, he should go for a take. There is a grave danger in the performance becoming stale if it is overrehearsed. Remember that there is a certain magic that takes over when the cameras roll, and especially when they roll for the first take. Steven Spielberg has said that he considers this magic important enough to print the first take of every scene regardless of any problems there may have been during that take.

When everything is ready to roll, the first assistant director calls "Quiet on the set, roll sound and roll camera." The director then calls "Action." If the director doesn't call "Cut" before the end of the scene, he may have a good first take. On the other hand, the dolly might have hit a bump, or the sound mixer might have picked up a car honking in the distance, or the camera assistant might have missed a focus mark, or. . . . With all of the possibilities for error, it's amazing it ever goes smoothly—even with all the specialists at work. If there are problems with the first take, shoot a second take, and a third, and a fourth, and so on until it's right. Then move on to the next setup.

It is important to run through the entire action for each setup before the camera, lighting, and sound crews move into position. The reason for this is to communicate precisely which portion of the scene will take place during the shot. It may be that only a very small segment will be covered by a particular setup and the crew will move much more efficiently if they limit their work to covering only that segment of the scene.

Follow this process, beginning with your largest shot and working down to the smallest shot until you've completed the scene. Then move on to the next scene and begin the process again. Continue this for each scene in the schedule until you've finished the film.

Pickups

Most people involved in film production are perfectionists. Directors are no exception. Budget and time limitations, however, make perfection almost impossible. Most filmmaking is a series of compromises in which you do the best you can. This is especially true on a modest- or low-budget picture with a tight shooting schedule.

Sometimes it isn't important to try for perfection from start to finish in a single take. If you're shooting a long master shot, it isn't necessary to shoot it over and over until it's perfect, or even acceptable, from start to finish in a single take. Suppose you've shot the scene three times and you're pleased with the first half of the scene in all three takes, but not with the second half. Instead of starting from the top on take four, you can shoot a pickup beginning with the middle of the scene and running to the end. In other words, concentrate on shooting the portion of the scene that's giving you trouble. Perhaps you'll get a pickup take of the last half of the scene in which everything works except one line. You can shoot *another* pickup of just that one line, over and over, until it's right.

In the finished film you can't cut from one take directly to another take from the same camera position without suffering a jump in the action. Consequently, in order to utilize your pickups, you must shoot close-ups and cutaways to cover the jump. A simple example: a man and a woman walking along the beach at water's edge. The master shot shows them walking toward the camera. The camera dollies back, keeping them both in frame. In take one, only the first half of their dialogue is acceptable. In take two, only the second half is acceptable. In the finished film, take one can't cut directly to take two without causing a jump in the action. In order to cover this, the director must shoot a cutaway such as a *point-of-view* shot—a handheld shot that shows what the couple sees as they walk down the beach. In the finished film, the audience will see the couple in take one for the first half of their dialogue. The scene will then cut to the point-of-view shot and when it cuts back to the couple for the remainder of their dialogue, the audience will be watching take two. The jump from take one to take two will be covered by the cutaway to the couple's point-of-view.

Pickups can be helpful when shooting any long takes, whether they're master shots or close-ups, but make sure they're covered with cutaways.

If you intend to run an entire scene in a master shot from beginning to end with no cutaways in the finished film, you must reshoot the master shot again and again until it's right, from start to finish, in a single take. But even then it's wise to move in for a cutaway or two, simply as a form of insurance. This allows you the option in the editing room of selecting portions from different takes, and of manipulating the pacing of the scene if it doesn't play well in the context of the finished film. A master shot that appears well paced during production may be dull as dust in the finished film. Unless you have the option of accelerating the pace with cutaways, perhaps even shortening the scene, you may be stuck with a dull scene, and you'll tear your hair out for not taking a few extra minutes during production to shoot protection cutaways.

It's helpful to tell the script supervisor which part of which take is acceptable immediately after the take. In this way you won't lose track of what you've got and where it is. You won't become confused about which pickups you need and you won't shoot unnecessary takes.

Production Sound

In addition to recording a clean, full dialogue track, the sound mixer must also record *room tone, production sound effects,* and *wild lines.*

Room tone is the ambient, background sound of each location. Each location will have a unique tone. It will be used to fill any holes in the dialogue tracks and to smooth out differences in level and equalization between voices in the final mix.

Production sound effects are sounds the mixer records for scenes in which there is no dialogue. For these scenes, he will record sync sound effects that may be used in the finished picture or used as a guide track for the sound effects editor.

In addition to sync sound effects, the mixer will record wild sound effects that can be cut to match the picture during the editing. Examples of wild sound effects are footsteps, dog barks, shattering glass, body hits, tire squeals, and gunshots. Production sound effects such as these are often more effective than stock library effects.

Wild lines are short words or phrases such as "Halt," "Let's go," or "Good day," which are often recorded "wild" (that is, off camera) when the quality of the sync recording is questionable. Also, if a character in a film such as a bank robber wears a mask, his lines will often be rerecorded wild after the sync take for better intelligibility. Wild lines must also be recorded for off-camera dialogue, such as a character's rambling thoughts in a dream sequence in which we don't see the actor speaking. Often these lines can be recorded during production, saving time and money in postproduction.

The Dailies

When shooting in 16mm, it is standard procedure to print every take; when shooting in 35mm, in order to avoid the expense of printing unwanted takes, the laboratory will print selectively. At the end of each take, the director will decide whether or not the take is worth printing. The takes that he selects will be circled on the script supervisor's copy of the screenplay, on the camera reports, and on the sound reports. Selected takes are also referred to as "circled takes." In the following sample camera and sound reports (Table 11), the selected takes are scene 77: takes one, four and five; scene 77A: take one; scene 78: takes one and three; scene 61: takes one, six, and seven.

At the end of each day a production assistant will run the exposed film and a copy of the camera reports to the laboratory, and the one-quarter inch tapes and a copy of the sound reports, to the sound house. During the night, the lab will process the film

Table 11   **Sample Camera and Sound Reports**

Camera Report				
Date ____ Title _____				
Company_____				
Director _____				
Cameraman _____				
Magazine 3_____				
Roll no. 16_____				
35mm color 16mm color				
35mm B & W 16mm B & W				
Emulsion 5247_____				
Remarks _____				

Print circled takes only:

Scene no.	Takes 1/5 2/6 3/7 4/8				Remarks
77	①	2	3	④	Ext. Day
	⑤				
77A	①				Ext. Day
78	①	2	③		Ext. Day
61	①	2	3	4	Nite effect
	5	⑥	⑦		

Good footage 383
N.G. footage 51
Waste footage 17
Total footage 400

Sound Report			
Date ____ Title _____			
Company_____			
Producer _____			
Director _____			
Mixer _____			
Boom Man _____			
Recordist_____			
Recorder no. __ Mike no. __			
Remarks _____			

Print circled takes only:

Scene no.	Take no.	Footage	Remarks
77	①		Sync
	2		
	3		
	④		
	⑤		
77A	①		
78	①		
	2		
	③		
61	①		
	2		
	3		
	4		
	5		
	⑥		
	⑦		

End of roll

and make a positive print, called a "daily," of the director's selected takes; the sound house will transfer the one-quarter inch tape from the same selected takes onto a sprocketed magnetic track. This is called a "sound daily." The stock used for a 16mm magnetic track is completely coated with magnetic oxide; 35mm magnetic stock for sound dailies is coated with two stripes of oxide and is referred to as "edit stripe." The sound from the original one-quarter inch recording will be transferred onto the wider of the two stripes. The narrow stripe is called a "balance stripe" since its purpose is to balance the thickness of the stock at both edges. If one edge were thicker than the other, the stock would have a tendency to "cone" as it's being wound onto a core or reel.

The following day, while the production team shoots the next series of scenes, an assistant editor will sync the dailies, lining up the sound track with the picture for an interlock screening that same evening. The picture and sound track are placed in sync by lining up the picture and sound of the clapstick at the beginning of each take. A sync signal system on the camera and tape recorder will ensure that they both run at the same speed. Consequently, when the picture and sound of the clapstick are in sync at the head of a take, the rest of the take will be in sync as well. After checking to make certain that each scene is in sync, the assistant editor will send the picture and sound track to be coded. *Coding* is the process of printing numbers (code numbers) on the edge of the picture at one-foot intervals and identical numbers at identical intervals on the corresponding sound track. These numbers will be used as a sync reference when the editor begins cutting the picture and tracks.

In addition to syncing the dailies, the assistant editor will log each take, listing the scene and take number, the code numbers at the beginning and end of each take, the print-through edge numbers (see Chapter 21) at the beginning and end of each take, and a brief description of each take. For a sample assistant editor's log sheet, see Table 12.

If you are shooting in close proximity to your lab and sound house, each day's shooting will be synced and ready for an interlock screening the following evening. The first day's dailies will be screened on the second night of production and a new set of dailies will be ready for screening every night thereafter.

Deviations in this schedule occur when the production goes on

Table 12 **Sample Editing Log**

Company ————		Page number————		
Title ————		Camera roll no. ————		
Producer ————		Edge no. prefix————		
Director————		Lab roll no. ————		
Editor ————		Order no. ————		

Code number	Edge number	Sc/Tk	Description	Remarks
BD0003–040	D9x36072–109	17–1	Ms Jack in garage, Rx to Mary enters	
BD0041–086	36110–155	17–2	Same	
BD0087–103	36156–172	17A–1	Cu Mary enters garage	
BD0104–125	36173–194	17A–4	Same (slower)	Tail slate
BD0126–173	36195–242	62–1	Ms Jack in garage, gets in car, exits	
BD0174–271	36243–340	62A–1	Ls ext. garage, car exits, drives off	
BD0272–362	36341–431	62A–6	Same (better traffic)	
BD0363–387	36432–456	62B–1	Cu electric garage door device (open and close)	MOS

distant location or switches to a night-time shooting schedule, or when the laboratory has difficulties, such as a printer breakdown. If you're shooting on distant locations it will take time to ship material to and from the lab. A lab technician will give you technical reports each morning by phone, which aids the director of photography but doesn't tell the director anything about the performances. Often a producer will not go to the location but will stay behind and screen dailies. This can be of great value to the director. In any case, the dailies will be sent as quickly as possible to wherever the production is shooting.

Some low-budget pictures are scheduled so tightly as to make daily screenings impossible. At the very least, however, dailies may be viewed on weekends or on the first available rest day.

The value of screening dailies cannot be overstated. For the director it is an opportunity to determine how the actors' performances and character interpretations translate to the screen. He will judge the accuracy of his communication with the director of photography and the camera operator, with the sound mixer, the makeup artist, and so forth. He will get a clear, overall feeling for how his picture is coming together.

For the crew, dailies offer an opportunity to evaluate their specific areas of responsibility. The director of photography and gaffer will judge their approach to lighting. The sound mixer will judge not only his original recordings, but also the quality of the transfers. The makeup artist will improve his approach to certain actors' makeup based on information he gets from the dailies. The script supervisor will double-check continuity within each scene. In short, everyone stands to learn from the dailies and improve his work on the film.

In addition, dailies are a terrific morale booster. Film almost always looks good in daily form, sometimes deceptively so. Francis Ford Coppola once said, "A finished film never looks as good as the dailies." The daily screenings are a time for congratulations and a pat on the back for the crew. It's exciting and gratifying to sit in a screening room and watch the previous day's work. It's usually verification that everyone has done a good job.

The same is often true of the actors, but there is a difference. Actors are not sitting back objectively watching their work; they are watching *themselves*. For some actors this is constructive but for others it is devastating. Should they not like their performance in a particular scene, or their interpretation of a character, they may suddenly change that character partway through the film. It may be that a scene out of context and unedited will strike a wrong note with an actor. Their trust in the director may decline. They may become timid and less willing to take chances. That same scene in the context of the finished film, completely edited, may work magnificently but it is often difficult for an actor to judge a scene out of context. In a sense, it requires reading the director's mind. For this reason many directors request that the cast not be permitted to attend dailies screenings. This is often sound policy and not necessarily a reflection on the director's sense of security about his work.

Another advantage to daily screenings is that if a scene doesn't work it can usually be reshot with minimum effort. Even if you've moved to a different location, you may be able to rewrite the scene to fit the new location. The sooner you know you've got a problem, the more flexibility you will have in solving it.

In addition to the cast and production crew, the film editor will usually attend daily screenings. The editor's role is discussed in Part IV, "Postproduction."

Sound Decisions

Before closing this chapter, I would like to offer a few additional thoughts about sound. Film is essentially a visual medium and many times it will be to the advantage of the film to compromise sound for the sake of improving the picture, for example, requiring the boom operator to stand in an awkward spot in order not to interfere with the lights.

However, I have witnessed many production crews working according to an unspoken, unbendable law: "picture at the expense of sound." When there is a compromise to be made, the automatic assumption is that sound comes second. I recall a scene in a florist shop in which the air-conditioning unit on the roof created sound problems. The sound man was unable to turn the unit off so he began fastening green sound blankets to the ceiling in order to dampen the air-conditioning noise. He had hung about three blankets when the gaffer came over and said, "You can't do that. I need the white ceiling to bounce light. Those blankets will make the lighting appear green and everyone in the scene will look sick." His assumption was that lighting took precedence over sound and that a compromise was out of the question. Fortunately, the director was more open-minded. He called the gaffer back and explained that the sound quality was important for the scene. He asked the gaffer at least to consider achieving the same lighting effect in another way, or possibly reach a compromise with the sound man. The minute the director opened up the possibility of an alternate solution, the gaffer had the answer. The sound man could put up his green sound blankets but the grips would hang a white silk cloth beneath them. The sound from the air conditioner would be dampened and the gaffer could bounce light off the white silk. This was a perfect solution without compromising either sound or picture.

The gaffer had all of the necessary information to solve the problem from the beginning but his immediate assumption was "picture at the expense of sound." It simply hadn't occurred to him to offer a compromise or an alternative.

Another problem sound men are faced with is that most producers and directors don't know much about sound. They judge a production mixer's work in the dailies, and if it doesn't sound like a finished movie, the naive assumption is that something's wrong. A production mixer's track *shouldn't* sound like a finished movie. In a finished movie, the postproduction mixers take great pains carefully to equalize, filter, and otherwise adjust the production track for the optimum balance of sound throughout the film. What the production mixer should strive for is the cleanest, fullest track he can get in order to give the postproduction mixers maximum flexibility in the final mix (see Chapter 20). It is in the final mix that the rerecording engineers carefully listen to the entire complement of sound, equalizing and balancing each track to its fullest potential. The problem is that many production mixers, knowing that their work will be evaluated in the dailies, equalize and filter the original recording to give the impression of better sound in the dailies. Ultimately, this restricts the flexibility of the postproduction mixers and the sound track in the finished film suffers.

When hiring a sound man, stress the importance of recording for the final mix, not for the dailies. If the sound mixer knows that you understand this problem, he'll respond accordingly and you will have a better original track for the final mix.

PART 4

Postproduction

CHAPTER 18

Picture Editing

Postproduction begins with the editing of the film and ends with the printing of the first trial composite answer print. This is the first color corrected print with a complete sound track. The principal steps that lead to the first trial print are picture editing; titles and optical effects; dialogue editing; sound effects editing; music scoring; music editing; the sound mix; the optical sound track; negative cutting; printing.

A number of these steps will be conducted simultaneously but each one is dependent upon the completion of the first, picture editing.

The Picture Editor

When building a house, a construction engineer begins with a blueprint and basic raw materials such as wood, nails, bricks, glass, etc. A good construction engineer will make the most out of whatever material he is given. He can't miraculously turn wire and straw into a Tudor mansion but he can turn them into a very good straw house. Like the construction engineer, a good film editor will make the most out of whatever material he is given, but there the similarity ends. A construction engineer can't work miracles but a good film editor often can.

I said earlier that a film often looks deceptively good in the dailies. The reason for this is that there is no story in the dailies. They are fragmented bits and pieces of random scenes. Any scene that is technically well executed will look good in the dailies. The problem for the editor is to make the most of each scene within the context of the story. *The primary function of the editor is to tell the story.* Technical expertise, such as matching cuts and making smooth transitions, is an assumed ability for any editor. Novice editors put tremendous emphasis on technical perfection. The best editors, however, will throw technique out the window in favor of telling the story.

The work of editors like Dede Allen, Sam O'Steen, and Verna Fields *transcends* technique. Their editing is geared exclusively to telling the story, not to advertising their flawless cutting ability. If the pacing of the story is improved by a cut that doesn't quite match, they will suffer the imperfect cut in favor of the story. In the final analysis, what matters to the audience is the story. A strong, well-told story can withstand technical flaws from top to bottom, but a weak or poorly told story, no matter how technically well edited, will always be weak. An editor must think *story* first, technique second.

This concept is extremely important for anyone hiring an editor for a feature film. It is dangerous to hire a feature editor on the basis of a sample reel that contains only isolated scenes. It is difficult enough to judge an editor's work without knowing what raw materials he had to start with; certainly the Academy Award for best editor would be more fairly judged if the voters could screen the dailies that were available for each picture prior to editing. But assuming an editor's sample reel contains random scenes cut from good raw material, the only judgment you will be able to make is whether he is competent to make technically good cuts and smooth transitions. You may also be able to judge his ability to pace an isolated scene or two, but this can be terribly misleading. An isolated scene that appears well cut and well paced in the sample reel may be dull as dust in the context of the finished film. Likewise, a scene that appears awkward, perhaps jarring, out of context may be an excellent deliberate statement about a character or situation in the finished film. Such scenes may be magnificent in the complete film but awkward out of context.

Editors who can effectively execute isolated scenes are not hard to find. What matters is an editor's ability to pace a feature film in such a way as to draw an audience in at the beginning, hold them, and let them go at the end, emotionally satisfied but wanting more. Occasionally, this ability will exhibit itself in a dramatic short, but more often than not you will need to screen an entire feature.

Look for a style in an editor's work that is appropriate for your picture. Does he have a sense for dramatic tension, for suspense, for slapstick comedy? Comedy almost more than any other genre is dependent on pacing and timing in the cutting room. Does the editor's sensitivity mesh with that of the director? Does he like the script? These are all questions to ask when searching for the best editor for your project. But first and foremost is finding an editor who thinks *story*.

If you are making an IA union picture you must hire and retain a union-affiliated editorial staff from the first day of principal photography through completion of the final dub. The final dub is the last step in the editorial postproduction process (see Chapter 20). The minimum editorial staff for an IA feature includes one editor and one assistant editor. There is no limit to the maximum number of editorial personnel a producer may hire as long as he hires at least one assistant for each editor. On a major feature with a rushed postproduction schedule a producer might have as many as fifteen people—editors, assistants, and apprentices—working simultaneously.

All IA editorial personnel belong to the Motion Picture Editor's Guild. The address and phone number of this guild may be found in the *Pacific Coast Studio Directory*. Minimum wage requirements for guild members may be found in *Brooks' Standard Rate Book* and in the *Hollywood Production Manual*. These publications are listed in Appendix E. Additional information regarding guild regulations may be obtained by contacting the guild office.

When an IA producer settles on one or more potential editors for his film (generally by word-of-mouth reputation and screening films) he will contact the guild for the most updated information regarding the editors' availability. Assuming the producer's choices are available, the guild will supply the producer either with contact information for the editors or, in order to maintain the confidentiality of its members, will often contact the editors directly and give them the producer's name and phone number. It's then up to the editor to follow through. The guild maintains a partial list of members' credits and will supply this information to signatory producers. A complete list of credits may be obtained either directly from the editor or from the editor's agent.

If a producer has signed a NABET contract for his film he must hire a NABET editorial staff. Since NABET has one office for all its below-the-line job categories, a NABET producer seeking an editorial staff should contact the NABET office at the address listed in the *Pacific Coast Directory*. NABET will supply him with a roster of names and phone numbers of all available editorial personnel.

If your picture is nonunion you must hire either a nonunion editor, a NABET editor for no less than NABET minimum terms, or an IA editor who is willing to moonlight. There is no structured organization for nonunion editorial personnel. The best way to locate such people is, first, by screening nonunion films and compiling a list of potential editors, and, second, by contacting the producers and/or directors of those films and asking their opinion of the editor's talent and temperament. The producer and/or director of a particular film can often be reached through the production company that made the film or through the distribution company that released it.

Most producers and directors are happy to recommend people with whom they have had a good experience and will undoubtedly put you in touch with such people either by giving you their address and phone number or by contacting them on your behalf and asking them (assuming they are interested and available) to contact you.

Other ways to locate nonunion editorial personnel are through recommendations by key members of your production crew such as the production manager and director of photography and by placing ads in trade publications such as *Variety* and the *Hollywood Reporter*.

Once you have selected an editor it is wise to let the editor select the assistant, provided the salary demands of the assistant fall within the limitations of your budget. This is an area of the postproduction budget to which close attention should be paid. A good editor will insist on a competent, experienced assistant, and such assistants are costly. However, an assistant who frees the editor from organizational details and allows him to concentrate on cutting the film is, from a budgetary standpoint, a producer's luxury.

In addition to the responsibilities described in the previous chapter, the assistant editor must maintain throughout postproduction the organization of the editor's leftover footage (trims and outs of both film and sound track) from every scene in the film.

At any given time the assistant should be able to locate quickly any piece of film or sound the editor requests. In addition, the assistant must communicate with the laboratory, optical house, and sound facility ordering reprints, opticals, supplies, etc.

Producers of nonunion films sometimes make the mistake of hiring an untrained assistant editor in order to save money. This is a mistake that inevitably *costs* money. An assistant who requires on-the-job training not only chews up the editor's valuable time but also breaks the flow of the editor's concentration on the picture. An organizational mistake by an untrained, inexperienced, or careless assistant can easily waste hours and sometimes days. For example, if the assistant misfiles a trim that the editor subsequently requests, the assistant may spend hours searching for the trim. During this time the editor will have to reorganize his cutting bench in order to move on to another scene, leaving the previous scene unfinished. Often a misfiled trim is never found and the entire shot must be reprinted, synced, coded, and several days later given to the editor for inclusion in the film.

It often makes sense to hire an untrained *apprentice* editor who can relieve the assistant of such tasks as running errands and rewinding reels of film. Apprentice editors are less expensive and usually less experienced than assistant editors. Often the assistant can teach an untrained apprentice the basic procedures in the cutting room during postproduction without interfering with the editor's schedule.

The Director's Role

The overall vision of the film belongs to the director and it is ultimately his responsibility to ensure that the editing reflects his interpretation of the screenplay. An editor is essential to the execution of the director's vision of the film, but a good director makes himself responsible for the character of the cut.

The most difficult, yet most important quality for a director to maintain during postproduction is objectivity. The editor allows the director the freedom to view his film from a greater distance and with more objectivity than a director who attempts to cut the film on his own.

An editor's skill is important but it is severely restricted without a clear, open line of communication with the director. If they have worked together in the past, if they have established a mutual understanding of their approaches to film, then chances are that they will communicate successfully. If not, the communication channel should be established before the cutting begins. The director must not only know what he's after but he must be able to *communicate* his thoughts to the editor. If a director finds himself working with an editor who is simply on a different wave-length, unable to comprehend and execute his vision of the film, he should get another editor. Not all editors are right for all directors. On the other hand, from the editor's point of view, there is nothing more frustrating than working with an indecisive director, trying a multitude of random combinations, hoping that one will strike a familiar chord.

There must be an open line of communication and a sense of mutual respect in order for the team to work effectively. In the making of any film, this relationship is of critical importance.

The manner in which a director and editor work together depends on the director's relationship with the editor, the budget and schedule, and the preferred working style of the director.

Some directors are frightened by the cutting room and avoid it like the plague while others continually stare over the editor's shoulder, commenting on every cut. Some directors will turn their film over to the editor on the first day of production without so much as a word of discussion until production is finished and the editor completes the first cut. Others won't allow a single cut to be made until production is finished and they have had several weeks or months to decide how they would like to begin. There is an enormous gray area between these extremes and no single book can begin to cover the entire spectrum. The next section, however, does describe an effective, efficient approach to the entire process of postproduction. A literal application of these procedures may or may not fit for you and your project. In any case, this can serve as a guide for organizing a postproduction process that best fits your needs.

From Dailies to Fine-Cut

The process begins on the second night of production during the screening of the first day's dailies. The director and editor sit together in a screening room and discuss the material. The director explains his intentions for each scene to the editor and also selects favored takes. The following day, the editor will begin editing the film. This process continues throughout production. Editors will often travel to the location with a portable cutting room in order to screen dailies with the director and begin the first cut. A good editor will be able to keep pace with most directors' shooting schedules. Given a shooting ratio of approximately 10:1, it is reasonable to expect a finished first cut one week after completion of principal photography. It may be three hours long but it will all be there, roughed in with selected takes from start to finish.

During the week following principal photography, as the editor is completing the first cut, the director may go on vacation—Hawaii, Singapore, South America, anywhere to get away. There are two advantages to this: first, the director will need to recuperate physically from the rigors of production. William Goldman once said about directing, "It's hard. I don't mean hard like it was hard for Van Gogh to fill a canvas or Kant to construct a universe. I mean hard like coal mining. Directing a film is one of the most brutally difficult occupations imaginable." At the end of production, a rest is in order. The second advantage to a week's hiatus for the director before viewing the first cut is to get some distance from the film, to gain some objectivity. Remember that if the director cares about his film (and the good ones care desperately), he has been living with it for seven days a week, eighteen hours a day, for several months and in some cases years and, of course, is biased in terms of the thoughts he has had during production. It is impossible to erase this bias, but a week at the beach can contribute immeasurably to a director's objectivity when viewing the first cut.

The first-cut screening will be the first opportunity to view the entire film uninterrupted, watching each scene in the context of surrounding scenes. For the first time, there will be a sense of continuity in the film. It is always best to view completed cuts of the film in an interlock screening room with changeovers. This is a screening room equipped with two projectors and two sound dubbers so that the projectionist doesn't need to stop and rethread between reels. Stopping between reels, as on an editing console, can so disrupt the continuity of the film as to make judgments about pacing and story structure practically impossible.

As the director, you will suggest changes based on the first-cut screening. The editor, also seeing the film uninterrupted for the first time, will offer additional suggestions. Together you will work on the second cut. Scenes will be moved around, shortened, lengthened, added, and deleted. The second cut will undoubtedly run long but it will be shorter than the first. When the second cut is completed, screen the picture again—only this time invite an audience of perhaps ten or more people. The kind of audience you invite will greatly affect the value of the screening. If you and the editor have trouble solving certain problems in the film, you may wish to screen it for other directors and editors. But if you have a handle on where you're going with it, the thing you will need most is objectivity, so invite an objective audience to your screening—ideally, people who know nothing about your film, nothing about making films, and nothing about you. The important thing to remember about screening for audiences is this: *The degree to which you will achieve objectivity is directly proportional to the objectivity of your audience.*

You are not necessarily looking to this objective audience for comments. Your film will run overlong; the picture will be dirty, scratched, and spliced; most of the sound, titles, and opticals will be missing. You will be screening a skeletal structure, not a fleshed-out film. Nobody at this stage, except the director and sometimes the editor, is in a position to fill in all these blanks. Consequently, any critical comments from the audience may have little or no meaning. Most of what you want from the audience you will glean simply by being in the room with them during the screening.

What happens in a screening of this kind is a sort of magic, and until you've experienced it for yourself, you probably will not truly understand it. What happens is that you see the film through the eyes of the audience. If your audience is comprised of cameramen, you will pay undue attention to the photography. If you screen for directors and editors, you will see the film through their biased eyes with an emphasis on the details of technique. But if you screen for an audience of nonfilm people who know nothing about your film, they will be essentially unbiased. The degree to which a director can achieve objectivity in this environment is truly remarkable. He is in the unique position of simultaneously seeing the film through the eyes of an unbiased audience *and* of filling in all of the missing blanks. He will see, in his mind's eye, the polished picture with titles, opticals, and a fully mixed sound track. And he will see it through the unbiased eyes of his audience. This is truly a magical experience. Again—the degree to which a director will achieve objectivity is directly proportional to the objectivity of the audience.

Francis Ford Coppola concluded his statement "A finished film never looks as good as the dailies" with, "or as bad as the first cut." If you listen to critical comments from the audience, your objectivity may be dampened as well as your spirits. All the audience sees is an incomplete patchwork skeleton of your film. Their comments will reflect this and they will often be painful to hear. However, in some cases, they may offer insights into problem areas. Audience comments must be carefully evaluated. Chances are that they will be vague, something like, "The ending didn't work." The audience probably won't be able to tell you *why*, they will simply know that for them it didn't work. It may be that a missing element such as music or an optical effect will solve the problem. Or it may be that some small change must be made clear back in reel one in order for the ending to satisfy the audience. The audience is by no means dictating the final cut. Rather, they are bringing potential problem areas to your attention. It is up to you, as the director, to solve the problems.

From a practical point of view, gathering a group of totally unbiased people for your audience is difficult. When you can't succeed entirely, do the best you can. The closer you get to this ideal, the better will be your judgment of the film.

Based on your experience screening with an audience, you will gain insights into how to modify and improve the picture. So it's back to the editing room for cut number three. Then another audience screening. With each screening bring in a new audience. You don't want people who are biased by the previous cut. Their view of the film will be far from objective. Continue this process of recutting and screening until your picture gels into a cohesive, well-paced structure close to your targeted final running time. Bear in mind that I'm not talking about the picture gelling into a cohesive structure for the audience. It's still unfinished, with many pieces missing, and it may still be a while before it plays well for an audience. But when it gels for you while viewing the picture with an unbiased audience, filling in the missing pieces in your mind, you will know you're close to a final cut. From this point on, the picture will probably require nothing but fine-tuning. You may or may not choose to screen the film for another audience; it depends on how certain you feel about the final cut.

When you've reached a decision to stop cutting, your picture will be considered locked. From this point on, the postproduction work will be targeted on making titles and optical effects, on the sound mix, and on the first trial composite answer print.

Titles, Opticals, and Special Photographic Effects

The titles and credits at the beginning and end of a film are called "main and end titles." They can be as simple as white letters on a black background or as elaborate as an animated television commercial. Generally, main titles are static colored words made up on cards and superimposed over a live-action background. End titles are usually in the form of a list of credits that moves up the screen, often superimposed over a live-action background. This moving list is called a "crawl."

Titles are designed and executed either by a company specializing in motion picture titles or by an optical effects house that has a title department. Many optical effects houses have such a department.

Optical effects (called "opticals") such as fades, dissolves, wipes, superimpositions, and split screens are effects made by modifying and manipulating existing images on film. A producer provides an optical effects house with an image on film and the optical house adds the desired effect to that image. Rarely will an optical house generate the original image.

Optical effects are made on a specialized camera called an "optical printer" that is designed to rephotograph images on film in such a way as to incorporate the desired effect. When the optical printing is finished, the new piece of film, which includes the original image and the optical effect, is sent to a laboratory for processing and printing.

Many laboratories are equipped to make simple optical effects such as fades and dissolves but more creative and complex effects such as a rippling dream sequence or split screens must be done by an optical house that specializes in such effects.

The unavoidable reality about most optical effects is that they require going several stages, or "generations," away from the original negative and consequently the picture quality suffers, usually with increased contrast and grain. Taking your work to a house with first-rate optical equipment and first-rate experienced technicians will minimize this problem, but it will still exist.

Another danger in making optical effects is that your original negative for those sequences will be exposed to extra handling, dust, and printing machines. A scratch on the negative or a badly torn perf is often irreparable. Optical effects are a complex, delicate, tricky business. Taking your work to a first-rate house increases the chances of its being executed correctly on the first pass, thus minimizing the handling of your negative.

Companies that make special photographic effects differ from optical effects houses in that they create and film original images (almost any images the producer and director can conjure up) such as landscapes, miniatures (models of spaceships, buildings, boats, etc.), matte paintings (usually used to simulate backgrounds for live-action scenes), and animation.

Animation is a process that creates the illusion of motion in a drawing or an inanimate object (model) by photographing it one frame at a time and redrawing the image or moving the model slightly between each exposure. The principal drawback to creating motion in this way, particularly for model animation, is that unlike photographing an object in motion at the conventional rate of twenty-four frames per second, in which case each image has a slight blur or trailing image that smoothes out the movement, animation results in hard, sharp images and consequently is often jerky when projected at twenty-four frames per second. In drawn animation the artist can airbrush a trailing blur on each drawing, thereby creating an illusion of smooth motion. In model animation the animator does not have this same flexibility.

There are some relatively new and highly sophisticated computer-controlled systems, generally referred to as "motion control" systems, that make it possible to photograph model animation with the model and/or the camera actually in motion, resulting in the desired trailing image behind each photograph of the model. The frame rate during this process varies, depending on the desired effect. Motion control systems are used for a variety of effects, but generally the term refers to the ability of the system to control and duplicate accurately, if necessary, the motion of the camera and/or the model being photographed. Such systems are available at many houses specializing in the production of special photographic effects.

A thorough discussion of optical and special photographic effects is beyond the scope of this book. However, persons interested in a greater understanding of these effects may refer to *The Technique of Special Effects Cinematography* by Raymond Fielding (see Appendix E). This book is updated regularly and is probably the most comprehensive text available on the subject.

The specific services offered by companies specializing in titles, optical effects, and special photographic effects vary enormously from house to house. Optical effects houses will often have the facilities to make a variety of special photographic effects. Special photographic effects facilities commonly have optical printers as part of their equipment. Even within a particular field such as optical effects, the services vary from house to house. Some specialize in 16mm work, others in 35mm work. A special photographic effects house may specialize in miniatures, motion control, front-screen projection, rear-screen projection, matte paintings, or animation.

The only way to be sure that a particular company can provide the effects you need is if that company can demonstrate that they have successfully made similar effects in the past. Some effects houses maintain a demonstration reel that contains samples of their past work. When screening a sample reel, look for effects similar to those your film will require. If you're making a feature film, screen the sample reel in a projection room or movie theater. A videotape viewed on a television screen may mask flaws in the effects that will show up on the big screen. Look for an acceptable level of quality. Ask yourself if the effects are believable. Are the images sharp? Grainy? Contrasting? If there is a sound track on the reel you might consider watching the reel a second time without the sound. Occasionally a carefully made sound track can distract the viewer from flaws in the effects.

Also bear in mind that even though the world of optical and special photographic effects is highly technical, it is ultimately the artist making the effects that matters. A company may have the most sophisticated equipment in the world, but unless they have seasoned professionals to operate it, the end result will probably be disappointing. If a company has a demonstration reel that indicates their ability to accomplish effects similar to those your film requires, it will be reassuring to know that the artists who made those effects are still with the company.

Occasionally, if a producer is uneasy about a company's ability to deliver a certain effect, the company will offer to make a sample test of the effect. Usually they will charge the producer only for their costs. In the case of an optical effect, say a blow-up of an image, the cost to the producer for the test would include the raw film stock and laboratory charges for processing and printing.

A producer or director beginning a project that requires optical or special photographic effects should consult a specialist—an effects artist experienced in the kind of effects the producer is seeking—before beginning principal photography. The specialist will almost certainly offer guidance that will save time, money, and ultimately result in superior effects. Budgets often go through the roof when a producer waits until principal photography is finished before consulting an effects specialist. In such cases the effects artists must work with footage that was shot without consideration for the effects instead of footage that was designed with the effects in mind from the start.

Another reason for consulting a specialist is that optical and special photographic effects work has evolved a language all its own. Common terms are *background plate, beam splitter, "d-x," raster, slit-screen, vector graphics, photo-repo, glass painting, articulate matte,* and *traveling matte.* An effects artist might describe a scene as follows: "We'll use blue screen to generate an articulate matte for the ship that will carry an "r-p" screen to display interior action; the background plate will be a vector graphic display of the space station; then we'll slit-scan and streak in the warp effects. Once we've roto'ed we'll "d-x" in glows and lasers." There is so much in-house jargon that without a specialist to guide him, a producer or director unfamiliar with this world might easily be intimidated and get lost in a labyrinth of confusion and misunderstanding.

There are several ways to find a specialist experienced in the kind of effects a particular film will require. The first is by watching for similar effects in other films and noting the effects artists who created them. Another way is through word-of-mouth recommendations within the film community. A third way is to visit several effects companies and consult with the specialists working for those companies about your particular effects requirements. Such companies may be found in the *Pacific Coast Studio Directory* (see Appendix E) or in the yellow pages under Motion Picture Special Effects.

Often there are a variety of methods by which one can attain a desired effect; the cost and ultimate quality of the finished product will vary depending on the method chosen. Spending a lot of money won't guarantee quality effects. They can be extremely complex, cost a lot, and look bad. Occasionally effects artists will add unnecessary complications to a particular effect in order to make it more interesting for them to work on. Usually such complications are appreciated by other effects artists but are lost on the general public. From the producer's point of view, the simplest solution is usually the best. When discussing your effects requirements with a particular company, inquire as to how the company intends to accomplish the effects. When the effects are inherently complex, discuss various approaches with several companies before committing yourself to a particular method.

The cost for various titles, opticals, and special photographic effects varies enormously from house to house, and it's worth doing some price-comparing before settling on a particular company. Many houses provide a price list for standard effects such as fades and dissolves, but more elaborate effects require careful planning and budgeting on the part of the effects house. Occasionally an effects house will offer a reduced price for an opportunity to do something new and intriguing.

When ordering titles and effects, spell out clearly and specifically what effects your picture will require. Some films require only main and end titles while others require far more elaborate effects. In any event, spell out the specifics and go for a flat, guaranteed fee in writing. Some houses, even some of the best houses, will purposely underestimate the cost of your titles and effects in order to get the work and then subsequently bill you for what the estimate *should* have been. Optical and special photographic effects work is often unpredictable, and effects houses shy away from a guaranteed fee in writing. But it becomes very difficult to budget a picture with variables that sometimes run 100 percent or more off the mark. If you can't get a guaranteed fee in writing, at least get a written estimate and insist that they inform you before incurring expenses beyond that estimate. In this way, unless you modify your requirements, you are assured of staying within your total title and effects budget.

Elaborate titles and effects, especially for a modestly budgeted film, should be approached with caution. They are both unpredictable and costly. It is usually a mistake to construct a low-budget screenplay that is dependent on elaborate effects. Their effectiveness can often be judged only when they are finished, and you may have to modify and reorder the effects several times before they really work, and you must pay for each modification. Further, a tight budget often eats up the entire contingency fund during principal photography and is consequently at its tightest during postproduction. If you get into postproduction and don't have quite enough in the kitty for quality effects, your whole picture will suffer.

If a producer consults with a competent specialist prior to beginning principal photography and works with the title and effects houses to plan and carefully budget his titles and effects, the end result stands a good chance of living up to his expectations.

Black and White Dupes

Once the picture is "locked" (i.e., picture editing is completed) and prior to beginning sound editing, you will need one or two black and white prints of the film. These are simply black and white copies of your spliced, scratched, dirty work print. They are referred to as "dirty dupes." Each sound editor and the composer must have a print of the film to work with and the black and white dupes allow the sound editors and the composer to work simultaneously. The sound effects editor may use the color work print, while the dialogue editor and composer work with the black and white dupes. This kind of parallel sound editing is the most efficient approach to postproduction sound.

A further and equally important use for a black and white dupe comes during the final mix (see Chapter 20). Unlike the color work print, the black and white dupe contains no splices, tears, or torn perfs. It contains photographic *pictures* of them printed from the work print, but the film itself is flawless. During the mix, the picture will be run back and forth many times, putting a great strain on the film. Weak spots, such as poor splices and torn perfs, will undoubtedly cause breaks in the film during the mix. This not only interrupts the flow of the work and the mixers' sense of continuity, but it is also expensive. The down time cost involved in repairing the film and getting things rolling again might easily run $50 to $100 per break.

CHAPTER 19

Postproduction Sound

All of the work involved in building the postproduction sound tracks for your film will be targeted on the final mix. Most of the sounds that you hear in a film were at one time separate from one another. *Mixing* is the process of blending together the isolated sounds—dialogue, sound effects, and music—onto a single track. The process is similar to multiple-track music recording in which each instrument is recorded on a separate track. An engineer subsequently rerecords the multiple tracks equalizing the instruments and blending them onto a single track. He may wish to boost the high frequencies of the snare drum or dial out the violins for an organ solo. The sound mix for a film follows the same technique. Sounds are separated in order to give the mixing engineers maximum flexibility when blending them all together.

The Director's Role

Postproduction sound is divided into three categories: dialogue, sound effects, and music. The specialists responsible for the construction of these sounds are the dialogue editor, the sound effects editor, the composer, and the music editor. Each of these individuals will bring to the picture a different point of view and each will emphasize his particular area of concern. The sound effects editor will view the picture with a prejudiced ear for sound effects; the composer will watch primarily for places where music will enhance the film. It is the responsibility of the director to maintain an overview of the entire sound structure. He must guide each of the specialists, keeping them all informed of his overall vision of the film so that their respective sounds, working together, will complement each other.

The important thing to remember about sound effects, music, and dialogue is that only one at a time can dominate; the others must be subordinate. If they are all running at full steam, the result will be confusion. If you want confusion, you can run them backward, forward, upside down and inside out, all at full volume. But if you're going for a controlled, dramatic impact, you must decide which will dominate, and you must not make the decision arbitrarily. Let the emotion you're seeking dictate the answer.

Consider a chase sequence with several car crashes. A composer who screens this sequence without the sound effects may "hear" an entire symphony orchestra, a cacophony of sound with kettle drums, horns, strings, cymbals, and more. However, if the director wishes to maintain a strong sense of reality he may request that the sound effects editors create this symphony out of sound effects —tire squeals, metal ripping, people screaming, glass breaking, etc. In such a case it would be inappropriate for the music to dominate the sound effects. A more appropriate score might involve a low-end undercurrent of tension such as a synthesized bass line with a nervous, staccato, almost subliminal percussion track.

If the director fails to inform the composer of his intentions regarding this sequence, the composer will very likely score the bombast of symphonic sound he originally "heard" and he will undoubtedly be disappointed in the mix. In order to achieve the feeling the director is after, it will be out of the question to run both the music and the sound effects at full volume. The symphony will be held down under the sound effects and its impact will be lost. It's possible that the symphony, even at low volume, will cause confusion and will finally be eliminated.

The Dialogue Editor

The original recording of the dialogue made during production will need a considerable amount of work before it is ready for the mix. The objective for the dialogue editor is to construct the tracks in such a way as to give the mixers clean tracks with maximum flexibility for modifying the equalization and level of each voice individually.

You will recall in the discussion on production sound recording that the production mixer will record room tone for each location, usually thirty to sixty seconds. This will be used by the dialogue cutter to replace any silence in the edited dialogue sequences or any unwanted sound between words in the dialogue, such as a distant car horn or an unwanted off-camera voice. There is no such thing as a silent location (unless you're shooting in a special anechoic chamber). Even the quietest location has some ambient sound or tone. Pure silence stands out like a sore thumb in a sound track and must be replaced with the correct tone for each location.

Production sound effects will be put on a separate track for the sound effects cutter and replaced with room tone on the dialogue tracks. This process is called "cleaning the tracks."

Finding room tone that matches precisely with the background tone during dialogue is sometimes difficult. Occasionally, when the match doesn't quite work, the dialogue cutter will resort to tone from dialogue out-takes, seeking quiet pauses between words to match the tone of the scene accurately.

Once the tracks are cleaned in this way, the dialogue cutter will split the voices onto separate tracks. This will allow the mixers to modify equalization and level for each voice without affecting the other voices. The process involves building dialogue tracks by "checkerboarding" between the original dialogue track and "fill." Fill is any sprocketed (usually nonmagnetic) film such as clear leader or salvaged prints from old films that are too badly scratched to be of use to a distributor. The latter, called "picture fill," is the most common. The important thing is that the fill contains no magnetic signal that might be picked up by a sound head. Inexpensive picture fill is available from any film salvage company.

The checkerboarding process for a scene involving two voices is shown in Figure 1.

The two tracks will be played simultaneously on separate playback machines during the mix. In this way, the mixer may modify one voice without affecting the other. The ideal of maximum flexibility means a separate track for each principal voice.

If the dialogue cutter foresees drastic equalization or level changes between voices, he will prepare the tracks with overlapping tone. In the case of Jason and Judy, assume that Judy's

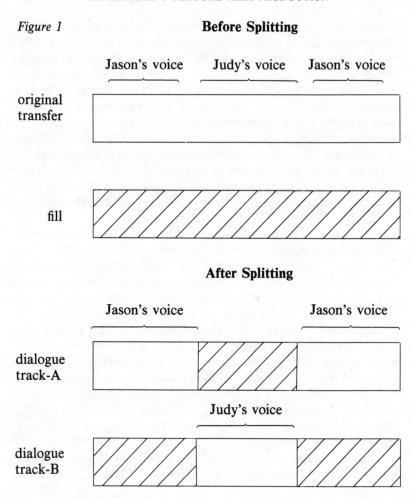

Figure 1

Before Splitting

Jason's voice   Judy's voice   Jason's voice

original transfer

fill

After Splitting

Jason's voice   Jason's voice

dialogue track-A

Judy's voice

dialogue track-B

volume in the original recording is much lower than Jason's. If the mixers raise the volume significantly on track B (Judy's voice), there will be a jump in the background sound whenever the voices (tracks) change. When room tone is added to overlap the background sound, the edited tracks will look as they do in Figure 2.

Figure 2

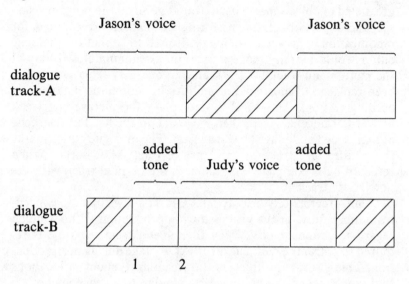

This allows the mixers to match Judy's tone with Jason's at point 1, and gradually increase the volume of track B to optimum level for Judy's voice when she begins speaking at point 2. A gradual, overlapping change in background tone will be far less disturbing than a direct jump from track A to track B and back again.

For additional insurance, the dialogue cutter will make closed loops of room tone for each sequence. If the mixers need to smooth over a rough transition that isn't adequately covered with overlaps, they will run the continuous loop of tone on a separate playback machine, gradually increasing its volume to mask out the rough transition, then gradually decreasing the volume of the loop back to zero. This process should not be confused with dialogue looping as described in the following section.

ADR (Looping)

Looping is a system for rerecording dialogue in synchronization with the picture during postproduction. This is done when the original recording is unacceptable for various reasons, such as a great deal of objectionable background noise on the track or when the audio portion of the performance must be rerecorded for modification of an actor's delivery. It used to be that the dialogue cutter would literally make a continuous running closed loop of the picture and track for the scenes in question. This system has been replaced in most sound facilities by automatic dialogue recording (ADR). The ADR system plays the picture and track forward at normal speed, then zips back to the head of the scene at high speed and plays forward again. The dialogue cutter marks the picture and track at the start of each ADR scene. When rerecording is completed, he replaces the original track with the new ADR track.

Some directors rely heavily on ADR. It allows them to concentrate more fully on the visuals during production without much regard to sound quality. They then spend whatever time is required to polish the dialogue on an ADR stage during postproduction. This also gives directors the freedom to shoot in locations that would otherwise be unacceptable due to extraneous noise.

The arguments against ADR are, first, that the quality of ADR sound tends to be sterile. ADR lines lack a dimension of reality. They sound like ADR lines. This is particularly noticeable in exterior scenes. Another disadvantage to ADR is the cost. If your budget is tight, go for the best production sound you can get. If you have to loop a line or two during postproduction, it won't break your bank but don't rely heavily on ADR work at the tail end unless you are sure you can afford it. A third disadvantage to ADR lines is that it is often difficult for an actor to match his ADR performance to his performance during production. The performance during production is usually more effective.

The Sound Effects Editor

The first step in sound effects editing is a detailed discussion, called a "sound effects spotting session," between the director and the sound effects editor. The director will communicate his overall vision of the sound structure, talking first in general terms and eventually narrowing the discussion down to specific sounds. He will also discuss which of the production effects are acceptable and which will need to be replaced.

A good sound effects editor approaches his work much like a composer approaches music. He will go far beyond the obvious sound effects that the picture demands; he will create moods and feelings such as suspense, joy, loneliness, or terror. The sound effects will have a tremendous influence on the audience's reaction to the film. A person walking down a country road will seem lonely if the sound effects contain a quiet wind, occasional buzzing insects, and the distant mooing of a cow. But if the track consists of birds singing in the trees and a small dog yapping nearby, the mood will shift to happiness.

Sound effects, like dialogue, are constructed to give the mixers maximum flexibility for manipulating individual sound effects. They are built on a multitude of checkerboarded tracks using fill for the spaces between sounds.

In addition to cleaning and splitting the production sound effects, the sound effects cutter will often embellish these production sounds. A crackling fire may need more crackle; a dull gunshot may need to be sharpened with an additional bang.

A sound effects editor sometimes will create entire sound effects sequences from scratch. There may be a badly recorded production track that he can use as a guide (called a "scratch track"), but often he will be asked to work with no reference material. In such cases, he will assemble all of the individual sounds needed for the sequence. He will either record original material, use wild sound effects recorded during production, or locate the sound effects in a stock library. He will then checkerboard them into a complete structure.

There are an infinite number of choices for each sound effect. How many ways can a gunshot sound? How many ways can crumpling paper sound? Breaking glass? Does it break on wood or on cement? Indoors or outdoors? Many of these decisions will be made by trial and error, listening to variations of a sound played in sync with the picture. The sound effects editor must construct sounds that complement one another, ones that will blend together smoothly in the mix. Most editing machines play only two or three sound tracks simultaneously and usually the first time the sound effects editor hears everything together is in the final mix. If he's in doubt about a certain combination, he will sometimes cut one or two alternatives for the director to choose from during the mix.

The following is a simple example of sound effects construction. Imagine the inside of a dingy hotel room. A man enters, turns on the light, drops his keys on the dresser, removes his coat revealing a splotch of blood on his shirt, tosses his coat on the chair, and flops onto the bed with a sigh. The list of sound effects needed for this scene are:

- distant city traffic
- key in lock
- doorknob turning
- door squeaking
- door closing
- light switch
- footsteps on carpet
- keys jingling
- keys hitting dresser top
- clothes rustling
- jacket dropping onto chair
- man flopping onto bed (squeaky bedsprings)
- man sighing

Depending on the mood of the scene, the sound effects editor may wish to add an angry car horn in the distance, a cat fight, a radio or television in the next room, a couple arguing upstairs, a fog horn, a police siren, a train whistle, a leaky faucet, or a toilet flushing. But assume for now that we're just concerned with the basics in the numbered list. Figure 3 shows the structure, checkerboarded across five sound effects tracks.

Each sound will be cut to synchronize precisely with the corresponding visual action in the picture. It is important to allow enough time (fill) between different sounds on a given track to allow the mixers enough time to make adjustments in equalization and level before each sound reaches the playback head. Similar sounds are kept on one track for easy reference in the mix.

A steady "hum" sound such as a motor boat engine is treated in a slightly different way. If the picture is cutting back and forth between long shots, medium shots, and close-up shots, it would seem logical to cut the sound effects as in Figure 4. However, the abrupt sound cuts will be too severe for the ear

Figure 3

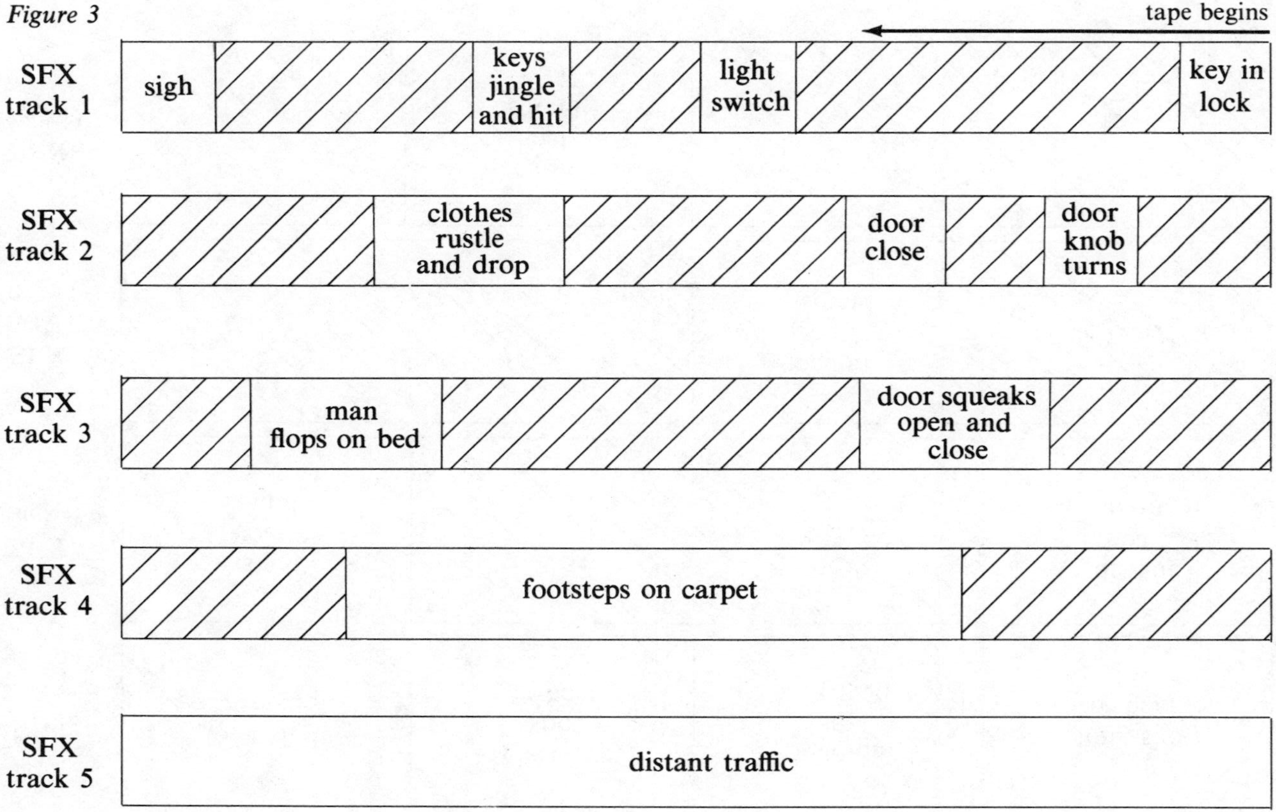

SFX track 1 | sigh | keys jingle and hit | light switch | | key in lock

SFX track 2 | | clothes rustle and drop | | door close | door knob turns

SFX track 3 | man flops on bed | | door squeaks open and close | |

SFX track 4 | | footsteps on carpet |

SFX track 5 | distant traffic |

tape begins

Figure 4

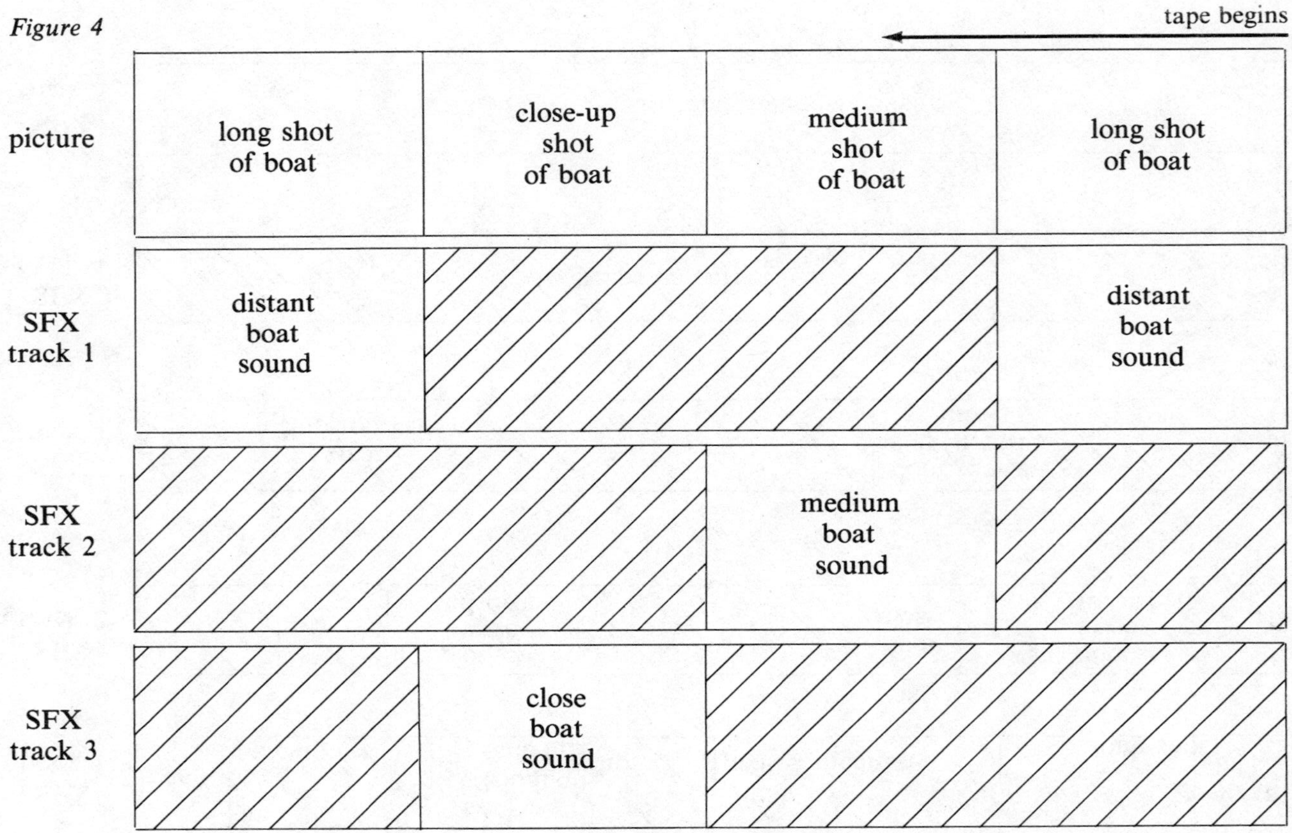

tape begins

| picture | long shot of boat | medium shot of boat | close-up shot of boat | long shot of boat |

| SFX track 1 | distant boat sound | | | distant boat sound |

| SFX track 2 | | medium boat sound | | |

| SFX track 3 | | close boat sound | | |

Figure 5

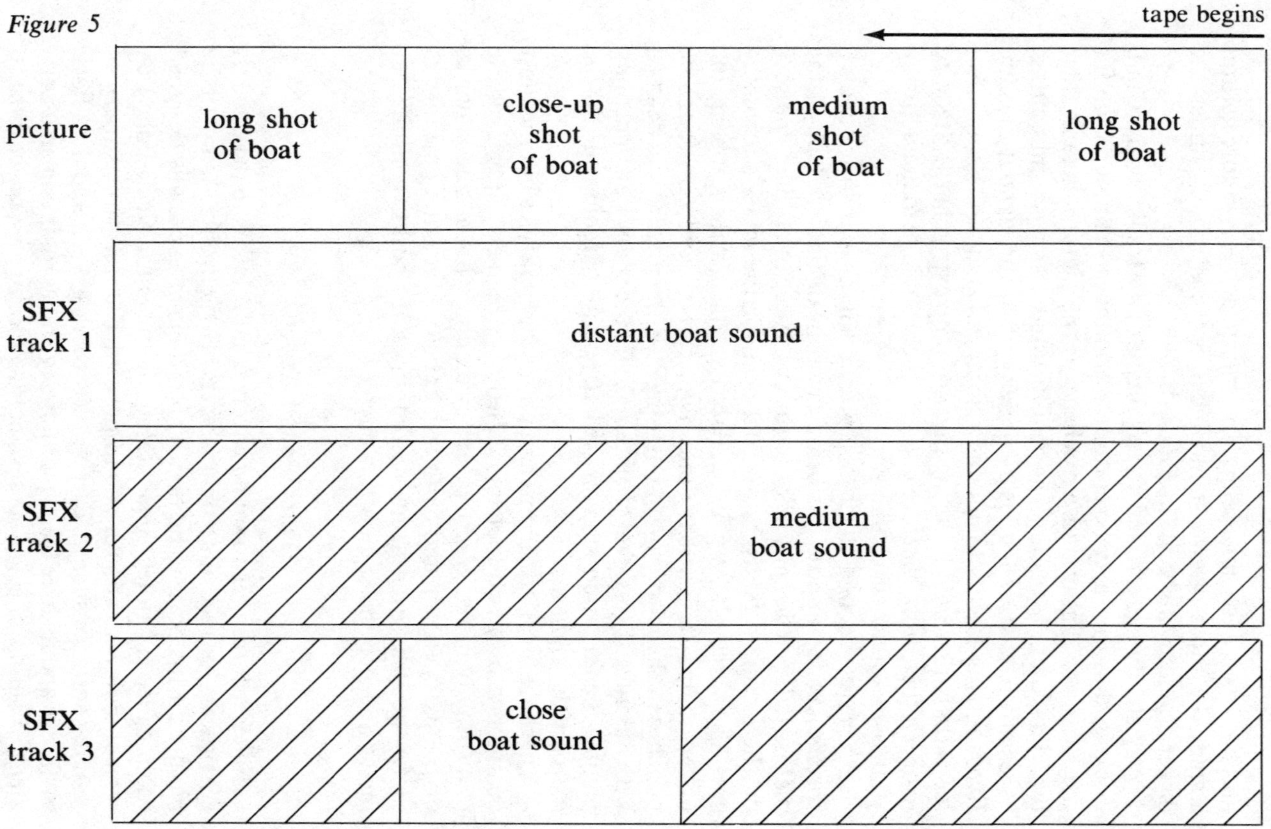

tape begins →

picture

| long shot of boat | close-up shot of boat | medium shot of boat | long shot of boat |

SFX track 1

distant boat sound

SFX track 2

medium boat sound

SFX track 3

close boat sound

and the mix will sound choppy. In order to achieve a more natural sound, the most distant sound must run continually under the closer sounds, as shown in Figure 5.

Any steady background sound such as city traffic, birds, wind, crickets, and rain may be cut into a continuous running loop for the mixers to dial in and out whenever the picture dictates their use. This often saves a great deal of unnecessary sound editing, especially if such a sound is used many times throughout the film. Every mixing facility maintains a library of standard sound effect loops that are available during the mix at no extra charge. It's wise to check their library before going to the trouble of manufacturing your own sound effect loops.

Whenever a sound effect loop must begin or end abruptly on a specific cut (as opposed to being faded in or out gradually), the picture will be cued just prior to the cut. A series of three "pluses" on the picture establishes a visual beat for the mixer's incoming cue. The three pluses will be spaced so that as they appear, the mixer counts to himself: "one, two, three," and on "four" he punches in the loop. For an outgoing cue, the picture will be cued with "minuses" instead of pluses. Figure 6 shows an incoming picture cue for a rain loop on the left, and an outgoing cue for the loop on the right.

There are a variety of plus and minus cueing styles but the most common uses a two-foot line called a "streamer" drawn on the film (usually in red grease pencil) preceding plus or minus marks on the sixth, eighth, and tenth frames before the cut. Some mixers prefer the fifth, seventh, and ninth frames. It's best to consult your mixer and use the style of his choice.

Foley Sound Effects

Foley recording is to sound effects what ADR is to dialogue. It is a process for recording sound effects in synchronization with the picture during postproduction. This is done in a specially designed room called a "Foley stage" (after the inventor, Jack Foley). A typical Foley stage is a sound-proofed room with a variety of walking surfaces such as carpet, tile, wood, gravel, and dirt. Each surface is about three feet square. Foley stages maintain an assortment of sound effects sources such as clothing, wooden blocks, matches, a dried tree branch, and a variety of metallic objects.

Figure 6

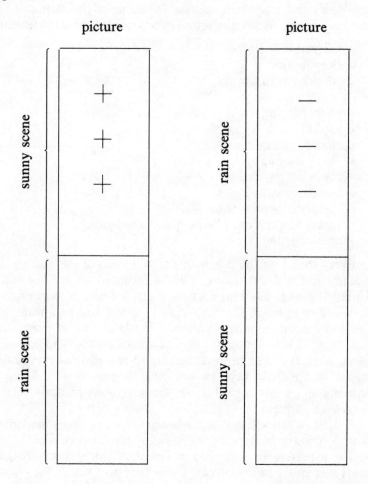

Most Foley jobs require special props in addition to the ones found in the stage.

During a Foley session, the picture will be projected through sound-proof glass onto a screen inside the stage. The Foley sound effects man will watch the picture a couple of times. Then, using his props, he will create the necessary sound effects in sync with the picture. He repeats this process, recording each take until he gets one right. For example, take the scene of the man entering the hotel room. Again, the sound effects needed for this scene are:

- distant city traffic
- key in lock
- doorknob turning
- door squeaking
- door closing
- light switch
- footsteps on carpet
- keys jingling
- keys hitting dresser top
- clothes rustling
- jacket dropping onto chair
- man flopping onto bed (squeaky bedsprings)
- man sighing

Every sound on the list, with the exception of the distant city traffic and the door closing, may be recorded on a Foley stage. Unless the stage has your particular kind of door as part of their standard equipment, the door closing sound will be impractical because a door mounted in a frame is too clumsy to move onto the stage. This sound may easily be recorded wild and edited in as on page 191. The props necessary to record the Foley sound effects will include keys on key ring; doorknob with keyhole; squeaky hinge; pile of clothes; section of squeaky bedsprings (perhaps four springs).

A light switch will not be necessary since a similar sound effect may be created by tapping a single key on the doorknob.

The experts who specialize in Foley recording work with remarkable speed and accuracy. Often they will watch the picture only once before attempting a first take, and often the first take will be flawless.

The recording of the hotel room scene on a Foley stage might go something like this: The Foley man will watch the picture to get a feel for the pacing. When he's got it down, he'll go for a take. He'll stand on the carpeted floor surface, hold the keys in one hand, the doorknob in the other, and the squeaky hinge in his teeth (the fewer times he picks up and puts down his props, the less chance there is for extraneous noise). When the film begins, he'll watch the action with intense concentration. At precisely the right moment, he'll shake the keys (possibly behind his back, away from the microphone, so they sound as though they're on the far side of the door as in the picture), then he'll place a key in the doorknob, turn the knob, and reach up to squeak the hinge as the door opens. As the man in the film enters the hotel room, the Foley man will walk (in place) on the carpeted floor surface, taking steps in sync with the man in the film. He'll squeak the hinge as the door closes, then gently tap a single key on the doorknob to simulate the sound of the light switch. He'll continue his footsteps as the man in the film walks into the room and at the right moment, he'll shake the keys and drop them on the wooden floor surface (for the sound of the keys dropping on the dresser in the picture). With his now-free hand, he'll pick up the pile of clothing and rub it against his body as the man in the picture takes off his jacket. He'll drop the pile of clothing on the floor (avoiding the keys that he dropped earlier), as the man in the picture tosses his jacket onto a chair. The Foley man will quietly set down the doorknob, pick up the section of bedsprings, and prepare to collapse physically onto the pile of clothing that he just dropped on the floor, as the man in the picture flops onto the bed. When the Foley man hits the clothing he'll squeak the springs to match the timing of the man settling on the bed. At the proper moment, he'll let out a tired sigh, pause for a moment, then call "Cut."

A Foley man looks frankly ridiculous operating his assortment of bizarre props, moving from one floor surface to another, staring intently at the screen, glancing away only to pick up the next prop, but the results are astonishingly accurate.

The advantages of Foley recording are, first, that it is an efficient way to construct a multitude of sound effects on a single track without editing. Further, additional time is saved in the mix since there will be fewer tracks for the mixers to deal with. The hotel room scene, instead of five edited tracks (see p. 200) will consist of three tracks as shown in Figure 7.

The only disadvantage to Foley recording is the cost of the stage (and a Foley man, if your sound effects require an expert). You must weigh these costs against the time you will save in editing and mixing.

Small, easily controlled sounds such as walking, clothes rustling, writing, breathing, scraping, hitting, clicking, and brushing

Figure 7

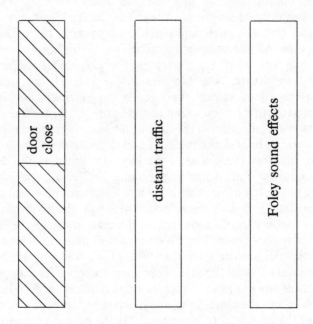

lend themselves to Foley recording. Sound effects such as traffic, cat fights, thunder, wind, tire squeals, and airplanes lend themselves to production recording or postproduction editing.

Selecting a Composer

In 1953 composers organized the Composers and Lyricists Guild of America. The guild received union status from the National Labor Relations Board approximately twenty years ago. At that time the guild negotiated a contract with studios and producers, establishing minimum wages and working conditions for composers and lyricists. However, their union status lapsed several years ago as a consequence of a lawsuit between the guild and major studios. Until such time as the guild reestablishes its union status, its minimum contract is not effective, and each contract must be negotiated separately. Additional information regarding the status of the guild may be obtained by contacting the guild office at the address and phone number in the *Pacific Coast Studio Directory* listed in Appendix E.

The musician's union, called the Musician's Mutual Protective Association, covers musicians, orchestrators, conductors, arrangers, contractors, and copyists (the composer writes the entire score across long single pages; the copyist copies each instrument onto its own part book). The union is associated with the American Federation of Musicians and has various locals throughout the country. Composers frequently function as orchestrators and/or conductors and in those capacities they are protected by the union.

The musician's union has a standard contract with producers establishing minimum wages and working conditions for their members. Since the vast majority of persons working in the above-mentioned union capacities are members of the union, it is very difficult for a producer to score a film properly without signing a union contract. In order to do so, a producer must supply the union with pertinent information regarding his project, such as the name of his production company, the principals in that company, the type of license for which he is applying (motion picture or television), and the picture's music budget. In addition, the union requires a financial statement, documented by a bank, that verifies the producer's ability to pay for the costs of his music. The union will send this information to the American Federation of Musicians for approval and, assuming it's approved, will sign a contract with the producer. The producer will then be required to post a bond equal to the amount of his total music budget as a guarantee that the union members will be paid.

Producers have a reputation for spending more than their anticipated budget during production, leaving very little for postproduction costs. The musician's union has a history of problems in this area and consequently requires the bond. For the same reason, agents who represent composers almost always insist that the producer pay a third or half of the composer's fee before the first note of music is written, an additional percentage on the day the music is scored (recorded), and the balance be paid when the music is dubbed (music is originally recorded on multiple tracks and is subsequently "dubbed down" or mixed onto a single track).

A picture's budget will often dictate which composers are most appropriate for the job. The minimum a producer should expect to pay for a composer who also functions as an orchestrator and conductor is $10,000.

Independent producers often have particular composers in mind for their projects. Their choices are generally based on a combination of past experience, scores that impressed them in other films, and recommendations from other producers. If a producer doesn't have a specific composer in mind he needn't worry. Composers commonly watch for announcements and advertisements in trade publications such as *Variety* and the *Hollywood Reporter* alerting them to pictures in various stages of production and postproduction. These composers will contact the producers of these films and offer their services. The majority of work for many composers comes about in this way.

Another approach to finding a composer is for the producer to contact agencies that represent composers. The principal agencies in Los Angeles include Bart-Millander Associates and the Carol Faith Agency. Some additional agencies that handle composers are the Barskin Agency, Richard Lee Emler Enterprises, and the Robert Light Agency. When contacting agencies, be prepared to discuss the music style you're seeking and your anticipated schedule. The agent may request information about your music budget in order to recommend an appropriate composer, but it is best not to divulge the details of that budget, especially the amount allotted for the composer's fee, since that fee is open to negotiation. The agencies will recommend composers, provide you with a list of the composers' credits, and in many cases will offer to send you a demo tape containing samples of the composer's past work.

A composer should be chosen based on considerations similar to those used for selecting any creative member of your team. Find someone whose work exhibits a style that complements your project; someone with whom you communicate well; someone with experience working within the framework of your budget and time schedule.

It is important to discuss your budget and time schedule with the composer as early in the project as possible. He must know how much he has to spend, the number of musicians available to him, and the amount of studio time he will have for scoring and dubbing. Each film has unique requirements but most pictures require thirty to forty minutes of music. If you are budgeting for a low-budget picture, allow for at least ten musicians, two three-hour recording sessions, and six hours of dubbing time. Consider fees for composing, orchestrating, conducting, muscians' salaries and union fees, studio rental, instrument rental, and copying fees. Before attempting to detail these costs, consult the composer and, if possible, the musician's contractor, and listen carefully to their advice.

Preparation for Music Scoring

When the picture editor cuts the film, he seeks maximum visual impact without regard to the music that will eventually accompany the picture. After the picture is cut, the composer must score the music to fit the picture. He must contribute to the mood of the scene and, when required, write music to accent highlights precisely in the scene's action. This requires a sophisticated combination of creative talent and technical skill.

The following terminology describes the various types of music scoring for films: *underscoring* (dominant or subordinate); *visual vocal* (on-camera singer); *background vocal* (off-camera singer); *source music* (music coming from a specific source such as a radio, television, PA system, or jukebox).

Before a director begins discussions with the composer, it is helpful for the composer to screen the film uninterrupted from start to finish in a screening room. In this way he will gain a sense of the overall pacing and feel of the picture. Ideally, he will be screening the final cut although schedules often require a composer to begin preliminary work based on a rough cut. Subsequent discussions begin in a music spotting session either in the screening room or in the cutting room. It is here that the director (and/or producer), music editor, and composer determine where music should be utilized in the film and what it should sound like. Again, it is important for the director to communicate his concept of the overall sound structure—dialogue, sound effects, and music. The composer is a part of the whole picture and the director must ensure that each part complements the whole. Spotting sessions begin with a general discussion about moods and feelings, and eventually narrow down to specific discussions about where music will be used and what it will sound like. Each unit of music is referred to as a "cue." Within each cue there may be important moments that the music will highlight. These, too, will be determined in the spotting session. It may take several sessions, if time allows, before the director and composer establish congruent thoughts about the music.

At the conclusion of the spotting sessions, the music editor or his assistant will time each scene that requires music. Each specific action, camera move, camera angle change, dialogue start and stop, will be described and timed to the hundredth of a second. The starting frame for each cue will be marked with a number. The first cue in reel one will be marked M-11 meaning, *music, reel one, first cue.* The second cue in reel one will be marked M-12. The first cue in reel two will be marked M-21, and so on throughout the picture.

The marked starting frame will be frame 1, and each timing in the scene will be counted in frames from that starting frame. The frame counts will then be converted into seconds by dividing the number of frames by twenty-four (film travels at the rate of twenty-four frames per second).

Music timing sheets will be made by the assistant music editor and will contain all of the timing information for each scene to be scored. Each timing sheet will begin with an introductory paragraph to orient the scene in the story. Each specific action will be described and timed. The director and composer will have previously determined during the spotting sessions which of these actions, if any, will be highlighted or accented by the music.

For the scene in which the man enters the hotel room, as described in the previous section on sound effects, we will assume that the music will start when the door opens and we first see the man entering the room. The director and composer decide to accent, first, the moment when the man removes his jacket and reveals the blood on his shirt and, second, the moment when the man hits the bed (perhaps the music will "sigh" with him). This is a very obvious use of music (called "mickey mousing") and the example is intended only to help communicate the technical problems of the composer. Current thought in the film world tends toward a more subtle approach, such as musically emphasizing emotions rather than mickey mousing the action in the picture as described here.

The timing sheet for the hotel scene mentioned above is shown in Table 13.

Table 13   **Music Timing**

M-52 (fifth reel, second cue) The man is returning from a bar where he was stabbed during a fight with two drunks. He ran from the bar and we now cut to the inside of his hotel room as the door opens and . . .

(seconds)	(frames)	(action)
0:00	(0 frames)	We first see the man.
0:03.96	(95 frames)	Door closes.
0:07.04	(169 frames)	Lights on.
0:13.04	(313 frames)	Drops keys on dresser.
0:17.13	(411 frames)	Removes jacket . . .
0:23.00	(552 frames)	revealing blood.
0:28.21	(677 frames)	Drops jacket onto chair.
0:31.88	(765 frames)	Flops onto bed and . . .
0:40.33	(968 frames)	sighs. Camera slowly moves in to close-up of man's face and we cut to . . .
0:48.38	(1161 frames)	next scene.

Note: Leave long tail on music to carry over cut to next scene.

Each music cue in the film is spotted and timed in this way.

It is common for directors to request a long tail, or long fade, in the music to allow leeway for a long music fade in the final mix (see Chapter 20). Often this long tail may be used to smooth the transition from one scene to another.

Free Timing and Click Track Recording

There are two conventional approaches to scoring music for films. The first, called *free timing,* is where the musicians in a scoring session play the music while watching the picture. This is a costly process. Running the picture involves additional studio time and it may take several tries before the musicians record an acceptable take.

The *click track* is a more controlled approach and is usually more efficient. When a composer decides to score a cue using a click track, he will select an electronic metronome "click" speed based on how the piece is paced in his mind. The metronome click number represents the number of clicks per minute; each click represents one-quarter note beat in the music. The late Carroll Knudson conceived and assembled a book that cross-references seconds with numbers of clicks for each click speed. Composers use this book as a guide when writing music for click track recording.

For example, if a composer scoring music for the hotel room scene (see p. 204) decides on a metronome click speed of 41.74 (i.e., 41.74 quarter-note beats per minute, or 34.5 frames per beat), he opens the click track book to the page for click 41.74 and cross-references the number of seconds for each timing on the music timing sheet with the corresponding number of clicks in the book to determine precisely how many beats into the music each timing will occur. The click track book will reveal that for a 41.74 metronome click count, the moment when the blood is seen (0:23.00 seconds on the timing sheet) is click number 17, or 17 beats from the start of the cue. The composer writes the music so that the proper effect for the "blood" timing occurs at precisely 17 clicks (0:23.00 seconds) from the start of the music. When the composer goes into the studio to record the music for the film, he will instruct the engineer to play the proper electronic metronome click speed for each cue into the headphones of the musicians. In the case of the hotel room cue,` that speed will be 41.74. The conductor/composer is the only person who *must* hear the click, since he will set the beat. The other musicians may or may not wish to hear it. In this way the musicians will play each piece of music at precisely the right speed. In the case of the hotel room cue, on the seventeenth click, exactly 0:23.00 seconds from the start of the piece, the music will accent the blood on the man's shirt. The composer will proceed to score the entire picture in this way, using a predetermined click for each piece of music.

The hotel room scene is a very simple example of film scoring. You will begin to appreciate the problems of music scoring for film if you consider the complexity of scoring three minutes or more of continuous music with twenty-five important accented highlights. Imagine the problems involved in writing not only an aesthetically effective piece but also one that meets the twenty-five musically arbitrary highlights.

It is not uncommon for a composer to combine free timing with the click track. In this way he benefits from recording directly to the picture while maintaining considerable control with the click track. This is a more time-consuming and costly approach than simple click track recording.

When organizing a scoring session, the composer will begin the session with the most fully orchestrated pieces of music. For example, if the scoring session requires thirty musicians for half of the music and fifteen musicians for the rest, he will score all of the thirty-man pieces first. He'll then keep only half of the orchestra in the studio for the remainder of the session. This avoids paying all of the musicians for the entire session.

The Music Editor

When original music is scored for a picture, there is little for the music editor to do besides laying in the music tracks opposite the appropriate places in the picture. When prerecorded music is used, such as stock library music (which is occasionally used when the budget is so tight that original music is not scored), the music editor's job becomes more difficult and more creative. He must select, with the director, pieces of music that best approximate the desired pacing and mood of the film. Since the accents in the music will come at arbitrary points, the music editor must select the most important visual action and line up an accent in the music with that action in the picture. He'll then run the piece back to heads and listen to the entire piece from the beginning. Many such trial and error placements will be required before he determines the most acceptable compromise. He may need to shorten a piece by cutting out a phrase of music, or lengthen a piece by adding, or *segueing* (dissolving) to another piece of music. One way to deal with this problem is to select key scenes that will require music and pick the music before cutting the picture. The picture may then be cut to fit the music. This may be the most effective way to deal with certain scenes, but it is still a compromise.

At best, library music for a feature film is a second-class way to go. It is certainly cheaper than original scoring but the inherently awkward score is an unpleasant trade-off. The principal disadvantages of library music are the lack of specific cuing for cuts and action, the lack of a theme or musical thread throughout the picture, and the inconsistency of instrumentation. Even an untrained ear will be aware of this inconsistency. The audience will hear the change in instrumentation from piece to piece, and the continuity of the film will suffer accordingly. The only advantage of library music is that it's cheaper.

Playback Recording

Playback recording is used primarily with on-camera musicians and singers when a live recording is impractical. For example, a location may have poor acoustics for live recording. Prior to beginning principal photography, the musicians will make a multitrack studio recording of the music. This will then be mixed down onto one-quarter inch tape. The one-quarter inch studio recording will be played back on location during each take and the musicians will play their music in time with the studio recording. Given a little practice, competent musicians will be able to match their movements accurately with the studio recording during location playback. This is sort of like looping in reverse.

The music that is actually recorded on location is called a "scratch track." It will be used for editing but will be replaced with the studio recording for the final mix (see Chapter 20).

It is crucial that each stage of recording in the playback process, including the original multitrack recording, contains a consistent sync signal (such as the one provided by a Nagra recorder), in order to maintain absolute synchronization with the final performance on film.

Cue Sheets

The dialogue editor, the sound effects editor, and the music editor will each prepare cue sheets for the final sound mix. The cue sheets will list each sound as it appears on each track with precise footage counts for the beginning and end of each sound. The cue sheets should be constructed as a quick-reference road map for the mixers. These sheets may be thought of as an on-paper model that parallels the construction of the edited sound tracks. A typical cue sheet, again using the hotel room sequence described previously, is shown in Table 14.

The numbers refer to footages. Head and tail footages are written for cues longer than approximately ten frames; shorter cues such as the door close sound at ten feet on track 2 require only

Table 14   **Sample Cue Sheet**

Title _____	Mixer _____	Page ___ of ___
Production Company _____	Director _____	

Track	Track	Track	Track	Track
SFX-1	SFX-2	SFX-3	SFX-4	SFX-5
				0 DISTANT
				TRAFFIC
3 KEY IN DOOR				
	5 DOORKNOB TURNING	'SQUEAKS'		
		6 DOOR OPENS		
		'SQUEAKS'		
		9 DOOR CLOSE		
	10 DOOR CLOSE		10 FOOTSTEPS ON CARPET	
12 LIGHT SWITCH				
20 KEYS JINGLE				
(HIT DRESSER)				
— 22	22 CLOTHES RUSTLING			
	— 24			
		26 MAN FLOPS ON BED	— 26	
		— 30		
32 "SIGH"				
				— 36

the head footage. The scene ends at thirty-six feet. Compare this cue sheet with the construction of the edited tracks on page 200 and you will see their parallel construction. Separate cue sheets will be written for dialogue, sound effects, and music.

There is no absolute standard format for writing cue sheets. In New York, for instance, where it is common to use only one mixer, footages are often listed *only* in the extreme left-hand column. Check with your mixer to determine the style he prefers.

CHAPTER 20

The Sound Mix
(or the Final Dub)

All of the postproduction sound work—dialogue, sound effects, and music—culminates in the mix. It is here that the isolated sounds become blended into a finished, integrated track. For many features, the process takes several weeks but low-budget films are often mixed in three or four days.

Selecting a Mixing Facility

A typical mixing facility is about the size of a modest movie theater without the seats. At one end of the room is a projection screen and footage counter. At the other end of the room is the mixing board, or console, that looks like the control panel for a futuristic spaceship. Around the console are chairs for the mixers, director, producer, composer, and sound editors. Between the screen and the console is an empty floor. In the back of the console is another room that houses a projector, a bank of playback machines, and the recording equipment. Personnel in this room are the projectionist, several machine operators who line up the edited sound tracks on the playback machines, and the recordist who operates the recording equipment and monitors the progress of the mix through headphones, listening for any defects in the recording.

Because of the time, effort, care, and expense that have gone into preparing your tracks, you will want to use a sound facility that will produce a first-rate mix. There are half a dozen studios that consistently mix major feature films. There are many others that mix smaller features, television shows, industrials, educational films, and commercials. When choosing a mixing facility, there are four equally important considerations: the mixers, technical capabilities, reputation, and cost.

The Mixers

The qualifications for a good mixer are technical competence, sensitivity, attitude, and experience. If you're mixing a feature, it is important to use mixers who regularly mix features. The problems involved in mixing a sixty-second commercial are very different from the problems involved in mixing a ninety-minute feature. In both cases, it's best to hire a specialist. When mixing a sixty-second commercial the mixer will spend many hours focusing on the optimum sound for that sixty seconds. There isn't as much time available for each minute in a feature film as there usually is for the single minute in a sixty-second commercial. Another principal difference between mixing features and mixing almost any other type of film is that feature mixers must maintain a continuity of sound over several reels of film mixed over a period of a week or more. This requires a special sensitivity that is developed by practice. Regardless of the facility you choose, it is best to work with mixers who regularly mix features.

Another qualification for a good mixer has to do with attitude. This varies all over the board and can be determined, first, by the mixer's reputation and, second, by meeting with him to discuss your project prior to committing your film to the facility.

The most skillful mixer in the world, if he has a jaded or prima donna attitude, may be a detriment to your project. There are many top-notch mixers to choose from who will cooperate with you to achieve the best possible results within your budget. The larger mixing facilities have several staff mixers to choose from and will occasionally borrow additional mixers from other facilities. Smaller facilities have fewer on-staff choices but they, too, often borrow mixers from other studios for specific projects.

A great morale booster for mixers at every facility is a thoughtful producer who supplies an assortment of donuts with coffee for the mixing crew at the start of each day. Many producers do this as a matter of routine and most mixers have come to expect it. Like the production crew during principal photography, many mixers will begin work disappointed if this simple protocol is overlooked.

Technical Capabilities

You must find a facility capable of meeting the special requirements for your project. If you have a complex mix with many edited sound tracks per reel, you will need a facility with an appropriate number of playback machines. If you intend to add distortion, echo, or other special sound modifications to your original tracks, the facility must have the appropriate equipment to do so. Often there is an extra charge for the use of special equipment. If the mixing facility of your choice doesn't have a particular piece of equipment necessary for your mix, they may be able to rent it specifically for your picture, but they will need advance notice in order to make such arrangements. Don't assume that every studio has the same equipment. Define your needs and make certain that you're covered.

Reputation and Cost

Reputation and cost considerations must be lumped together. You will need a facility with a reputation for efficiently mixing feature films with consistent professional quality. Such a reputation will reflect the competence of their mixers, as well as the quality and maintenance of their equipment. The facility must also have a reputation for working with producers to stay within the production budget. It is unusual to find a mixing facility that offers a guaranteed flat fee for a mix. The reason is that it is impossible to determine in advance the complexity of the tracks and the degree of perfection that the producer and director will demand of the mixers. Every mix requires a continuous stream of compromises, but an open-ended flat fee schedule encourages producers and directors to become unreasonably demanding in their search for perfection. When the time clock is ticking away minutes and dollars, everyone is far more willing to accept reasonable compromises. If a facility does agree to a flat fee, there will almost certainly be a limit set on the maximum time allowed.

When mixing feature films, it is common to use three mixers—

one for dialogue, one for sound effects, and one for music. Depending on the complexity of your mix and your budget limitations, you may wish to use only one or two mixers. Mixing studios charge an hourly rate that varies depending on the number of mixers involved. Using one mixer is not necessarily the least expensive way to mix your film. You must estimate the amount of studio time you will save by using additional mixers and weigh this against the additional cost for the added mixers. For example, if the studio charges are $200 per hour for one mixer, $250 per hour for two mixers, and $300 per hour for three mixers, and you are mixing a simple, ten-minute sequence with one dialogue track, two sound effects tracks, and one music track, one mixer will probably do the entire job in two hours. Using two mixers might save fifteen minutes and using three mixers might save another fifteen minutes. In this case, it is more efficient to use one mixer. However, if this same ten-minute sequence has four dialogue tracks, eight sound effects tracks, and three music tracks, it may take one mixer six hours, two mixers four hours, and three mixers two hours. In this instance, it is least expensive to use three mixers.

Most feature films have enough tracks to warrant the use of three mixers. When operating on a small budget, however, it is sometimes sensible to use one or two mixers for portions of the film, bringing in a third man only if necessary for the most difficult reels. If you are using union mixers, however, bear in mind that the minimum amount of time for which a mixer must be paid is a full nine-hour day.

There is also a question of preference when determining the number of mixers you will use. Some directors, especially in New York, feel that one mixer is preferable for two reasons. First, the director has only one person with whom to communicate. Second, one mixer may be able to achieve a more consistent balance in the sound than two or three mixers. The one-man mixing system is most successful in studios utilizing an automated console. This is one in which a computer memory records the mix *information* as opposed to recording the sound itself. This recording is called *the program* as opposed to the *premix* (see p. 220). Information for any one sound in the program can be changed without affecting the information for any other sound whereas a premix often blends sounds together.

Most directors in Los Angeles prefer to work with three mixers.

When to Book the Facility

Once you have selected a studio, estimate when you will be ready to begin your mix and book the facility for that date. You should do this early in your postproduction schedule since the better facilities are tied up for months in advance. Also, setting a target date for the mix will give your postproduction team a specific goal. If your first-choice studio is booked so solidly that you can't get in, put your name on the waiting list in the hope that someone else cancels and book yourself into another facility for protection. Most mixing facilities won't require a holding deposit until very close to the mix date.

Three-Stripe Mixing

35mm feature films are mixed onto 35mm sprocketed full-coat magnetic stock. This is similar to 35mm edit stripe stock, only instead of two stripes, the entire surface is coated with magnetic oxide. Hence the term "full-coat." The full-coat mag travels over three separate, parallel sound heads that record three parallel stripes of sound—one for dialogue, one for music, and one for sound effects. Each stripe will have equalization and blending modifications built into it during the mix so that when all three stripes are played back simultaneously, they will sound like one integrated sound track.

There are two advantages to the three-stripe system of recording. First, this system makes it possible to make changes during the mix on one stripe without affecting the other two. This saves an enormous amount of time, especially when mixing complex sequences. If one mixer achieves an acceptable mix for a given portion of the film, he may punch out of the record mode for his stripe while the other mixers go back to the start of the sequence and rerecord only on the stripes that need improvement. For example, consider a sequence involving three dialogue tracks, five music tracks, and eight sound effects tracks. Assume that each of the sixteen edited sound tracks contains several tricky cues and the mixers have made seven passes through the scene in an effort to get an acceptable blend. On the seventh pass, the dialogue mixer and the sound effects mixer hit every cue magnificently, but the music mixer is still a shade off the mark. Instead of all three mixers starting again from scratch, the dialogue and sound effects mixers may simply punch out of the record mode for their stripes, keeping their portions of the mix intact while the music mixer goes back to the start and continues working until he achieves an acceptable mix for the music.

The second advantage to three-stripe mixing will come further down the road when you sell your picture to foreign countries. If the foreign distributor wishes to rerecord the dialogue in a different language, as opposed to printing subtitles, he will request a music and effects (M & E) track. This is a transfer of your three-stripe mix onto another piece of 35mm full-coat stock, leaving the dialogue stripe blank. The foreign distributor then records the new language onto the empty stripe of the full-coat; he will not be burdened with the cost of remixing the music and sound effects tracks as well.

Most films have some production sound effects married to the dialogue track such as footsteps recorded during a walking dialogue sequence. Some foreign contracts require only a one-to-one M & E transfer, in which case any production sound effects on the dialogue track will be added by the foreign buyer. Other contracts require every sound effect to be on the M & E track. Often such contracts will additionally require room tone on the sound effects track during dialogue sequences to be used as background tone for those sequences.

There are few studios that use a four-stripe mixing system. The fourth stripe is used for final "sweetening" of the sound, such as a last-minute decision to boost the level of a gunshot. Rather than remixing the sound effects for the entire sequence, the louder gunshot is simply recorded onto the fourth stripe.

Temps and Trials

If the budget and time allow, it is common to make "temp" (temporary) mixes during postproduction in order to evaluate the picture more fully during screenings. Temp mixes tend to have "thin" tracks, utilizing minimum sound effects and whatever prerecorded music approximates what the composer will write for the finished picture.

Once all of the sound tracks are edited, it may be of value to take the picture and all of the sound tracks into the mixing studio for a trial run a week or so before the mix date. This will be a quick run-through, without recording, in order to gain a sense for how the tracks are fitting together. It isn't necessary to stop and start a great deal during the trial run-through, since you're not attempting to finalize the sound. You're looking only for glaring errors such as out-of-sync dialogue and ill-chosen sound effects. You may also become aware of a scene that needs a fuller track than you had originally expected. Perhaps a sequence for which you had intended to use nothing but music may need a few sound effects. The trial run will allow you to make any such changes before the mix.

The trial run will be of greatest value if the mixers who will do the final dub are present. This will give them an overall feeling for the flow of the film. When they begin the mix, they will have a clear understanding of where the picture is going. They will also have an opportunity to offer suggestions for improving the tracks prior to the mix.

On small-budget films, where a trial run is an unaffordable luxury, the director must ensure that the sound editors have meticulously checked and double-checked their work. He must also spend whatever time is necessary with the sound editors, listening to their tracks and discussing various selections and combinations of sounds so that when he enters the mix he knows precisely what he's working with. The more decisions that can be made during the editing, the more time will be saved in the mix. When there is doubt as to the most appropriate sound effect, or the most effective combination of sounds, a good sound editor will allow for choices in the mix, cutting more than one combination. There is nothing more frustrating than being caught short in the mix. Always bring too much, never not enough. A director will often request that the composer write one or two pieces of optional music for sequences that may or may not require music in the final mix. Such optional pieces will be cut into the music tracks, but a final decision as to whether or not they will be used will be reserved until the director hears the entire complement of sound in the mix.

The Procedure

35mm feature films are mixed in reels of 1,000 feet or less. One thousand feet is a little over ten minutes of film. This reel size is more convenient for the editors and mixers than the standard 2,000-foot reels that make up release prints. Consequently, a feature film is generally broken down into ten or more reels for mixing.

Before starting the mix, the sound cutters will review the cue sheets for the first reel with their respective mixers. They will synopsize the construction of the tracks and point out any special areas of concern. During this time, the machine operators in the back room will line up the edited tracks for reel one on the playback machines, the projectionist will thread reel one picture onto the projector, and the sound recordist will load a reel of 35mm full-coat onto the three-stripe recorder.

The chief mixer is the dialogue mixer. He will sit in the center of the board with the music and sound effects mixers on either side. In addition to mixing dialogue, the dialogue mixer will operate the controls that interlock and operate all of the machines in the back room. At the push of a button, he can run everything simultaneously forward or backward. He will also operate the push buttons that determine the record and playback modes for each of the three stripes on the recorder. The dialogue mixer must listen for the blending of *all* the tracks, not just the dialogue. The music and sound effects mixers will be more concerned with their individual responsibilities.

Once the mixers have been briefed on the content and construction of the tracks and the men in the back room have signaled their readiness to go, the dialogue mixer hits a button and everything starts to roll. This is a very exciting moment. It is the start of the culmination of months of work.

As in all phases of production, it is the director who must maintain an overall vision of the completed picture. He is responsible for guiding the mixers through each scene, communicating precisely what he's after. The director must also, however, listen carefully to the opinions and suggestions of the mixers before making final decisions. Each mixer is a specialist and each will bring to the film a unique experience, knowledge, and skill. If a director feels that a sound is too loud, or that the music is coming in too early, or that a voice is sounding thin, he must say so. If there is disagreement, the director must carefully weigh the options, make a decision, and stick with it. The opinions in a mix are largely subjective and ultimately one voice must make the final decisions. There is nothing more comfortable for a mixer than a single voice of authority, a director who exhibits both a respect for other's ideas and confidence in his own final decisions.

There is nothing more *frustrating* for a mixer than mixing by committee, when the producer, director, composer, sound cutters, and mixers each express different opinions and interpretations and nobody seems able to make an intelligent, final decision. The mixers need *direction* from a single voice of authority. The ideal situation is one in which everyone's subjective opinions are funneled through the director.

At the beginning of the first day, the mixers will view the entire first reel, listening to all of the tracks, then return to the head of the reel and begin mixing, one sequence at a time. As the picture rolls forward on the screen, the mixers watch the action, the footage counter, the cue sheets, the VU (level) meters, and the myriad of dials, buttons, slides, and switches on the control panel. They must stay one step ahead of the picture, anticipating footage cues, listening carefully and modifying each sound for the proper overall blend. Very few cues will sound right the first time through. It often takes several passes before the mixers find the correct level and equalization for each sound.

Most contemporary mixing facilities have a system of "rock 'n roll" mixing that allows the dialogue mixer to start the mix, stop, back up, stop, and start again. Some facilities have a high-speed backup system that runs several times faster than normal sound speed. During a take, the mixers will record onto the three-stripe mag until one of the mixers misses a cue. Instead of going back to the beginning of the reel and remixing everything up to the missed cue, the dialogue mixer will simply punch out of the record mode, rock back a short distance, stop, roll forward, and punch back into the record mode prior to reaching the missed cue. If the mixer hits it right this time, they will keep going. If not, they'll back up and do it again. Experienced mixers are skillful at punching in and out of the record mode without causing any observable change in the sound.

Using the hotel room scene (see p. 192) as an example, the mixers begin this portion of the film on the cut to the interior of the empty hotel room, as they wait for the man to enter. As the scene plays, the mixers hit their cues, setting proper level and equalization for each sound until something goes wrong. Perhaps they get to the keys falling on the dresser and it sounds more like a pailfull of nuts and bolts dropping from a second-story window. The mixers stop, punch out of record, back up past the key drop, stop again, roll forward, and punch back into the record mode prior to the key drop. The sound effects mixer lowers the level for the keys and this time it sounds like keys dropping on a dresser. They continue recording and stop again whenever there's another problem.

It is the dialogue mixer who determines whether or not to stop. If the sound effects mixer runs into a problem, as with the keys, but the dialogue mixer and music mixer are doing fine, the dialogue mixer may wish to finish out the scene, laying down the dialogue and music, then returning to correct the key sound by rerecording on the sound effects stripe only.

The entire mix follows this procedure. The mixers start at the beginning of reel one and rock 'n roll through the film, stopping, reversing, starting, stopping again, and so forth, inching their way to the close of the final reel.

Premixing

A feature film will often have more edited sound tracks per reel than the mixing facility has playback machines or more edited tracks than the mixers can comfortably handle at one time. For example, if you are mixing in a studio with twenty-five playback machines and you have a reel in your film with twenty-seven edited sound tracks—eighteen sound effects tracks, four music tracks, and five dialogue tracks—you can't put them all up on playback machines at the same time. Even if you could, chances are that the mixers would be unable efficiently to mix twenty-seven tracks simultaneously. In situations such as this, the mixers will select several of the edited tracks and premix them, combining the sounds from several edited tracks onto a single premixed track. They will use the premixed track in place of the original edited tracks in the final mix. In this way they will reduce the total number of tracks to a manageable number.

An absolute judgment about level and equalization for most sounds can't be made until all of the sounds are heard together. The danger in premixing is that certain sounds will be blended together that you may wish to modify separately in the final mix.

Consequently, premixes will often be recorded onto a three-stripe track, blending together only the sounds that are "safe" to combine on a single stripe. The mixers will separate the remaining sounds and premix them onto the other two stripes. Sounds that are safe to blend in the premix are those that will require identical modification in the final mix. In other words, their relative differences will be established in the premix. As a simple example, imagine a scene that takes place in downtown city traffic. A businessman is screaming (dialogue) at a trio of street musicians (music). The musicians ignore him but their dog barks back furiously (sound effects). The sequence was shot on a sound stage so the city traffic sounds must be created with edited sound tracks. The sound effects editor has edited the following tracks: track 1, dog barking; track 2, distant city traffic; track 3, sound of cars passing close to scene; track 4, occasional car horns; track 5, distant police siren.

All of these sound effects tracks may be blended together in a premix except for track 1, the dog barking. The modifications for tracks 2, 3, 4, and 5 will be dictated by their relative differences. If the mixers combine tracks 2, 3, 4, and 5 in a premix, creating a single big-city traffic sound effect, the overall volume of the track may be raised and lowered accordingly in the final mix, but the relative differences between the sounds in tracks 2, 3, 4, and 5 will remain the same. Track 1, the dog barking, must remain separate until final mix because it will be modified to blend with the dialogue and music, not with the city traffic. If the mixers had married the dog bark to the city traffic in the premix, and discovered in the final mix that the traffic was fine but the dog was barking much too softly to blend well with the dialogue and music, they would have been unable to increase the volume of the dog barking without also raising the volume of traffic to an objectionable level.

In the situation described on page 220 with twenty-seven sound tracks—eighteen sound effects tracks, four music tracks, and five dialogue tracks—the mixers might choose to premix the eighteen sound effects tracks. If so, they could spread the eighteen tracks across the board, giving six to the dialogue mixer, six to the music mixer, and six to the sound effects mixer. They could then mix the tracks onto a 35mm three-stripe track, keeping certain predetermined sounds separated for individual modification during the final mix. Once they had completed the sound effects premix, they would make a final mix using the three premixed sound effects stripes, the four edited music tracks, and the five edited dialogue tracks. Since they have twenty playback machines, it isn't technically necessary to premix all eighteen sound effects tracks, but doing so brings the total number of tracks down to a more manageable number. If they had more than three simultaneous sounds that they wished to keep separate for the final mix, they would have premixed fewer than eighteen tracks. During the final mix, the sound effects mixer would have used the three-stripe premix plus whichever edited sound effects tracks were not used in the premix.

CHAPTER 21

The First Print

The Optical Sound Track

Upon completion of the mix, the magnetic signal on the three-stripe mixed track will be translated into an optical signal and printed onto the edge of a special role of 35mm film. The optical representation of your sound track is similar to the pattern in the grooves of a phonograph record or laser disc. It is simply a line that varies in such a way as to represent the total sound in the film.

The optical track is an excellent medium for reproducing sound; its frequency response is almost equivalent to that of FM broadcast stereo. However, the quality of the optical track is diminished in the printing process, especially in laboratories using high-speed printers. The printed track usually suffers further when reproduced through theater playback systems. Since the three-stripe magnetic track reproduces a wider range of sound than the printed optical track as it is reproduced in theaters, mixing facilities have available in their playback systems filters that cut off the highs and lows in the sound at the points that match the inherent limitations of the optical reproduction. This cut-off is the standard Society of Motion Picture and Television Engineers (SMPTE) curve, also called the "academy rolloff." In this way, during the mix, the sound one hears from the three-stripe magnetic track will be almost identical to the sound that will be reproduced by the optical track.

The making of an optical track is a delicate process. In order to obtain maximum results, the track should be processed within hours of exposure. If you complete your mix on a Friday and the lab isn't processing optical tracks until Monday, wait until Monday to make the transfer to optical and have the track processed the same day.

There is a special system for mixing called "Dolby" that is currently used only for stereo mixes. Using this system, the sound is mixed through a special box called a "Dolby matrix." Its purpose is to minimize extraneous noise such as hiss and rumble. Not only does the Dolby system improve the quality of the mix, the optical track made from a Dolby mix is also improved. First, because a Dolby mix does *not* use the SMPTE academy rolloff curve so the optical track has an extended frequency response. Second, optical recorders for printing Dolby optical tracks print a wider frequency response than standard optical recorders.

The Dolby system has provided several advances in the quality of motion picture sound but it has many limitations. Better systems have recently been tested and will soon be marketed.

Negative Cutting

The negative cutter edits the original camera negative to match precisely the edited work print and lines up the optical sound track in synchronization with the cut negative. The original negative has numbers on the edge of the film at intervals of sixteen frames. These numbers are built into the negative at the factory and are subsequently printed onto the dailies. The negative cutter will give each roll of negative film a number and will list on a log sheet the print-through edge numbers (see Chapter 17) that correspond with each roll number. As he prepares to cut each scene, the negative cutter locates the edge number on the work print and finds the same edge number in the log sheets. This tells him which negative roll contains the shot he's after.

When syncing the optical track with the picture, the negative cutter locates a "pop" sound at the head of each roll of optical sound and lines it up with the number 2 on the picture academy leader at the head of each picture roll. The pop sound is built into the edited sound tracks by the sound cutters opposite number 2 on the picture academy leader of the work print and is subsequently transferred to the optical track as a sync reference for the negative cutter. Actually, the negative cutter will advance the pop sound by twenty frames since the optical sound head in a projector is twenty frames ahead of the picture lens. Advancing the pop sound by twenty frames will cause the pop to pass the sound head in the projector as the number 2 on the academy leader passes the lens. Hence, the audible pop will be heard when number 2 of the academy leader appears on the screen. Every sound thereafter will be in sync with the picture.

The First Trial Composite Answer Print

Once the negative has been cut and the optical track lined up accordingly, the laboratory will make a first trial composite answer print. This will be the first print that combines the fully mixed track with the first color print from your cut negative. Screening the first trial is a most exciting experience but very often a disappointing one. After all the time and effort that has gone into making the film, one enters a first trial screening expecting to see a finished, polished film. This is unrealistic since the film is really not yet finished. The principal function of the answer print is to determine the proper color balance and density for each scene in the film. Rarely will the color and density be correct throughout the film on the first trial print. A laboratory timer will screen the print with the director to discuss the proper color and density for each scene. The timer's overall objective is to maintain a pleasing visual continuity throughout the film. Often a director will wish to deviate from this continuity and he must communicate these thoughts to the timer. It is also helpful to involve the director of photography in first trial screenings and discussions as this phase of production reflects directly on his efforts to light each scene for a particular effect.

Among the additional problems that you may encounter in first trial screenings are misaligned optical tracks, and negative cutting problems such as black leader slugs in place of scenes that the negative cutter has not yet found, or wrong scenes cut into the picture due to duplicate edge numbers on the original negative. On films where 100,000 feet or more of original negative is shot, it is common to have a few duplicate edge numbers. Since the negative cutter depends primarily on matching edge numbers, he may select the wrong set of matching numbers when there are duplicates to choose from. Another discouraging factor to bear in mind when screening a first trial print is that the sound is often disappointing. This is partly due to the fact that optical tracks that have been equalized reproduce sound less effectively than the magnetic tracks you're used to hearing in the mix. But the principal reason is that laboratory screening rooms, where first trial prints are viewed, have notoriously poor sound systems. The laboratory's concern is with the visual image, not with the sound. The labs will go to great lengths to ensure that their projection systems are the best on the market, that the projector bulbs are accurately matched from projector to projector, that an exact sixteen foot-candles falls on the screen from each projector, and so forth. But the sound system in a laboratory is given far less attention. Labs will often let it slide until someone complains.

Mixing facilities routinely receive calls from distraught producers complaining about the drastic difference between the three-stripe magnetic mix and the optical track. This call usually follows the first trial screening. The first thing the producer will be asked is, "Where did you screen it?" If the answer is, "At the lab," the mixing facility will invite the producer to screen the print in *their* screening room. Nearly always, the producer is satisfied and quite astonished at the drastic difference between sound systems. I would like to add that when screening at the sound facility, the producer may be pleased with the sound quality but disappointed in the picture quality. Again, the emphasis in a sound facility will be on the sound, not on the picture.

These are some of the reasons that a first trial print is often disappointing. Remember, however, that a first trial is a *trial.* Most laboratories guarantee the quality of the answer print and will retime and reprint it several times until it's right. In fact, they base their price for the answer print on the assumption that they will have to make more than one print in order to get a final answer print of acceptable commercial quality.

Once you have worked with the laboratory to fine-tune the answer print and once you've achieved the perfection you're after, another disappointment may come when you see the film in a movie theater. Very few theaters maintain their projection and sound systems up to industry standards. The light level in movie houses is often 20 percent below the standard sixteen footcandles. Drive-ins are even worse. Occasionally a distributor will make a special set of "light" prints for showing only at drive-ins. Also, you can imagine what those three-inch drive-in speakers will do to your beautiful sound track.

Upon completion of postproduction, you will have one composite answer print made from your original negative and optical sound track. If you have made distribution arrangements prior to completing your picture, you will move right into marketing. If not, you will be in the sometimes enviable, sometimes terrifying position of a producer who has successfully financed and produced an entire motion picture without ties for distribution. Part V, "Distribution and Marketing," discusses the pros and cons of approaching distributors during various stages of production and outlines the distribution avenues available to the independent producer.

PART 5

Distribution and Marketing

CHAPTER 22

Distribution

Writing a thorough document on motion picture distribution is an impossible task, since each distribution agreement is tailored to fit the specific requirements of each project. Therefore I have written this part as an exploration of some of the avenues of distribution available to independent producers, not as a guide for negotiating deals.

The first and most important rule for an independent producer is to involve legal and accounting counsel substantially *experienced* in motion picture contracts prior to approaching distributors. I emphasize the word "experienced" because distribution agreements have evolved a language of their own that often means in practice something different from what it appears to mean on paper.

The following quote from *Legal and Business Problems of Financing Motion Pictures* (a publication of the Practicing Law Institute—see Appendix E) illustrates this disparity: "The beginning of wisdom in understanding distribution agreements is to recognize that the terms 'net profits' and 'gross receipts,' when incorporated in a distribution agreement, take on meanings totally different than those associated with these terms by accountants or the general financial community." In other words, these terms are redefined in distribution agreements.

Unless a distributor purchases a film outright for a flat fee, a distribution agreement will provide for profit participation by the producer. The definition of *profits* is the most elusive term to pin down and define in a distribution agreement. The best deal for a producer is a gross deal since there is little room to manipulate what that means. A net deal is almost impossible to define and rarely pays off to the net participant. According to *Legal and Business Problems of Financing Motion Pictures:* "It is apparent that variations in the standard 'net' agreements make defining a participation as 'net' difficult, if not impossible." This is just one example to emphasize the importance of involving experienced legal and accounting counsel in your distribution negotiations who will know what the distribution agreement will mean in *practice*.

The Distribution Deal

In addition to many boilerplate provisions, the guts of a standard distribution deal usually involves:

- an advance paid to the producer by the distributor in exchange for the right to distribute the film. This advance will usually be deducted from the producer's profit participation in the film. There are also distribution agreements in which the producer receives no advance.
- a complete definition of how the box office receipts will be disbursed.
- a commitment by the distributor to spend a specified minimum amount of money on prints and advertising.
- a definition of the territories covered by the agreement and certain minimum box office guarantees for these territories.

The Worst Deal

The worst deal is not getting a deal at all. The second worst deal, from the producer's point of view, is when a film is completed and a distributor takes it on with reluctance. In such cases the producer will get little or no advance, little or no guarantees, and a small commitment to prints and advertising. The distributor will send the picture out with little support and if it doesn't perform, he'll pull the picture and call it quits. Hopefully, the distribution agreement will provide the producer with an option to regain control of the picture if the distributor puts it on the shelf. Remember that unless a distributor feels quite certain that a picture will perform well at the box office, he won't commit large sums to advances, guarantees, prints, and advertising. He'll send the picture out with minimum support, which is minimum risk for himself and he'll see how it does. Only if it performs well at the box office will he begin to push it. Consequently, the picture is forced to prove itself to the distributor without the benefit of a reasonable advertising campaign. This process is self-defeating, since even the best pictures will rarely perform well in the first two weeks without a strong campaign. For any film in any location the box office receipts for the first two weeks are almost entirely a matter of the campaign and have little to do with the film itself. If the distributor sends a picture out with little support, it will almost certainly take a nose dive.

A worst deal situation occurs only when a producer is desperate and willing to accept minimum terms. The distributor has almost nothing at stake, which makes it very easy for him to pull the picture and quit trying.

Another dangerous distribution deal is one in which the producer is offered a modest advance and an enormous profit participation, but little commitment to guarantees or prints and ads. It's a "trust me" deal and one the producer should be wary of. In a case like this the distributor may have little hope for a film's box office success but doesn't want some other distributor to come along and prove him wrong. Chances are that he will contractually commit to nothing more than a "reasonable efforts" clause in the distribution agreement that gives him far greater leeway than a "best efforts" clause. If, for example, he spends $25,000 to open the film in three territories and recoups only $20,000, he can argue that he has made a reasonable effort, perhaps not his best effort, but certainly a reasonable effort to market the film.

Although it rarely happens, it is also possible for a distributor to offer a trust me deal as described above *in order to keep a producer's film on the shelf.* Let's say that you bring a distributor a $700,000 picture about motorcycle gangs and he says, "This picture will make a fortune. I'll give you a huge chunk of the gross and a $200,000 advance. The only thing I ask is that you don't tie my hands with regard to prints, ads, guarantees, and the rest. Just trust me and you'll make a fortune." Suppose, however, that this same distributor had picked up a similar motorcycle picture six weeks earlier for a $500,000 advance, substantial guarantees, and a sizable commitment to prints and ads. To him it may be worth $200,000 simply to keep your picture out of circulation and offering you a large chunk of an imaginary gross costs him nothing. Again I stress the importance of obtaining substantially experienced legal and accounting counsel prior to entering negotiations with a distributor.

The Best Deal

The best distribution deal is one in which the distributor is enthusiastic about the film and is willing to make a substantial commitment to its marketing. In this situation, the producer may receive a large advance, strong guarantees, a substantial commitment to prints and ads, and a reasonable percentage profit participation. This is a deal in which the distributor has a great deal at stake and will suffer a sizable loss if the picture dies. The distributor must push the picture by developing a strong campaign, testing the campaign, and opening the picture with a large enough advertising budget to draw people in for the first two weeks. From then on, if the picture clicks with the public, the distributor will cut back on the advertising and let word-of-mouth carry the film during subsequent weeks. A further discussion of this marketing procedure is found in Chapter 24.

When to Approach a Distributor

An independent producer may approach distributors at any step in the development of a project—concept level, preproduction packaging, completion of principal photography, rough-cut editing, or finished film. As discussed in Part I, "Legal Structuring and Financing," the ideal arrangement for a producer is to assemble a strong enough package consisting of script, director, and cast to obtain a favorable distribution deal prior to beginning production.

The commercial success of any film is dependent upon distribution and since many independent films never find a distributor, independent producers often feel that the risk of beginning a project without a distribution deal is simply too great. Max E. Youngstein, chairman of the board and chief executive officer of Taft International Pictures, has counseled independent producers for many years in the development, production, and distribution of their films. It is his present policy to encourage producers to have a distribution deal set prior to committing any substantial money to a project. "That is because of the current state of the market," says Mr. Youngstein. "The fact is that only two years ago I would have been willing, if I thought the other ingredients of the package were correct, to take my chances on a distribution deal after the picture was finished. That is not the case today." Milton Goldstein, president and chief operating officer of Melvin Simon Productions, spoke at a recent conference on independent motion picture production. He cited two successes out of eleven attempts by Melvin Simon Productions over the past several years and said, "The biggest risk you could possibly take is to be at the mercy of a distributor without having a deal up front. Don't make your film unless you have that distribution deal first!"

However, many independent producers, especially beginning producers with modest- or low-budget projects, are not in a position to assemble a strong package of preproduction elements and consequently it is difficult for them to negotiate for distribution prior to making their film. These producers believe just as strongly as any other producers that their film will be a box office success. But a producer in this position is forced either to accept an unfavorable distribution deal or to finance and produce the film on his own. A producer who opts for proceeding without a distributor runs the risk of never finding a distributor, but he also maintains the freedom to offer his finished, or partially finished, film to several distributors, hopefully creating a bidding situation among them.

The kind of distribution deal you get will depend first, on the film and, second, on the stage of its development. If you began production without a distribution deal you will be offering the distributor a finished, or partially finished, film. Regardless of the stage of completion, remember that a distributor cannot afford *not* to look at your film. Their business is distributing films and they do need marketable products.

Assuming a producer makes a film that distributors want, he is in an optimum bargaining position if he completes the film independently. First, because he will be showing distributors a polished, finely tuned product. Second, because he isn't asking distributors to finance the completion of the film. He's simply offering them an opportunity to market it. This position becomes even more powerful if there are several distributors interested and the producer establishes a bidding situation among them.

Distributors should not be shown an incomplete film unless absolutely necessary. The only reason to show distributors a partially finished film is because you need money. Distributors know this and will use it to advantage in negotiating a deal—*if* it ever gets that far. Selling a partially finished film in order to get completion money is not easy. One of the reasons is that a rough-cut looks bad. The picture has scratches, dirt, splices, and often lacks titles and opticals. The sound will be incomplete, often missing music and sound effects. Be wary of a distributor who says, "I know it's not finished, but it doesn't matter. I've seen hundreds of rough-cuts." Don't believe him, it *does* matter.

The only person who can successfully fill in the missing blanks is the director and sometimes the editor. A person walking into a screening with little or no prior knowledge of a partially completed picture is in no position to judge the potential emotional impact of the completed product. This problem is compounded further because a screening room is similar to a commercial movie theater and the environment says, "finished film." The immediate conditioned response to sitting in a screening room is the expectation of seeing a completed film. No matter how many rough-cuts a person has seen, when he enters a screening room and the lights go down and the curtain opens, a portion of his understanding for your unfinished film will vanish.

If, at this screening, a distributor turns your picture down, chances are that his decision will be final. He won't give you a second shot if you finish the picture on your own and approach him for a second screening. First impressions count for a lot and a first impression based on a cold screening of an unfinished film is most unfair to the film.

There is a simple way to minimize these problems. If you must screen an unfinished version for a distributor, do it in the cutting room on a flatbed editing machine such as a Kem or Steenbeck. Distributors won't like the inconvenience and maybe they will insist on a screening room, but try to screen in a cutting room. Tell them the work print isn't double-spliced and won't travel through a projector, or tell them the perfs are weak. Tell them anything, because this screening may be extremely important and you want to stack the deck as much in your favor as possible. The advantages to screening in a cutting room are, first, there is no conditioned "finished film" response associated with the cutting room. The environment says "work in progress." Second, you can stop the film at any point and explain how the music and sound effects will be used. You can explain missing titles and opticals. You can even high-speed through the roughest sequences. In short, you can talk your way through the film with the distributor so that when he leaves, he takes with him a significant understanding of the picture's potential emotional impact. He probably won't *feel* the emotional impact any more than he would in a screening room but at least he'll understand it.

In this setting, it is unlikely that a distributor will close the door on your project. You can expect one of two reactions: "I'm unable to make a decision based on this viewing but I would like to screen the finished film." (the door's still open), or "Let's negotiate." At which point, if you read the beginning of this chapter, you will call your attorney.

CHAPTER 23

The Distributors

There are four distribution routes available to the independent producer: the "majors," the "minimajors," the independent distributors, and the producer ("four-walling").

For domestic distribution, the United States has been divided into thirty-two territories or exchanges, such as the Chicago exchange, the New England exchange, the Philadelphia exchange, the Dallas/Fort Worth exchange, and the Carolinas exchange. In each exchange, there are several states righters, or subdistributors (called "subs"), to choose from who book films into the theaters in their exchange. Subs are paid a percentage of the box office, usually 25 percent.

In the old days, major distributors maintained sales offices in all thirty-two exchanges. Today, however, because of the advances in communication and shipping technology, they have sales offices only in the principal exchanges. In the remaining territories, they operate subdepots that function as shipping offices for their films and related promotional material. The minimajors, such as New World, are in a state of transition. They maintain sales offices in several territories and are currently in the process of purchasing outright, or at least purchasing the controlling interest in, subdistribution companies in the remaining territories. The principal differences between the majors and minimajors are:

- the quality of the pictures they distribute
- the amount of capital they have for in-house production
- the quality of the films they produce
- the number of exchanges they control through their own sales offices

Independent distributors, such as Crown International, Group I and Compass International use independent subs for practically all of the country. They generally book directly with theaters only in their home territory. All national distributors work closely with their subs to ensure optimum release patterns for their films.

A producer who opts to distribute his film on his own, using the four-wall technique, will rent theaters for a flat weekly fee. He may do this entirely on his own or in conjunction with an independent distributor or a local subdistributor.

When evaluating these four approaches—majors, minimajors, independents, and four-walling—it is important to bear in mind that every distributor, from the corporate conglomerate major to the smallest independent, competes for the *same theaters.* The following is a look at some of the pros and cons for the three most conventional approaches: majors, minimajors, and independents. Four-wall distribution is discussed later in this chapter.

The Majors

Major distributors offer the most prestigious route for an independent producer. The majors handle virtually all of the important films and consequently wield the greatest power. They command the best theaters at the best times of year. They also wield the greatest collection power. A major distributor who withholds product from an exhibitor who is slow in paying, puts a sizable dent in the exhibitor's business.

The majors are strong enough financially to offer a producer a large advance and to mount an impressive national advertising campaign. The advance is generally paid back to the distributor out of the producer's share of profits. The standard division of receipts that a producer can expect from a major distributor for distribution in the United States and Canada is 70 percent to the producer and 30 percent to the distributor. On the surface, a 70/30 split in favor of the producer sounds terrific. But what this actually means is that the distributor will take 30¢ off the top of every dollar that comes in. He will then deduct the distribution expenses from the remaining 70¢. If anything is left over, he will give it to the producer. Since all of the expenses are deducted from the producer's share, there is often nothing left for the producer. Consequently many producers negotiate primarily for the largest advance they can get. They believe it's all they will ever see. Even if the picture is a blockbuster, they question whether they will ever see a cut of the profits, and they question with good reason.

Consider a film that cost $6,940,890 (detailed in Appendix B). Assume that this film has returned $40 million to the distributor. This is a very successful film since it will have had to gross nearly $100 million at the box office to return $40 million to the distributor. Table 15 is a sample studio accounting sheet that outlines where this $40 million might go before the producer sees a penny.

It doesn't always work out this way but, as you can see, even an extremely successful film may have a difficult time digging its way out of the studio's accounting hole. Tom Pollack, one of the most successful entertainment lawyers in Los Angeles, recommends that his clients audit any picture that has any likelihood of going into profits. An audit of studio books for U.S. and Canadian expenditures costs about $15,000. However, says Pollack, "I have never, in all the pictures I have had audited, seen an audit that didn't pay for itself. We have had audits of major studios that have uncovered millions of dollars in errors. Most errors seem to be in the studio's favor."

Some producers, on the other hand, will give up their entire advance in favor of a greater percentage of the profits. This leaves the distributor with more cash on hand to spend promoting the film. Whether you choose to negotiate for a large advance or a large percentage of the profits, or some meeting ground in between, will depend largely on your faith in the picture and the definition of profits in your distribution agreement.

Should you go with a major, be prepared to lose control of your picture. The marketing department will determine how the picture will be sold, including the concept for the campaign and the marketing strategy for where to open the picture and when. They will not, as a rule, care to hear the producer's opinion on these matters.

The biggest drawback with major distributors comes with low-budget pictures. The majors generally aren't very interested. They are not interested in simply making a profit. They are interested in making an enormous profit. Sources close to the distribution industry say that the majors are interested only in pictures that they believe will gross $10 million or more. Apparently anything less than that isn't worth their effort. From the producer's point

Table 15   **Sample Studio Accounting Statement**

Gross film rental

Domestic	
Theatrical	$ 20,000,000
Nontheatrical	4,000,000
Foreign	
United Kingdom and Continental	
Europe	4,900,000
Additional international territories	11,000,000
Net trailer rentals (theaters generally rent a promotional trailer from the distributor that they run as a preview of coming attractions)	100,000
Total gross receipts	40,000,000
Less distribution fees (This is the distributor's fee for marketing the film. It is deducted off the top—before expenses—and is calculated in percentages ranging from 30% to 40% in each category)	13,200,000
Balance	26,800,000
Less distribution expenses	
Costs for checking theater box office attendance and collecting payments	235,000
Trade association fees and assessments	200,000
Advertising costs	15,000,000
Costs for making foreign language versions	350,000
International taxes, duties, and government fees	1,000,000
Prints and reediting costs (occasionally a distributor will reedit a film, perhaps modifying the ending or adding special optical effects prior to release)	3,200,000
Shipping and delivery costs	115,000
Miscellaneous expenses	250,000
Total distribution expenses	20,350,000
Net receipts	6,450,000
Less	
Negative cost	6,940,890

Table 15 (cont.)

Interest charged by the distributor on the film's negative cost (generally 125% of prime)	1,110,000
Agreed overbudget deduction (penalty against the producer for going over budget as defined in the distribution agreement)	1,000,000
Net Profits (Loss)	$ (2,600,890)

of view, a low-budget film needs only to gross a fraction of that amount to return a reasonable profit to the investors. The standard industry rule of thumb says that a film must gross three times its negative cost to break even. This means that for a $500,000 film, everything over a $1.5 million gross will pay profits. These figures look terrific to the low-budget producer but to the major distributors, they mean almost nothing. As a consequence, there is very little meeting ground for major distributors and low-budget films.

The Minimajors

These distributors are more approachable and more interested in smaller independent pictures than the major distributors. They are in a position to offer reasonable advances and to mount a strong national advertising campaign. They too, however, are reluctant to take on anything that isn't a pretty good bet for a large commercial success. Mounting a national campaign is a huge job and the picture must warrant the effort. Even though the minimajors are more approachable than the majors and more likely to take on independent products, they will rarely accept a low-budget film. When they do, however, they may offer more flexibility in structuring the distribution deal than the majors. This depends entirely on their enthusiasm for the picture.

One possible variation from the standard 70/30 major deal is a sliding scale whereby the distributor pays for all promotional costs and receives 70 percent from the first million, 60 percent from the second million, and 50 percent thereafter. The argument in favor of the sliding scale is that the majority of the distributor's expenses for prints and advertising is incurred during the initial opening of the film. These costs are usually covered during the first million dollars of gross receipts. Promotional costs are reduced during the second and third million dollars of gross receipts.

Another variation is a 50/50 split from the first dollar with no advance. The theory here is that since the producer financed the film, and the distributor is financing the distribution, they are taking an approximately equal risk and should therefore share equally from first dollar. These are two examples to illustrate some of the ways in which distribution deals may vary.

The Independent Distributors

This is the marketplace for most low-budget features. Independent distributors offer less prestige, less promotional capital, smaller advances, and less clout with exhibitors than either the majors or the minimajors. But they are willing to take on pictures that will make money on a smaller scale than the majors' $10 million minimum. The standard independent domestic distribution deal is a 50/50 split between the producer and the distributor. The principal difference between this split and the majors' 70/30 split is that expenses come off the top and the balance is split 50/50. In other words, the distributor and producer share equally in distribution expenses such as prints and advertising, whereas the major distributor generally takes 30 percent off the top as profit and deducts distribution expenses entirely out of the producer's 70 percent share.

Independent distributors have less product than the majors and minimajors and can therefore give more personal attention to each film. They are also smaller and less bureaucratic. An independent producer will probably find independent distributors reasonably receptive to his opinions about the campaign concept and marketing strategy.

The down side of the independent distributors is that they have less promotional capital available to launch a film than either the majors or minimajors. A national campaign is often out of the question. Instead they will often strike a minimum number of prints and open the picture in one exchange at a time.

There are many theories about the best marketing strategy

when playing one territory at a time. Some distributors believe it's best to begin in major cities and branch out from there. Others prefer to start small, honing the campaign in less important territories, allowing the picture to build up steam gradually before hitting the major markets, such as New York, Chicago, and Los Angeles. The strategy will vary depending on the marketplace orientation of the film, the distributor's promotional budget, the time of year, and the distributor's intuitive sense for the most effective approach.

Another downside consideration with independent distributors is their lack of clout for commanding good theaters at good playtimes. The best theaters will be booked during peak seasons by the majors. In order to book a good theater, an independent distributor must wait for an opening between major releases and will probably be stuck with a statistically unfavorable time of year to open.

In a strange way, this may work to the independent distributor's advantage. If a small, independent film opens during the Christmas season, which is a peak moviegoing time, chances are it will die at the box office because so many of the major releases will open in direct competition. Opening in a good theater during a statistically slow season may be an advantage since there will be very few major releases opening at the same time. There may be fewer people going to the movies but there are fewer movies to choose from.

If an independent distributor believes in a film and is tenacious in his efforts to open it in the best theaters, he must settle for whatever times those theaters become available. This lack of booking clout takes considerable marketing control away from the distributor. Only if the film becomes a hit will the distributor gain power for negotiating competitive playdates.

In addition to having less booking power than the majors and minimajors, the independent distributors have less collection power. If a theater is late in paying, there is little the independent distributor can do. His threat to withhold a low-budget exploitation picture is far less powerful than a major distributor threatening to withhold a multimillion dollar all-star Christmas show.

In addition to the conventional independent distributors, there is a cooperative organization called First Run Features, Inc. devoted exclusively to booking American independent features. This organization supplies no money for prints or advertising; that's up to the filmmaker. What they will do, in exchange for a small fee, and assuming they agree to handle a particular film, is get the film booked into theaters. Examples of films which have been distributed through First Run Features include Gal Young Un, Joe and Maxi, The Life and Times of Rosie the Riveter, Northern Lights, and Soldier Girls. The amount of money spent on prints and advertising is up to the filmmaker. In the case of Gal Young Un, Victor Nunez restricted his entire marketing and distribution expenses to $28,000. In an effort to ease the financial burden on filmmakers, First Run Features often groups several films together in a series format. The promotional costs for the series are then shared among several filmmakers. First Run Features can be contacted at 144 Bleecker St., New York, N.Y. 10012, (212) 673-6881.

Another organization which is devoted to supporting independent production is the Independent Feature Project. It is comprised of approximately eight hundred people who are associated, in one way or another, with independent film production. The principal purpose of the organization is to pool together information and resources for the mutual benefit of its members. Each year the Independent Feature Project sponsors the Independent Feature Market, during which members have an opportunity to screen their films for domestic and European buyers for both theatrical distribution and television sales. The Independent Feature Market is held in New York and coincides each year with the New York Film Festival. Membership in the Independent Feature Project is $35 per year. For more information contact the Independent Feature Project at 80 East 11th St., New York, N.Y. 10003, (212) 674-6655.

How to Choose

There are several ways for an independent producer to determine which distribution pattern, and specifically which distributors, would be suitable for his film. The first is to seek the advice of an entertainment attorney experienced in motion picture distribution. He may be able to offer suggestions regarding appropriate distributors, and in some cases may act as a direct contact with those distributors. There are some entertainment attorneys who function as producers' representatives by contacting distributors, arranging screenings of films, and negotiating contracts. Such attorneys may be found either through word-of-mouth recommendations within the film community or by following the procedure outlined in Chapter 1.

Another approach is for the producer to make a list of other films that have successfully reached his intended market and to approach the distribution companies that handled those films. This requires going through back issues of *Weekly Variety* as described in Chapter 4.

It is helpful to discuss the distribution of such films with the producers who made them. Their experience working with distributors may greatly influence a producer's selection. Such producers may be contacted either through the distribution companies who handled their films, the Producers Guild of America, or the companies for whom they work. They may also be listed in the *Pacific Coast Directory,* which is listed in Appendix E, or in the yellow pages under Motion Picture Producers and Studios.

Should you find yourself in the envious position of choosing among several interested distributors, your decision will undoubtedly be based on which distributor you feel will return the greatest profit to your investors. This by no means suggests an automatic decision to choose a major over a minimajor or an independent. You may sacrifice some prestige by going with an independent but if he has a solid reputation, a sensible marketing strategy, and an obvious enthusiasm for your picture, he may be your best choice. As with every step in the process of distribution, an experienced attorney will be your most effective guide in evaluating the pros and cons of various offers.

Money Coming Back

A motion picture goes from the producer to the distributor, who sends it to territorial subdistributors, who send it to theaters. The box office receipts generated by the film travel this same route in reverse. The exhibitor takes a cut and sends the balance to the sub, who takes a cut and sends the balance to the distributor, who takes a cut and sends the balance to the producer. The inequity in this system is that the investors, who have had their money at risk for the longest time, are at the tail end of the chain.

A sad but unavoidable truth about motion picture distribution is the problem of stealing. This exists on all levels, from the ticket salesperson on down. At its worst, the process goes something like this: The cashier is in cahoots with the doorman. Together they steal from the theater owner. The theater owner reports only 80 percent of his sales to the subdistributor. The subdistributor in turn skims a little off the top before reporting to the distributor, and the distributor does the same before reporting to the producer. There are cases in which distributors have been found keeping two separate books of account—one for the producer to examine and one for themselves. The producer's set is adjusted dishonestly to hide a portion of the film's profits.

Not everyone in the distribution business is dishonest and the situation is certainly unfair to those who are trying to make an honest living. But the ones who suffer most are the investors who come at the end of the line. Even a crooked investor gets the short end of the stick, since the money reaching him has no place else to go. The only cut of the pie that passes through his hands is his own, whereas his share of the profits have passed through the hands of everyone else in the chain.

Some of the safeguards against this behavior are numbered tickets and a contractual right to audit books of account. Hopefully, they will be honest books of account. Distributors routinely hire checkers who go to the theater and count the attendance, either by purchasing the first and last ticket of the day and comparing ticket numbers or by counting each person entering the theater. There are companies that specialize in checking services for producers and distributors.

The bottom line is that stealing is illegal and one can lay a strong foundation for protection against it in the initial distribution agreement. Again, experienced legal and accounting counsel are essential when negotiating for such safeguards.

Four-Wall Distribution

As stated earlier, this technique involves renting theaters for a flat weekly fee. A producer may do this on his own or in conjunction with an independent distributor or subdistributors. The rental fee for the theater includes the theater staff—projectionist, ticket salesperson, manager, and candycounter salesperson. If the producer rents the theater without the aid of a distributor or subdistributor, the entire box office is paid to him and anything beyond the rental fee and advertising expenses is profit.

Four-wall distribution on any meaningful scale is a dangerous and risky proposition. However, it has been demonstrated that four-walling can result in a sizable profit. In order to initiate a four-wall operation, a producer or distributor must have an advertising campaign (see Chapter 24), a thorough knowledge of the value of various theaters at different times of the year, and a substantial amount of money to spend on promotion. Many of the family "adventure/wilderness" films have been successfully distributed using the four-wall technique. The films are often made for under $100,000 and are usually not very interesting, but they contain enough exciting highlights to make a terrific television advertising campaign. The producer or distributor will enter a territory, rent many theaters in neighborhoods throughout the area, then saturate the territory with television advertising. Since each television ad reaches all of the neighborhoods where the film is playing, the cost of the television time may be amortized among all of the theaters playing the film, thus greatly reducing the advertising cost per theater. It is common to spend much more on the saturation television campaigns than was spent to make the film. Since the films themselves rarely live up to audience expectations, they get poor word-of-mouth and most of them die after the first two weeks. But that's expected. The producer or distributor relies on an expensive saturation television campaign to draw large enough crowds in the first two weeks to return a profit. He will rarely stay for a third week. It's a hit-and-run technique that is sometimes profitable, sometimes not, but always risky.

Foreign Distribution

A domestic distribution deal usually refers to the distribution of a film to theaters in the United States and Canada. Foreign distribution refers to the rest of the world. It is common for a producer to make separate distribution deals with separate distributors for domestic and foreign release. For example, a producer may make a domestic distribution deal with United Artists and a foreign distribution deal with Warner Bros.; or, in the case of smaller independent distributors, a domestic deal with Dimension Pictures and a foreign deal with Manson International. Major distributors will usually charge a 37.5 to 40 percent distribution fee for distribution in foreign countries. Independent distributors' fees are often more negotiable.

The foreign market for major motion pictures is worth approximately 50 percent of the total world market. The following key foreign territories are listed with an approximate percentage of their value in the world market: Italy, 10.5 percent; Germany, 8 percent; United Kingdom, 8 percent; France, 7.5 percent; Japan, 7.5 percent; Australia, 7 percent. These figures can be deceptive to an independent producer since they represent across-the-board average values. The relative worth of each territory will vary enormously from picture to picture. A major motion picture with an all-star cast may be worth many millions of dollars in foreign advances, often before the film is shot. This is how Joseph E. Levine turned his personal $22 million gamble on the epic war film, *A Bridge Too Far,* into profits before it ever reached the screen. On the other hand, total foreign advances for low-budget, independent exploitation films rarely exceed $200,000.

Sales to foreign countries are often initiated at film festivals such as the Cannes Film Festival, the Milan Film Festival (MIFED), and the Canadian Film Festival. A large portion of these festivals is devoted to a buying market. Distributors come from around the world to view films, whether they are in competition or not. Foreign distributors will also evaluate preproduction packages for possible foreign presales. A distributor selects the films he would like to distribute in his country and negotiates the deals. Foreign sales usually involve an advance against a percentage. In other words, a foreign buyer will pay an advance to the producer that will be paid back out of the producer's percentage participation of the film's profits in that country. A portion of the advance will be paid upon signing the agreement, another portion when the film passes the country's censorship board, usually within ninety days, and the balance upon receipt by the foreign distributor of materials necessary to make prints and promotional materials. Such materials include the picture negative, an M & E sound track as described in Chapter 20 under "Three-Stripe Mixing," and a set of advertising materials, such as still photographs, posters, and a promotional trailer.

Keeping track of box office receipts is a problem in the United

States but it is a doubly difficult problem abroad. It is rare for an independent producer to realize foreign profits beyond the initial advance. A film must take off significantly at the foreign box office before a producer will realize any additional gain from profit participation.

Release Prints

Upon completion of distribution negotiations and the signing of a distribution agreement, the producer will give the distributor all materials necessary for making release prints. This will include the cut original negative and the optical sound track. The distributor will then make an internegative from which the release prints will be made. The purpose of the internegative is to protect the original negative from wear and tear during release printing. One common form of internegative is called a color reversal internegative (CRI). The reversal process is one in which the film, after exposure, contains a positive image that reverses itself during processing to become a negative image.

A somewhat older method of obtaining an internegative for release printing is by first making a separate interpositive (IP) and then making an internegative from the IP. Debate within the industry as to which is the optimum method has gone on for years and probably will continue. Even the top film laboratory experts do not agree on this subject and opinions are constantly shifting. The choice depends on a number of factors including cost, the characteristics of the original footage, and the experience of the laboratory you choose to work with.

Like the first print from the original negative, the first print from the internegative is called a "first trial." Its purpose is to check color and density prior to striking release prints. When the laboratory produces an acceptable first trial from the internegative, the distributor will order release prints.

If the distributor intends to open the picture in a small way, perhaps on a territory-by-territory basis, he may order only fifty release prints. A national distribution pattern, however, will require several hundred prints, and in some cases, 1,000 or more. Release prints for foreign versions of the film are generally the responsibility of the foreign buyer for each country.

Television Sales

Television sales include network showings, syndication, cable TV, other forms of pay TV, video cassettes, video discs, and new technologies, some of which are currently in development and may soon provide additional outlets. These rights are generally granted to a major or minimajor distributor as a part of the initial distribution agreement. They should not, however, be lightly given away; they are negotiable and should be used to advantage. Many of the smaller independent distributors don't have facilities to handle sales to television and in such cases the producer may bargain for retaining such rights. The distributor, however, will request a contractual restriction in the distribution agreement that prevents the producer from exercising television rights for a given period of time. Thus the film will not be shown on television before the distributor has had time to give the film thorough theater exposure.

The most significant television money is paid for prime-time network showings and the bulk of this money goes to the major studio releases. In order for a low-budget independent film to gain clout in television negotiations, it must first prove itself at the box office. The few independent films that have broken out to become hits command major release status in a television sale.

Films are often shown on television within two years of their initial release, although the sale may be made much earlier. One of the essential factors in determining a film's worth on television is its theatrical box office gross. One theory is that the sale price be 20 to 25 percent of that gross for two prime-time network showings, with a bottom-line figure around $250,000. Generally, 10 percent is paid upon signing the contract and the balance is paid when the film is first aired.

Most films, whether or not they are picked up by the networks for prime-time showing, are sold for nonprime-time showing, as well as cable TV, other forms of pay TV, syndication, video cassettes, and video discs. These often prove to be lucrative markets even for low-budget films with a bottom-line figure for all these rights being around $150,000.

If your picture contains scenes that may not pass the television censors, such as those involving nudity, excessive violence, or unacceptable language, it is important to shoot television "cover" shots during production. This means that after you've shot the theatrical version of such a scene, modify it to comply with television censorship and shoot it again. When you make your sale to television, simply replace the objectionable scenes with your cover shots.

Ancillary Rights

These include any additional rights to the original literary property that the producer may own, such as the right to produce a remake, sequel, television series, or stage play. Ancillary rights are potentially worth a great deal of money and distributors will generally attempt to negotiate for their ownership. As with television rights, ancillary rights are subject to bargaining and can take many forms in a distribution agreement. In some cases these rights are frozen with neither the producer nor the distributor free to exercise them without the consent of the other party.

Nontheatrical Distribution Rights

These rights include distribution to ships, airlines, and trains that depart from territories covered in the distribution agreement, hotel movies, U.S. military installations throughout the world, the Red Cross, colleges, clubs, religious groups, etc. Independent producers allow millions of dollars in potential revenues to go uncollected in the U.S. market each year because they lack the expertise to take proper advantage of the nontheatrical market. If, as a producer, you retain control of nontheatrical rights to your film, you should contact distributors who specialize in nontheatrical sales. An experienced entertainment attorney will be able to guide you in the selection of the best nontheatrical distributor for your film.

Merchandising Rights

Characters and events in films often lend themselves to exploitation beyond the motion picture market. Books, posters, jewelry, games, dolls, toys, and T-shirts can reap enormous royalty profits. For the most part these merchandising rights are valuable only for major pictures with name-star casts and large promotional budgets. It is rare for a low-budget independent film, even a successful one, to realize a meaningful return from merchandising rights.

Sound Track Albums and Music Publishing Rights

Most major distributors have their own record companies and will bargain to retain the right to manufacture and market a film's sound track album. The distribution agreement will specify the percentage of album sales that will be included in the distributor's gross receipts. This figure will usually be around 8 percent of the album's retail selling price.

Most major distributors also have their own music publishing companies and will insist on music publishing rights as well. Usually between 10 and 25 percent of the income from music publishing will be included in the distributor's gross receipts.

If a sound track album or a song from a film becomes popular, these rights may be worth a great deal and a producer should bargain for as large a percentage of these rights as he can get. Often smaller distribution companies, without ties to record and music publishing companies, will agree to concede these rights entirely to the producer.

CHAPTER 24

Marketing

The Importance of the Campaign

Unless a producer is four-walling a picture on his own, his film will be in the hands of a distributor. Hopefully, the distributor will listen to the opinions of the producer when assembling the elements for the campaign, but it is important for the producer to recognize that the distributor is paying for the campaign and consequently has the final say. Remember this when selecting the distributor for your film. Settle on one who understands your film and whom you trust to make sound marketing decisions.

The more you, as a producer, understand about the distributor's problems, the more helpful and supportive you will be during distribution. This final chapter will examine some of those problems, especially the process of assembling the elements for a motion picture advertising campaign.

The problems for a distributor involve more than just selling tickets to the public. He must sell subdistributors and exhibitors on showing the picture in the first place. Once he establishes a good box office track record for the film in any one territory, he can use those box office figures to sell subs and exhibitors in other territories. Until that time, he must rely on his sales ability and on the film's campaign. Exhibitors know how all important the campaign is to the success of a film and they will sometimes pay more attention to the campaign than they will to the film. Sales to theaters are often made solely on the strength of the campaign.

The reason such emphasis is placed on the campaign is that for the first two weeks theater patrons decide whether or not to buy tickets based on the campaign alone. The initial box office income has nothing to do with the film. A successful film is ultimately sold by word-of-mouth. However, in order to generate word-of-mouth, an exhibitor must entice the initial audience into the theater with the campaign. The initial audience hopefully will say good things about the film, their friends will then come to see it and they will tell *their* friends about it, and their friends will tell their friends, and so on. This kind of snowballing effect can take up to two weeks to get rolling. Consequently, the campaign must be strong enough on its own to draw people for the first two weeks. Often this requires substantial and costly promotion during this time. But if the film clicks with the public and word-of-mouth comment is strong, the expense is worthwhile.

By the third week, the promotional budget may often be cut back drastically, letting word-of-mouth advertising carry the film into its fourth, fifth, sixth week or even longer. A film that generates its own audience by word-of-mouth advertising, maintaining a strong box office over several weeks or months, is said to have "legs."

The exhibition of a film will usually follow one of three patterns. First, a film that opens weak at the box office will probably stay weak. The distributor should consider changing the campaign. Second, if a film opens strong but drops rapidly after the second week, the campaign is succeeding in drawing the initial crowd but the film isn't generating positive word-of-mouth. It may be that the campaign is misleading the public and drawing in the wrong initial audience. For example, if a sophisticated psychological drama is sold to the public as an action exploitation picture, the campaign may draw a large number of thrill-seekers in the initial audience. But these people are expecting something they're not going to get and will probably be disappointed. The result will be poor word-of-mouth. Another audience for the same film, if sold as psychological drama, may leave entirely satisfied and their praise for the film will generate subsequent audiences. A person's mental set upon entering a theater greatly influences his response to a film. This challenges distributors to create innovative ways to market each picture so that the campaign reasonably represents the film and also succeeds in drawing a strong initial audience during the first two weeks. A third pattern that a film may follow at the box office is a strong opening and healthy legs. If this happens, you've got a good campaign and a successful film. It is important to add that simply because a film doesn't have legs, doesn't mean it's a bad film. It may be a good film that is not commercially successful. The commercial success of a film relies on many things that are entirely out of the producer's hands. Such things as public taste at the time of release, unpredictable critical reviews, and the total thrust of the campaign greatly affect a film's chances at the box office and may have nothing to do with whether the film is good or bad.

The Elements of the Campaign

The campaign package will be sent first to subdistributors to sell them on representing the film. Subsequently, it will be sent to exhibitors who will use the campaign materials to sell the film to the public. This section describes the standard elements in a motion picture advertising campaign. Each of these elements must be approved by the Motion Picture Association of America (MPAA), 8480 Beverly Boulevard, Los Angeles, California 90048.

The *press book* is a pamphlet that contains all of the newspaper ads for the film. It also contains a synopsis of the story, the film's running time, and a complete list of the cast and crew. This not only gives subdistributors and exhibitors a feeling for what the film is about, it also provides them with information that reporters and critics may ask for.

The *one-sheet* is a standard-size color poster for display in front of theaters. The one-sheet usually contains the basic elements from which the newspaper ads are made. These elements include a graphic design such as a photograph or drawing, a custom title treatment (this often becomes a logo for the film), a lead line to accompany the title such as, "A story of love and power!", credits for principal cast and crew (usually contractual), and, finally, any outstanding quotes from critical reviews.

The *trailer* is a short promotional film exhibited in theaters as a preview of coming attractions prior to a film's exhibition. A trailer usually contains highlights from the film, although special material such as interviews with the cast and director may be used as well. Trailers usually run less than three minutes. The MPAA has four ratings for motion pictures: G for general audiences, PG for parental guidance, R for restricted audiences (under seventeen must be accompanied by an adult), and X for exclusively adult material. However, for trailers, they offer only two ratings: G for general audiences and R for restricted audiences (under seventeen must be accompanied by an adult). The reasons for this have to do with the difficulty of keeping track of which trailer is playing in which theater with which films. In order to run a trailer with a PG film, the trailer must have a G rating. Since the majority of films are rated PG, this is an important audience for a trailer. Consequently, a producer with an R-rated film should make a G-rated trailer in order to reach a maximum number of people prior to the film's release. This presents quite a challenge to the trailer maker. He must strive for a trailer with maximum impact, yet "soft" enough to be suitable for five year olds watching a G-rated family film. Occasionally, in addition to the G-rated trailer, a distributor will make a second R-rated trailer for showing only in theaters exhibiting R- or X-rated pictures.

Trailers must have an MPAA rating tag that runs for three seconds and gives the rating for the trailer. If the rating for the trailer is different from the rating for the film, such as a G-rated trailer for an R-rated film, the trailer must have a second tag that specifies the rating for the film. It is wise to screen a trailer for the MPAA in rough-cut interlock form prior to mixing the sound and cutting the original negative. There are specific guidelines that the MPAA follows when rating films and trailers and they will tell you at the interlock stage if your material violates their limitations. The MPAA is most cooperative in working with producers and distributors to achieve maximum impact with their campaigns, yet remain within the limitations of their rating system.

Television ads are similar to trailers, only shorter. The most common running time for a television spot is thirty seconds. Release prints for television spots are distributed in 16mm format as opposed to the theater 35mm format of the trailer. In order to minimize the expense involved in making television spots, the trailer may be constructed in a modular format so that entire sections may be removed intact, providing ready-made television spots.

Producing an effective *radio spot* presents a somewhat different problem from producing a television spot. On radio, you are selling a motion picture without the pictures. If you're lucky, the same audio elements used in the trailer will work effectively on radio. But there's a good chance they won't work without visual support. It is not uncommon to start entirely from scratch in an effort to produce an effective radio campaign. Running times for radio spots are usually ten, thirty, and sixty seconds. They are sent to subdistributors and exhibitors on cassettes as part of the initial sales package. However, when they are sent to radio stations, the standard format is one-quarter inch reel to reel tape.

Half a dozen carefully chosen 8 × 10 production *stills* (still photographs) will go a long way toward stimulating interest from subdistributors and exhibitors. They will also be used in front of the theater to attract the attention of pedestrian traffic. Foreign distributors often request many more stills than are used for domestic distribution. It is wise to prepare for this and have an assortment of approximately twenty-five different stills, both color and black and white, available upon request.

In addition to the basic campaign package, a distributor may include an *alternate campaign*. This will be used to spur new interest and give the film a fresh look in its sixth or seventh week at one location. An alternate campaign often appeals to a different market from the primary campaign. When *Taxidriver* was first released, the lead line promoted the brilliance of Robert DeNiro. It was a sophisticated marketing approach. The campaign that followed in a subsequent release emphasized the relationship between a taxidriver and a teenage prostitute. The second approach is exploitative and appeals to a different audience than the first.

Another reason for an alternate campaign is if the primary campaign contains a graphic design that may be censored by newspapers in certain territories. The alternate campaign will utilize a more conservative graphic design in order to provide exhibitors everywhere with an acceptable newspaper ad.

The Promotional Concept

Most films contain a multitude of potentially commercial elements and it's easy for an ambitious producer, anxious to sell tickets, to get bogged down trying to devise a campaign that contains "something for everyone." A far more effective approach will be to define a specific audience for your film and tailor your campaign to appeal to that audience. An analogy can be found in the automotive industry. A manufacturer once designed a car based on the concept that no one would find anything to dislike about it. He was certain he would please everyone. Based on this concept, he produced the Edsel. On the other hand, prior to launching the most successful automotive campaign in history, the Ford Motor Company defined the potential buyer in great detail, down to the brand of Scotch he drank. The resulting campaign lifted Ford into the black and made their Mustang the number one selling car in America.

It is important to define your audience as specifically as possible. Don't be afraid of controversy and don't be afraid to take a stand. You can't possibly please everyone and, if you try, you'll fail. Without a strong, definite position, chances are you will get no one into the theater, but with a well-defined approach, you stand a good chance of drawing a specific, well-defined audience. If the film satisfies their expectations, word-of-mouth will carry it from there.

Those of you who have read this book from cover to cover have experienced, vicariously, the entire process of independent feature production from concept through distribution. Norman Mailer once described this process as ". . . a cross between a circus, a military campaign, a nightmare, an orgy, and a high." Certainly no one who successfully completes an independent feature looks back over the experience and says it was easy.

Every filmmaker enters into production with the hope that his film will become a success and maybe even a hit. In striving for that goal every filmmaker does the best he can. Those who succeed deserve congratulations and every bit of praise they receive. But those whose films, for whatever reasons, are simply not accepted by the movie-going public, also deserve recognition. They have taken a risk for something they believed in and they did the best they could. The variables involved in the success of a feature film are so tenuous and unpredictable that no filmmaker can guarantee success from the start. The history of the industry is filled with examples of films made by seasoned professionals for budgets of $10 million or more that were not accepted by the public, and other small independent films that achieved outstanding success.

If there is a single theme that resonates throughout this book it is the importance of setting one's sights high and firmly sticking to one's convictions. In the introduction, I talked about several successful independent feature films that achieved great success. In virtually every case, at some point along the way, the people responsible for those films were faced with awesome challenges. Had they lacked the strength to meet those challenges their films would be nothing more than unrealized dreams. Suppose David Puttnam, after trying unsuccessfully for two years to finance *Chariots of Fire,* had simply given up? Suppose John Sayles had accepted the studios' refusal to let him direct a film? What if Raphael and Joan Micklin Silver, after suffering three rounds of rejections from the major studios to distribute *Hester Street,* had abandoned their project? What if Ben Efraim had taken the easy route and agreed with everyone else that the early version of *Private Lessons* was unsalvageable? Each of these people went on to achieve great success because they had the courage and stamina to pursue their goals with unrelenting vigor.

There are thousands of independent features with less happy endings. Some never get beyond the concept stage or, if they do, never make it to the screen. This is either because the filmmakers failed to translate the ideas in their heads to images and sounds on film effectively, or because they lacked the strength to face the seemingly insurmountable difficulties of independent feature production. Even a brilliant filmmaker with a thorough knowledge of the filmmaking process will not succeed unless he can face disappointment, discouragement, and rejection with strength, fortitude, and courage. The only filmmakers who successfully realize their dreams are those who cling tenaciously to their convictions and simply refuse to accept defeat.

What I have provided in this book is the information necessary to guide a picture through the entire process of feature production from concept to distribution. What no book can provide is courage and tenacity in the soul of the filmmaker. That part is up to you.

Articles of
Limited Partnership

The following typical articles of limited partnership are included for general information and not for use without appropriate legal counsel.

_____ Company, a California general partnership, as general partner (hereinafter referred to as the "general partner"), and all persons, partnerships, or corporations whose names are subscribed to a counterpart hereof and designated as limited partners one or more of whom being hereinafter sometimes referred to as "limited partner" or "limited partners," respectively (hereinafter the general partner and the limited partners are sometimes collectively referred to as the "parties" or the "partners"), hereby form a limited partnership (herein referred to as the "partnership") pursuant to the provisions of Chapter 2, Title 2, of the Corporations Code of the State of California, known as the Uniform Limited Partnership Act of California.

ARTICLE I

Name

The name of the partnership shall be _____.

ARTICLE II

Documents

The partners shall promptly execute all certificates or other documents, and the general partner shall perform such filings and recordings and other acts conforming hereto as shall constitute a compliance with all requirements for the formation of a limited partnership under the laws of the State of California and for such other states in which the partnership elects to do business. The general partner shall be authorized to execute and file with the proper offices any and all certificates as required by the fictitious name or assumed name statute of California or similar statute in effect in any states in which the partnership elects to do business.

ARTICLE III

Business of the Partnership

The nature of the partnership business shall be the production, development, financing, and distribution arrangements for a motion picture tentatively entitled _____ (hereinafter referred to as the "picture"). It is intended that the picture will obtain a _____ rating from the Motion Picture Association of America. It is understood that the total budget for the picture will be set at _____, which includes legal, accounting, and administrative fees to be incurred by the partnership. It is also understood that the quality of the picture and its estimated costs are only opinions of the general partner and are not warranted or guaranteed.

ARTICLE IV

Location

The location of the principal place of business of the partnership shall be at _____, or at such other places as may be determined from time to time by the general partner.

ARTICLE V

Commencement

The partnership shall commence business on the date on which the limited partners have contributed the sum of _____ to the partnership; provided, however, if the sum of _____ shall not be contributed by the limited partners to the partnership on or before _____, this partnership shall not commence business and the capital contributed shall be returned to the limited partners as provided in section 2 of Article VI hereof.

ARTICLE VI

Contributions to the Partnership

Section 1. *Contributions of the general partner.* The general partner shall not be required to contribute cash to the partnership but shall contribute time and services to the business of the partnership as well as accepting its unlimited liability.

Section 2. *Contributions of the limited partners.* Contributions by the limited partners of cash to the capital of the partnership shall be separately set forth opposite their respective signatures on any counterpart of this agreement (hereinafter referred to as each limited partner's "participation"). Contributions to the partnership by the limited partners prior to the date on which the partnership shall commence doing business pursuant to Article V hereof, shall be deposited into an interest-bearing trust account at a commercial banking institution. Such contributions shall not be available for use by the general partner until such time as the partnership shall commence doing business pursuant to Article V hereof. If the sum of _____ shall not be contributed by the limited partners to the partnership on or before _____, the contributions to the partnership, if any, shall be returned no later than _____ to the limited partners together with any interest earned on such contributions less bank charges, if any. If the partnership shall commence doing business, any interest earned on a contribution by a limited partner, less bank charges, if any, shall be promptly paid over to the limited partner making such contribution.

Section 3. *Time of payment.* Payment from the limited partners is required upon the execution of these articles by the limited partners.

Section 4. *Assessments.* No limited partner shall be assessed for additional contributions.

Section 5. *Loans.* In the event that the partnership shall borrow any funds from any partner, above and beyond his capital account, such partner shall be paid such reasonable interest for the loan as shall then be agreed upon and such loan shall be accounted for as a liability of the partnership.

Section 6. *Capital accounts.* An individual capital account shall be maintained for each partner and shall reflect the participation of each partner. Each partner's proportionate share of the net profits and net losses (hereinafter defined) of the partnership to the date of the computation less any and all withdrawals by or distributions to each such partner shall be reflected in his capital account (each such partner's capital account hereinafter being referred to as a "capital account").

Section 7. *Admission of limited partners.* The general partner is authorized to admit limited partners to the partnership without approval of the other limited partners until the aggregate participation of the limited partners equals _____; thereafter, the general partner may only admit additional limited partners with the consent of all the other partners.

ARTICLE VII

Accounting

Section 1. *Distribution of revenues.* Revenues derived from the motion picture and actually received by the distributor will be considered gross film rental. The gross film rental will be subject to distribution and merchandising costs and the Distributor's percentage. After these deductions the film rental shall equal net film rental and shall be subject to production costs beyond the limited partnership investment capital such as loans, extended credit, and deferred payments to talent and technical facilities, and partnership overhead expenses. After the foregoing deductions the balance of net film rental shall equal partnership distributable cash.

Section 2. *Allocation of net profits and net losses.* The net profits and net losses, as hereinafter defined, of the partnership shall be divided as follows.

Net losses of the partnership shall be divided among all of the partners on the basis of relative capital account balances at the end of the partnership accounting year (before allocation of such net loss). Net profits of the partnership business shall be divided to the general partner, ____ percent, to the limited partners, ____ percent.

Section 3. *Specific allocation among the limited partners.* Net profits or net losses, as hereinafter defined, of the partnership that shall be credited to or borne by the limited partners shall be allocated among the limited partners on the basis of their relative participation in the partnership.

Section 4. *Cash flow.* The cash flow of the partnership shall mean all cash received by the partnership from any source (including partnership borrowings and the net proceeds from the sale of partnership assets) unless needed to pay partnership debts and expenses or otherwise required, in the sole discretion of the general partner for the partnership business.

Section 5. *Distribution of cash flow.* Until such time as the limited partners shall have received aggregate cash distributions equal to their initial cash contribution to the partnership, the cash flow of the partnership shall be distributed to the general partner, _____ percent, to the limited partners, _____ percent. After the limited partners have received aggregate cash distributions equal to their initial cash contribution to the partnership, the cash flow of the partnership shall be distributed to the general partner, _____ percent, to the limited partners, _____ percent. Distributions of cash flow to the limited partners shall be allocated on the basis of their relative capital account balances on the date of such distribution (before allocation of cash flow on such date). Once a distribution of cash has been made, a partner cannot be required to return any such distribution to the partnership.

Section 6. *Net profits and net losses.* For the purposes hereof, "net profits" or "net losses" shall mean the net income or loss of the partnership for federal income tax purposes as determined in accordance with generally accepted accounting principles.

Section 7. *Books of account.* At all times during the continuance of the partnership, the general partner shall cause proper and true books of account to be kept wherein there shall be entered particulars of all monies, goods, or effects belonging to or owing to or by the partnership, or paid, received, sold, or purchased in accordance with the partnership's business, and all such other transactions, matters, and things relating to the business of the partnership as are usually entered into the books of account kept by persons engaged in a business of like kind or character. Each partner shall at all reasonable times have free access and the right to inspect, at his own expense, said books of account.

Section 8. *Allocation of investment tax credit.* If the partnership shall make an investment during a taxable year of the partnership that qualifies for investment tax credit under the Internal Revenue Code of 1954 (as amended), the total amount of said investment shall be allocated among the partners on the basis of relative capital account balances as of the close of the taxable year in which the property qualifying for the investment tax credit is first placed in service.

ARTICLE VIII
Partnership Management

The business of the partnership shall be conducted and managed solely by the general partner in accordance with the provisions of this article and the provisions of the Uniform Limited Partnership Act of California. A limited partner shall contribute no services and shall take no part in or have any voice in the conduct or control of the partnership business or have any authority to act for or bind the partnership.

ARTICLE IX
Salaries and Reimbursement for Expenses of General Partner

Except as specified below, the general partner shall not be entitled to be paid a salary, fee, or other compensation for services other than its respective share of the net profits of the partnership. The following specific payments for services rendered shall be made to the general partner: ————.

ARTICLE X
Sale or Transfer of a Limited Partner's Interest

Section 1. *Withdrawal of capital.* No limited partner may withdraw his capital from the partnership without the consent of the general partner. Upon such withdrawal, the schedule of partnership assets shall be amended, and the certificate of limited partnership shall be amended in accordance with the provisions of section 15524(2)(a) of the California Corporations Code.

Section 2. *Amendment of certificate after termination of interest.* If, by reason of retirement, expulsion, disablement, bankruptcy, insanity, or any other reason whatsoever, a partner shall cease to be associated with this partnership, the remaining partners shall immediately amend the certificate of limited partnership as required by sections 15524, 15525, and 15525.5 of the California Corporations Code.

Section 3. *Substituted limited partner.* No assignee, legatee, distributee, or transferee (by operation of law or otherwise) of the whole or any portion of a limited partner's interest in the partnership shall have the right to become a "substituted limited partner" as that term is defined in the California Corporations Code without the written consent of the general partner except in the following circumstance. Upon the death of a limited partner, or if he be adjudicated insane or incompetent, his executors, administrators, trustees, committee, conservator, or representative (hereinafter sometimes called his "successor" or "successors"), shall have the same rights and obligations that such limited partner would have had if he had not died or been adjudicated insane or incompetent, except that his successor shall become a substituted limited partner as that term is defined in the California Corporations Code, section 15519, without the written consent of all of the partners.

Section 4. *Documents.* No sale or other disposition by a limited partner or his limited partnership interest (by operation of law or otherwise) shall be effective to constitute such assignee or successor a substituted limited partner as that term is defined above until all documents and acts required therewith under the laws of the State of California and all other states in which the partnership is doing business have been filed or taken. Each partner agrees upon request of the general partner to execute any such necessary documents and to perform such acts.

ARTICLE XI

Restriction of the General Partner

Section 1. *Admission of general partners.* No additional general partners shall be admitted to the partnership without the consent of all partners. Upon admission of an additional general partner all references in this agreement to the general partner shall be deemed to include the new general partner. The general partner shall determine what rights and voice an additional general partner shall have in the management of the partnership.

Section 2. *Death, incompetence, retirement, withdrawal, or expulsion of a general partner.*

The death, adjudication of incompetency, retirement, withdrawal, or expulsion (as hereinafter set forth) of any general partner shall not terminate the partnership (except as herein provided), but such deceased, incompetent, retired, withdrawn, or expelled general partner's entire interest or share of the partnership shall be converted from that of a general partner to that of a limited partner and, if there is then any remaining general partner or general partners, such general partner or general partners shall continue the business of the partnership.

The withdrawal or retirement of a general partner, unless consented to by all the partners, shall be deemed and shall constitute a wrongful withdrawal as defined in the California Uniform Partnership Act. In such event, all expenses, if any, of reconstruction of the partnership, including but not limited to reasonable attorney's fees, shall be borne by the wrongfully withdrawing general partner. If any general partner shall elect to withdraw or retire from the partnership, he shall serve written notice of such election upon all of the remaining general partners. Upon receipt of such notice of election to withdraw or retire from the partnership, the withdrawing or retiring general partner shall become a limited partner as hereinabove stated.

ARTICLE XII

Termination and Dissolution

Section 1. *Termination.* The partnership shall continue until _____, unless sooner terminated as herein provided.

Section 2. *Dissolution.* The Partnership shall be dissolved upon the earliest of the expiration of its term; the death or adjudication of incompetency of all the general partners; the wrongful withdrawal, bankruptcy, or insolvency of all of the general partners that is not reconstructed, discharged, or vacated within ninety (90) days from the date thereof; or the agreement of all of the partners. Upon dissolution and termination of the partnership, the general partner will proceed to liquidate the partnership. The partnership shall engage in no further business thereafter other than that necessary to wind up the business and distribute the assets. The proceeds from the liquidation of partnership assets shall be divided in the following order. The expenses of liquidation and the debts of the partnership other than debts owing to the partners shall be paid. Such debts as are owing to the partners, including unpaid salaries, loans, and advances made to or for the benefit of the partnership shall be paid. Such profits as shall be attributable to the interests of the limited partners shall be paid to said limited partners. Such profits as shall be attributable to the interests of the general partner shall be paid to said general partner. The balance of each limited partner's capital account shall be paid to said limited partners. The balance in the general partner's capital account shall be paid to said general partner.

Section 3. *Gain or loss during distribution.* The partners shall continue to divide profits and losses during the winding-up period in the manner provided in Article VII hereof; provided, however, any and all losses incurred on account of the abandonment of all or any of the assets of the partnership shall first be allocated among all of the partners having a credit balance in their capital accounts on the basis of relative capital account balances.

Section 4. *Tangible assets.* Upon dissolution of the partnership, a partner, either general or limited, shall have the right to demand back in kind any tangible assets that said individual partner has contributed to the partnership. The partners shall evaluate such asset or assets according to the fair market value at the time of distribution, and distribution shall then proceed as if the asset were being distributed in cash.

Section 5. *Accounting.* In case of the dissolution and termination of the partnership, a proper accounting shall be made of the capital account of each partner from the date of the last previous accounting to the date of dissolution.

Section 6. *Amendment of certificate and agreement.* The certificate of limited partnership and the articles of limited partnership shall be amended whenever: there is a change in the name of the partnership or the amount or character of the contribution of any limited partner; a person is substituted as a limited partner; an additional limited partner is admitted; a person is admitted as a general partner; a general partner retires, dies, or is declared insane, and the business is continued; there is a change in the nature of the partnership business; there is a false or erroneous statement in the certificate of limited partnership or the articles of limited partnership; there is a change in the time as stated in the certificate of limited partnership or the articles of limited partnership for dissolution of the partnership or for the return of a contribution; there is a change in the right to vote upon any of the matters affecting the structure of the partnership; the members desire to make a change in any other statement in the certificate of limited partnership or the articles of limited partnership in order that it shall accurately represent the agreement among them.

Section 7. *Distribution in kind.* After all of the debts of the partnership have been paid, the partners may elect, by mutual agreement, to distribute the assets of the partnership in kind. The general partner shall evaluate such assets according to their fair market value at the time of distribution, and distribution shall then proceed as if the assets were being distributed in cash. In determining the fair market value of the assets, the general partner may use whatever reasonable method of evaluation may be available, including but not limited to offering an asset for sale to persons or entities not related to the general partner and taking bids thereon, the highest such bid being deemed the fair market value of the asset.

Section 8. *Notice of dissolution.* The partners shall cause to have a notice of dissolution published in a newspaper of general circulation in the place where the partnership business was regularly carried on. A copy of such notice shall be mailed to each of the partnership creditors, and an affidavit of publication and mailing shall be filed with the county clerk within thirty (30) days after such publication.

ARTICLE XIII

Rights and Obligations of the Limited Partners

No limited partner shall be personally liable for any of the debts of the partnership or any of the losses of the partnership beyond the amount contributed by him to the initial capital of the partnership. No limited partner, as such, shall take part in the management of the business or transact any business for the partnership. No limited partner shall have the power to sign for, or bind the partnership. No limited partner shall be entitled to the return of his contribution except to the extent provided for in this agreement. Each of the limited partners agrees that he has not been induced to enter into this agreement by any warranties, guarantees, promises, statements, or representations, whether express or implied, except those that may be expressly set forth herein, and each limited partner acknowledges that he relies only on the good faith and integrity of the general partner and has subscribed hereto based upon such independent investigation as he deems sufficient, or upon no investigation whatever, but deems himself sufficiently informed to subscribe hereto.

ARTICLE XIV

Powers of the General Partners

Section 1. *Power of attorney.* Each limited partner agrees that, concurrent with the execution of this agreement, he will appoint each general partner as his true and lawful attorney coupled with an interest, in his name, place, and stead to sign, execute, acknowledge, swear to, and file any and all documents that in the discretion of such attorney are required to be signed, executed, acknowledged, sworn to, or filed by a limited partner solely to discharge the purposes of the partnership as herein stated.

Section 2. *Grant of authority.* The grant of authority set forth in section 2 of Article XIV is a special power of attorney coupled with an interest, is irrevocable, and shall survive the death of the limited partner. It may be exercised by either general partner for each limited partner by a facsimile signature or by listing all of the limited partners executing any instrument with his single signature as attorney-in-fact for all of them; and shall survive the delivery of an assignment by a limited partner of the whole or any portion of his interest, except that where the assignee has been approved by the general partners for admission to the partnership as a substitute limited partner, the power of attorney shall survive the delivery of such assignment for the sole purpose of enabling the general partners to execute, acknowledge, and file any instrument necessary to effect such substitution.

Section 3. *Responsibilities of the general partners.* The management and control of the business of the partnership for the purpose herein stated shall be vested exclusively in the general partner. The general partner shall use his best efforts to carry out the purpose of the partnership as set forth herein.

Section 4. *General authority.* Except as herein expressly stated, the general partner shall have all the rights and powers permitted under the provisions of the Uniform Limited Partnership Act of California.

Section 5. *Proscriptions.* Without the written consent of all of the limited partners, the general partners shall have no authority to: do any act in contravention of this agreement; do any act that would make it impossible to carry on the business of the partnership; confess a judgment against the partnership; or possess partnership property or assign partners' rights in specific partnership property for other than a partnership purpose.

ARTICLE XV

General Provisions

Section 1. *Notices.* All communications required or permitted to be given pursuant to this agreement shall be in writing and shall be sent by certified or registered U.S. mail, postage prepaid, or by prepaid telegram and addressed, if to the general partner, to the address of the partnership, and if to a limited partner, to such limited partner at his last known address. Any limited partner may change his address by stating his new address to the general partner. The general partner may change his address by giving notice to all of the limited partners. Such newly designated address shall be such partner's address for all purposes herein.

Section 2. *Successors.* This agreement and all the terms and provisions hereof shall be binding upon and shall inure to the benefit of the general partner, all limited partners, and their respective successors, except as otherwise provided herein.

Section 3. *Limitation of liability.* The execution of this agreement by the trustee of any trust shall be in his capacity as trustee in the exercise of the power and authority vested in him as trustee and not individually. It is understood and agreed that nothing herein contained shall be construed as creating any liability or obligation to perform any covenant, either express or implied, contained herein, on the part of the trustee individually hereunder, all such liability and obligation being expressly limited to the trustee's capacity as trustee.

Section 4. *Severability.* In the event any provision of this agreement shall be held invalid or unenforceable by any court of competent jurisdiction, such holding shall not invalidate or render unenforceable any other provision herein.

Section 5. *Gender.* All words denoting gender herein, shall be deemed to refer to the masculine, feminine, or neuter, singular or plural, as the context requires.

Section 6. *Headings.* The descriptive headings of the articles and sections of this agreement are inserted for convenience only and shall not control or effect the meaning of any of the provisions hereof.

In witness hereof, the partners hereto have executed this agreement this ___ day of ____, 19__, and each of the Partners whose name appears on the Register of Limited Partners has executed this agreement and has subscribed hereto the sum set forth opposite his name on the day and year stated.

Print or type name, address, and taxpayer identification number below.

General partner

by _____

Limited partners

_____

_____

_____

_____

_____

_____

_____

_____

Register of Limited Partners

Name	Date	Amount invested	Percent participation

Power of Attorney

Know all men by these presents that the undersigned, as a limited partner, does hereby appoint _____, as the general partner of _____, a California limited partnership (the "partnership"), created under a written agreement dated _____, (the "agreement") his true and lawful attorney coupled with an interest to sign, execute, acknowledge, swear to, and file any and all documents that in the discretion of said attorney are required to be signed, executed, acknowledged, sworn to, or filed by a limited partner of the partnership to discharge the purposes of the partnership as stated in the agreement, including, without limitation, a certificate of limited partnership for the partnership and all amendments thereto required by law or the agreement. In addition, said attorney shall specifically have the power to amend the agreement on the terms and conditions contained in section 1 of Article XIV of the agreement. All of the above shall be done in the name and stead, and as the act of, and as fully as the undersigned might do himself.

Said attorney shall not have the power to substitute and appoint from time to time an attorney or attorneys under him, the said attorney, but any substitute or additional general partners of the partnership shall, upon qualification as such under the agreement, become an additional true and lawful attorney of the undersigned and have the same powers as the said attorney.

The signing, execution, acknowledgement, swearing to, and/or filing of any of the above in pursuance of these presents shall be as binding upon the undersigned to all intents and purposes as if they had been duly signed, executed, acknowledged, sworn to, and/or filed in his own person.

In witness whereof, the undersigned has hereunto set his hand this __ day of ____, 19__.

————————

Subscribed and *sworn to*
before me this __ day of
____, 19__.

_____ *(Seal)*
Notary public

Sample Budget for a Studio Feature

Budget Recap

Title _____ Producer _____
Production company _____ Director _____
Production manager _____ Script dated _____

Above-the-line costs

1100	Story rights and continuity	$ 48,695	
1200	Producer's unit	213,921	
1300	Direction	155,500	
1400	Cast	1,039,972	
1500	Traveling and living cost	52,204	
1600	Fringe benefits	100,618	
	Total above-the-line		$1,610,910

Below-the-line costs
  Production period

2000	Production staff	169,525
2100	Extra talent	92,708
2200	Set design	122,150
2300	Set construction	741,610
2400	Set striking	20,000
2500	Set operations	119,900
2600	Special effects	103,700
2700	Set dressing	121,300
2800	Property	188,900
2900	Men's wardrobe	102,000
3000	Women's wardrobe	incl.
3100	Makeup and hairdressing	73,850
3200	Lighting	126,800
3300	Camera	201,850
3400	Production sound	50,961
3500	Transportation	362,800
3600	Locations	677,520

3700	Film and laboratory	109,863	
3800	Process	20,000	
3900	Second unit	—	
4000	Tests	6,000	
4100	Miscellaneous expenses	—	
4200	Fringe benefits	626,062	4,037,499

Editing period

4500	Film editing	157,300	
4600	Music	85,000	
4700	Sound	40,000	
4800	Film and laboratory	47,500	
4900	Main and end titles	6,000	
5000	Fringe benefits	65,000	400,800

Other costs

6700	Insurance	140,000	
6800	General Expense	60,464	
6900	Retroactive salaries		200,464
	Total below-the-line		4,638,763
	Total direct costs		6,249,673
	1.5% Legal		93,745
	Add 10% Contingency (below-the-line only)		461,376
	Add 2% finder's fee		136,096
	Total budget		$6,940,890

Budget Detail

Detail		Account	Total
1100 Story rights and continuity			
1101 Writers			
Treatment	$15,000		
First draft	15,000		
Second draft	10,000		
Polish $1,500 × 3 weeks	4,500	$44,500	
1103 Rights purchased			
MPAA title registration	300		
Copyright	695	995	
1106 Mimeograph		350	
1107 Secretaries			
1185 Other costs			
Production board/crossplot	1,000		
Script timing	350	1,350	
1199 Fringe Benefits and payroll taxes			
Payroll taxes and compensation insurance			
Pension @ %			
Health and welfare @			$48,695
1200 Producers unit			
1201 Executive producer			
1202 Producer		200,000	
1203 Associates			
1207 Secretaries			
wks. @			
wks. @		8,000	
1208 Legal and auditing expenses			
Legal fee			
Auditing fee			
Expenses			
1285 Other costs			
Research	5,921		
		5,921	213,921
1300 Direction			
1301 Director and associates		125,000	

	Detail	Account	Total
1302 Dialogue director			
Fee		9,000	
1303 Dance director and assistants			
1304 Casting director			
Fee		10,000	
1307 Secretaries			
16 weeks prep	4,000		
10 weeks shoot	2,500		
20 weeks finish	5,000	11,500	
1385 Other costs			
			155,500
1400 Cast			
1401 Stars and leads			
see 1401 detail		990,000	
1402 Supporting cast			
see 1402 detail		25,000	
1403 Day players			
see 1403 detail		4,500	
1404 Stuntmen			
see 1404 detail		20,472	
1406 Looping and overtime			
allowance		—	
1485 Other costs			
			1,039,972

1401 Stars and leads, detail

Character	Player	Start date	Finish date	Elapsed time	Guarantee	Amount
Alexis				pic		250,000
Richard				× 6		10,000
Monroe				× 4		75,000
King Nellis				× 4		50,000
Anna				× 4		45,000
Jagg				× 4		400,000
Jeremy				× 2		10,000
Arthur				× 3		30,000
Teliman				× 4		60,000
Tessie				× 3		50,000
Jobo				× 1		10,000
						990,000

	Detail		Account	Total

1402 Supporting cast detail

Character	Player	Start date	Finish date	Elapsed time	Guarantee	Amount
Mandy				× 1		
Illana				× 1		
King Jarnod				× 1		
Queen Arana				× 1		
Gandar				× 1		
Gorman				× 2		
Ladia				× 2		
Jordan				× 2		
Queen Julia				× 1		
Andrew				× 1 day		
Thoman				× 1		
Mathew				× 1		
Fishing girl				× 1		
Sister				× 1		
Kay				× 2		
Aknar				× 2		
Antony				× 1		
Ricardo				× 1		
Garth				× 1		

Total 24 weeks,
allow $25,000

	Detail		Account	Total

1403 Day players detail

10 × 2 days	days @ 225	4,500
	days @	
	days @	
	days @	
	days @	
	days @	
	days @	
	days @	
	days @	
	days @	
	days @	
	days @	
	days @	
	days @	
	days @	
	days @	

	Detail			Account	Total
	days @				
	days @				
	days @				
	days @				
	days @				
	days @				
	days @				
	days @				
	days @				
	days @				
	days @			4,500	

1404 Stunt men detail

1 Gaffer	4 wks. @	1,000	4,000	
5 Stunt men	3 wks. @	842	12,630	
1 Youth stunt	1 wk. @	842	842	
	weeks @			
	weeks @			
Allow for horsemen			3,000	
	weeks @			
	weeks @			
	weeks @			
	weeks @			
	weeks @			
	weeks @			
	weeks @			
	weeks @			
	weeks @			
	weeks @			
	weeks @			
	weeks @			
	weeks @			
	weeks @			
	weeks @			
	weeks @			
	weeks @			20,472

1500 Traveling and living costs

1501 Traveling and living costs

15 London–Los Angeles–London @ 2,012	30,180	
2 Los Angeles–London–Los Angeles for casting @ 2,012	4,024	
Living expenses @ 1,000 per week	18,000	
		52,204

	Detail		Account	Total

1600   Fringe benefits and payroll taxes

1601   Above-the-line, less story costs
Payroll taxes and comp. ins.
Pension per $1,000 @   %
Health and welfare per $1,000 @   %
Health and welfare   wks. @

		Detail	Account	Total
Director		13,375		
Cast		57,000		
Payroll		26,100		
Stunts		4,143		100,618

Total above-the-line   1,635,910

2000   Production staff

2001   Unit production manager

		Detail	Account
Preparation	4 wks. @ 1,400	5,600	
	12 wks. @ 1,900	22,800	
	10 wks. @ 1,900	19,000	
(including severance)			
	4 wks. @ 1,400	5,600	
	wks. @		53,000

2002   First assistant directors

		Detail	Account
	4 wks. @ 1,750	7,000	
	10 wks. @ 1,750	17,500	
(severance)	1 wk. @ 1,750	1,750	
	wks. @		
	wks. @		
	wks. @		
	wks. @		26,250

2003   Second assistant directors

		Detail	Account
	3 wks. @ 1,200	3,600	
	10 wks. @ 1,200	12,000	
(severance)	1 wk. @ 850	850	
	wks. @		
	wks. @		
Additional 2nd AD			
	10 wks. @ 910	9,100	
	wks. @		
	wks. @		
	wks. @		
	wks. @		25,550

	Detail			Account	Total
2004	Script supervisors				
	1 wk. @ 1,225	1,225			
	10 wks. @ 1,225	12,250			
	1 wk. @ 1,050	1,050			
				14,525	
2006	Technical advisors/coordinator				
	Sword training wks. @	8,000			
	Boating coordination				
	wks. @	4,000			
	wks. @				
				12,000	
2007	Secretaries and typists				
	16 wks. @ 350	5,600			
	10 wks. @ 400	4,000			
	4 wks. @ 350	1,400			
				11,000	
2085	Other costs				
	Location manager				
	16 weeks @ 350	12,000			
	12 weeks @ 800	9,600			
	2 production assistants				
	@ 140 × 20	5,600			
				27,200	169,525
2100	Extra talent				
2101	Extras and stand-ins				
	per detail				
	4 stand-ins × 60 days @ 30			7,200	
	crowd days 2500 @ 30			75,000	
2103	Sideline musicians				
	per detail				
2104	Welfare workers				
	per detail				
	Local × 4 weeks @ 520			2,080	
2116	Atmosphere cars				
	per detail				
2185	Other costs				
	Fringes @ 10%			8,428	
					92,708

		Detail			Account	Total

2100 Extra talent, detail

Scheduled date	Set	Days	Rate	2101 Extras	2103 Sideline	2104 Welfare worker	2116 Atmos. cars
		2	crowd	500			
		3	crowd	200			
		2		150			
		6		50			
		5		5			
		15		3			
					Total	2,270	
					Allow		2,500

	Detail			Account	Total

2200 Set design

2201 Art directors and assistants

Designer 16 + 10 wks. @ 1,500	39,000			
Assistant 12 + 10 wks. @ 950	20,400			
wks. @				
wks. @		59,900		

2202 Draftsmen

Chief 12 + 8 wks. @ 850	17,000		
2 other 12 + 8 wks. @	15,000		
wks. @		32,000	

2203 Model makers

1 × 15 wks. @ 750	11,250	
wks. @		11,250

2204 Sketch artists

1 × 12 wks. @ 850	10,200	
wks. @		10,200

2205 Set estimator

wks. @	
wks. @	

2216 Purchases

2,800	
	2,800

2285 Other costs

6,000	122,150

2300 Set construction (see 2300 detail)

2301 Labor	Coordinator 16 + 11 @ 1,400	37,800
	Assistant coordinator 25 @ 1,000	25,000

	Detail	Account	Total
2305	Scaffolds		
2316	Purchases building materials	} 351,210	
2317	Rentals road building, cherry picker, etc.		

2395 Studio charges

	Detail		Account	Total
3 plasterers 10 @ 750	22,500			
30 construction 10 @ 750	225,000			
5 local labor 10 @ 450	22,500			
1 master painter 12 @ 950	11,400			
4 painters 12 @ 750	36,000			
1 welder 12 @ 850	10,200	—	327,600	741,610

	Detail	Account	Total
2400	Set striking		
2401	Labor		
2416	Materials	}	
2485	Other costs		20,000
2495	Studio charges		
2300	Set construction detail		

		2301	2305	2316	2317	2395	
Number	Description	Labor	Scaffold	Material	Rentals	Studio charges	Total

	Detail		Account	Total
2500	Set operations			
2501	First company grip			
	13 wks. @ 1,200	15,600		
	wks. @			
	wks. @		15,600	
2502	Second company grips			
	12 wks. @ 1,000	12,000		
	wks. @			
	wks. @		12,000	
2503	Other company grips			
Dolly grips	11 wks. @ 950	10,450		
Hammer	11 wks. @ 850	9,350		
	wks. @			
	wks. @			
	wks. @		19,800	
2504	Prop shop/plumbers			
	wks. @			
	wks. @			

	Detail			Account	Total

2505 Greensmen, standby
Local   10 wks. @   850
                 wks. @   8,500

2506 Standby painter
                 wks. @
                 wks. @

2508 Craft servicemen
             10 wks. @   650
                 wks. @
                               6,500

2509 Miscellaneous labor
Utility men ( )   wks. @
Stage police   wks. @
Other labor   wks. @

2510 Reset walls, repairs   1,700

2516 Purchases
                                         7,000

2517 Rentals
Titan crane   wks. @
Nike   wks. @
Miscellaneous: helicopter
                 wks. @
                                       4,700

2586 First Aid studio
             10 wks. @ 650   6,500

2595 Studio charges
Dressing rooms 2 Portable toilets

	11 wks. @	950	20,900		
Air conditioning 6 wks. @		400	2,400		
Grip equipment 11 wks. @ 1,300			14,300		
				37,600	119,900

2600 Special effects

2601 Foreman and operating crew

8 wks. @ 1,000	8,000		
12 wks. @ 1,950	23,400		
14 wks. @ 1,200	16,800		
wks. @			
wks. @			
wks. @	48,200		

2602 Manufacturing labor
per detail Local 3 × 2 weeks   2,500

	Detail	Account	Total
2603	Rigging labor per detail		
2604	Striking labor per detail		
2609	Other departments per detail	35,000	
2616	Purchases per detail		
2617	Rentals per detail workshop @ 150 per day	18,000	
2685	Other costs		
2695	Studio charges		103,700

		2602	2603	2604	2616	2617	
Unit	Description	Manufacture	Rigging	Striking	Purchases	Rentals	Total

	Detail	Account	Total
2700	Set dressing		
2701	Set decorator		
	6 + 10 + 1 wks. @ 1,000	17,000	
	wks. @		17,000
2702	Other set dressing labor		
	Leadman 15 wks. @ 800	12,000	
	wks. @		
	8 men local 14 wks. @ 650	27,300	
			39,300
2711	Manufacturing labor		
2712	Manufacturing material		
2716	Purchases		
2717	Rentals	65,000	
2748	Loss and damage		
2785	Other costs		
2795	Studio charges		121,300

			Set dressing detail			
		2711–2712	2716	2711–2712	2717	
Set Number	Description	Manufacture	Purchases	Drapes	Rentals	Total

	Detail		Account	Total

2800 Property

2801 Property master
10 + 10 + 2   wks. @ 1,000   22,000
               wks. @
                                         22,000

2802 Other property labor
2 assistants   wks. @
8 + 10 + 1   wks. @   850   32,300
               wks. @
                                         32,300

2804 Animal handlers, wranglers,
        special operators
Head trainer   6 wks. @ 1,300   7,800
2 assistants   6 wks. @ 1,200   14,400
               wks. @
               wks. @
               wks. @
               wks. @
                                         22,200

2811 Manufacturing labor
Prop makers 4 @ 650 × 10   26,000

2812 Manufacturing material

2816 Purchases   40,000

2817 Rentals

2837 Animals and wagons
Bird, deer, wild pony, 6 cats,
4 caged bats, 6 pigs, 12 pigeons,   } 26,400
allow 24 @ 1,100

40 horses for kings, Alexis, and   }
battles, 40 × 12 days allow   }   20,000

2841 Picture vehicles
Alexis's cart, Jeremy's cart,   }
Jagg's cart, Richard's cart   } included above
King Nellis's wooden chariot   }

2848 Loss and damage

2885 Other costs

                                                  188,900

Detail	Account	Total
2900 Men's wardrobe		
2901 Operating labor		
Designer/coordinator		
8 + 10 wks. @ 1,200 21,600		
Assistant		
5 + 10 + 1 wks. @ 850 13,600		
wks. @		
2 local assistants 10 wks. @ 750 15,000		
	50,200	
2911 Manufacturing labor		
2912 Manufacturing material	46,000	
2916 Purchases		
2917 Rentals		
2921 Alterations and repairs		
2934 Other departments		
2946 Cleaning and dyeing	2,800	
2948 Loss and damage		
2985 Other costs		
Crowd dressing 6 locals × 1 week @ 500		
	3,000	102,000
3000 Women's wardrobe		
3001 Operating labor		
wks. @		
wks. @		
wks. @		
wks. @		
wks. @		
3002 Designers and assistants		
wks. @		
wks. @		
3011 Manufacturing labor		
3012 Manufacturing material		
3016 Purchases		
3017 Rentals		
3021 Alterations and repairs		
3034 Other departments		

	Detail			Account	Total
3046	Cleaning and dyeing				
3048	Loss and damage				
3085	Other costs				
					included above
3100	Makeup and hairdressing				
3101	Makeup artists				
	1 + 10 wks. @ 1,400			15,400	
Assistant	10 wks. @ 1,250			12,500	
	wks. @				
Assistants for	wks. @				
crowd allow	wks. @			4,800	
	wks. @				
	wks. @				
	wks. @				
					32,700
3102	Hairdressers				
	1 + 10 wks. @ 1,250			13,750	
Assistant	10 wks. @ 1,100			11,000	
	wks. @				
Assistants for	wks. @				
crowd allow	wks. @			3,700	
	wks. @				
	wks. @				
	wks. @				
					28,450
3103	Body makeup				
	wks. @				
	wks. @				
					1,800
3116	Purchases				
					900
3117	Rentals				
Wigs, chairs, etc.				8,000	
2 boxes @ 100 per week × 10				2,000	
					10,000
3185	Other costs				
					73,850
3200	Lighting				
3201	Rigging				
	allow				3,500

	Detail		Account	Total
3202	Striking			
	allow		3,500	
3203	Gaffer			
	13	wks. @ 1,200	15,600	
		wks. @		
			15,600	
3204	Best boy			
	12	wks. @ 1,000	12,000	
		wks. @		
			12,000	

3205 Operating labor

Electricians × 11	wks. @ 850	9,350
Electricians × 11	wks. @ 850	9,350
Electricians	wks. @	
Electricians	wks. @	
	wks. @	
Generator operator		
× 11	wks. @ 850	9,350
Generator operator	wks. @	
		28,050

3209	Lamps, carbons, gelatins	⎫	
3212	Gas/oil generators	⎬	11,000
3216	Purchases	⎭	

3217 Rentals

Equipment @ 3,000 × 11	33,000	
Box @ 100 × 10	1,000	
		34,000

3285 Other costs
Allow for night work

| | | 6,800 |

3295 Studio charges

Current studio	days @		
Generator	11 weeks @ 850	9,350	
Equipment rentals for nights 3,000	3,000		
		12,350	126,800

3300 Camera

3301 First cameraman

2 + 10	wks. @ 4,000	48,000	
	wks. @		
		48,000	

	Detail			Account	Total
3302	Operators				
	10¼	wks. @ 1,815	18,755		
		wks. @			
		wks. @			
		wks. @			
		wks. @			
				18,755	
3303	Assistant cameramen				
First					
	1 + 10 + 1	wks. @ 1,515	18,180		
		wks. @			
Second					
	1 + 10 + 1	wks. @ 1,310	15,720		
		wks. @			
		wks. @			
		wks. @			
		wks. @			
				33,900	
3304	Machinists, loaders				
		wks. @			
		wks. @			
3305	Stillman				
	5 wks. @ 1,815		9,075		
		wks. @			
				9,075	
3316	Purchases				
				2,700	
3317	Rentals				
	Panavision × 3				
	compliments of lenses, heads,				
	etc. @ 5,200 per week		52,000		
	Plus tax @ 6%		3,120	55,120	
3385	Other costs				
	Still camera @ 200 per week × 5		1,000		
				1,000	
3395	Second unit				
	Operator @ 1,815 × 10		18,150		
	Assistant @ 1,515 × 10		15,150		
				33,300	201,850
3400	Production sound				
3401	Recording crew				
	Mixer	10½ wks. @ 2,082	21,861		
		wks. @			
		wks. @			

Detail			Account	Total
Boom man 10½ wks. @ 1,600		16,800		
wks. @				
wks. @				
Recorder wks. @				
wks. @				
wks. @				
Cableman/Playback operator				
wks. @				
wks. @				
wks. @				
wks. @				
			38,661	

3410 Transfer costs
Dailies   M ft. @

3416 Purchases

¼″ tape	Rolls @	600		
Magnetic stripe 1,000 ft. @		1,800		
Batteries etc.		400		
			2,800	

3417 Rentals

Sound package @ 400 × 11	4,400		
Extra mikes etc. allow	1,800		
Walkie-talkies 6 @ 50 × 11	3,300		
		9,500	

3485 Other costs

3495 Studio charges
days @
days @
days @
days @
days @
days @
days @

				50,961

3500 Transportation

3501 Studio drivers
Captain

16 + 10 + 2 wks. @ 1,100	30,800	
Cocaptain		
14 + 10 + 1 wks. @ 975	25,350	
Camera/sound 11 wks. @ 850	9,350	
Props 15 wks. @ 850	12,750	

	Detail			Account	Total
Honey wagon #1					
	10 wks. @	900	9,000		
Honey wagon #2					
	11 wks. @	900	9,900		
Construction × 3					
	10 wks. @	850	25,500		
Set decorating	15 wks. @	850	12,750		
Grip/electric	11 wks. @	850	9,350		
Swing truck	11 wks. @	850	9,350		
Wardrobe van	11 wks. @	850	9,350		
Art department car					
	12 + 10 wks. @	850	18,700		
Cast minibus	11 wks. @	850	9,350		
Unit Bus (large)	wks. @				
	66 days @	850	9,350		
Construction minibus					
	10 wks. @	850	8,500		
Production car #1	wks. @				
	16 + 10 wks. @	900	23,400		
Production car #2	wks. @				
	14 + 10 wks. @	900	21,600	254,350	

3502	Local hire drivers			
		wks. @		
		wks. @		
		wks. @		
		wks. @		
		wks. @		

3542	Outside equipment				
	Constr. minibus	10 wks. @	200	2,000	
	Prod. car #1	26 wks. @	175	4,550	
	Prod. car #2	24 wks. @	175	4,200	
	Camera/sound	11 wks. @	200	2,200	
	Props	15 wks. @	250	3,750	
	Special effects	11 days @	200	14,400	(including driver)
	Const. × 3	10 wks. @	750	7,500	
	Set decor.	15 wks. @	250	2,750	
	Honey wagon	11 wks. @	950	10,450	
	Grip/elec.	11 wks. @	450	4,950	
	Swing truck	11 wks. @	200	2,200	
	Wardrobe van	11 wks. @	200	2,200	
	Art Dept. car	22 wks. @	175	3,850	
	Cast minibus	11 wks. @	200	2,200	
	Unit bus (large)	66 days @	85	5,610	
				73,850	

	Detail	Account	Total

3543 Local hire equipment
day/wks. @
day/wks. @
day/wks. @
day/wks. @
day/wks. @
day/wks. @

3544 Gas and oil   18,000

3585 Other costs
Cabs, mileage   4,600
Self-drive cars   12,000   16,600

3595 Studio charges
day/wks. @
day/wks. @
day/wks. @
day/wks. @
day/wks. @
day/wks. @
day/wks. @
day/wks. @
day/wks. @
day/wks. @
day/wks. @   362,800

3600 Locations

3601 Fares, public carrier
Preproduction   7,200
30 × first class   7,500
50 × economy class   9,600
Allow additional   1,700   26,000

3602 Site rentals, permits
Locations, hangar, offices,
security, police, firemen
         Allow   85,000
               85,000

3603 Hotels and motels
80 rooms @ $30 × 70   168,000
Prep and wrap
allow 2,100 nights @ $30   63,000
Per diems @ 25   140,000
Prep and wrap @ 25   50,000
Stuntmen allow 140 days @ 55   7,700
             428,700

3604 Meals
80 @ $8.50 (including tax) × 60   40,800

	Detail		Account	Total
Additional day players and crowd 2,250		21,420		
Night catering		3,000		
			65,220	
3605 Survey costs				
60 air fares		15,000		
Hotel, transportation, meals 10 × 6 visits		7,800	22,800	
3606 Shipping and forwarding costs			7,800	
3607 First aid and medical costs wks. @				
3623 Out-of-state set construction				
3628 Studio employees				
Auditor 30 wks. @ 800		24,000		
Location representative wks. @			24,000	
3634 Miscellaneous local employees				
Cashier 20 wks. @ 650		13,000		
Secretary 20 wks. @ 250		5,000		
wks. @				
wks. @				
wks. @				
wks. @			18,000	
3685 Other costs				
Employee mileage				
				677,520
3700 Production film and laboratory				
3702 Negative film				
250,000 M ft. @ .190		47,500		
+ 6% − 2%		+ 2,850		
		= 50,350	49,343	
		− 1,007		
3704 Negative developed				
250,000 M ft. @ .1093			27,325	
3706 Daily prints				
One lite 175,000 M ft. @ .1754				
Corrected M ft. @				
			30,695	
3728 Process plates				
M ft. @			2,500	

	Detail	Account	Total

3729 Still costs
3785 Other costs

			109,863

3800 Process
3801 Projectionists and cameraman
    Cameraman   days @
    Projectionists ( ) days @
3802 Set up and strike
3885 Other costs
3895 Studio charges

			20,000

3900 Second units/miniatures
4000 Tests/rehearsal costs
4001 Operating labor
    Camera ( )   days @
    Operations ( )   days @
    Props ( )   days @
    Wardrobe ( )   days @
    Makeup and hair ( )days @
    Lighting ( )   days @
    Sound ( )   days @
    Set dressing ( )   days @

	Allow	6,000	

4014 Negative film and laboratory
    Film   M ft. @
    Develop   M ft. @
    Print   M ft. @
4015 Sound tape and transfer
    Tape ¼"   Rolls @
    Tape, stripe M ft. @
    Transfer
4016 Purchases
4085 Other costs
4095 Studio charges

			6,000

4100 Miscellaneous production expense
4101 Cast insurance
  Million ( ) people for days @   ¢
4102 Stage rentals
             days @
             days @
             days @

	Detail	Account	Total

4185 Other costs

4195 Studio charges
Handling charge

4200 Production period fringe benefits

4299 Fringe benefits and payroll taxes

				Account	Total
Payroll taxes	M @		DGA	33,536	
Payroll taxes	@		IATSE	591,526	
Comp. insurance	M @				
Fringe benefits	M @				
	M @				626,062

4500 Film editing

4501 Film editor

Shoot	10	wks. @ 1,500	15,000		
Finish	24	wks. @ 1,500	36,000		
		wks. @		51,000	

4502 Assistant editors

Shoot 10	wks. @	950	9,500	
Finish 24	wks. @	950	22,800	
	wks. @		32,300	

4503 Looping editor and assistants
               wks. @
               wks. @

4504 Music editors and assistants
               wks. @
               wks. @

4505 Sound effects editors and assistants
               wks. @
               wks. @

4509 Coding
               reels @

4510 Projection
               hrs. @   74,000

4585 Other costs
Continuity
Supplies
Preview costs

4595 Studio charges
Cutting rooms and equip. wks. @
Music and sound effects library

                                              157,300

	Detail	Account	Total

4600	Music		
4601	Musicians		
4602	Composers, lyricists		
4603	Arrangers, orchestrators		
4604	Copyists		
4608	Singers	85,000	
4609	Other personnel		
4646	Music rights		
4647	Instrument rentals		
4685	Other costs		
	Contract		
			85,000

4700	Postproduction sound		
4703	Transfer cost		
	M ft. @		
	M ft. @		
4704	Dubbing crew and facilities		
	hrs. @ 305.20		
4705	Scoring crew and facilities		
	hrs. @ 285.00		
	hrs. @		
4706	Looping crew and facilities		
	hrs. @ 166.00	40,000	
4707	Film stock, reprints		
4708	Film stock, looping		
4709	Film stock, music prints		
4710	Film stock, dubbed master		
	and optical		
4785	Other costs		
			40,000

4800	Postproduction film and laboratory		
4810	Stock footage		
4813	Negative film, leader		
4814	Reversal prints, b & w		
	M ft. @		
4819	Editorial reprints		

Detail	Account	Total
4820 Sound negative develop and print		
Film M ft. @		
Develop and print		
4823 Inserts	47,500	
4825 Matte shots		
4826 Answer print and protection		
PM-CRI M ft. @		
Answer print M ft. @		
A & B printing M ft. @		
4827 Opticals manufacture		
4828 Miscellaneous lab costs		
4830 Negative cutting and breakdown		
Reels @		
4885 Other costs		47,500
4900 Main and end titles		
4901 Main and end titles		
		6,464
5000 Postproduction fringe benefits		
5099 Fringe benefits and payroll taxes		
Payroll taxes M @ IATSE		
Payroll taxes @		
Comp. ins. M @		
Fringe benefits @		
Fringe benefits		65,000
6700 Insurance		
6702 Negative insurance		
6703 Errors and omissions		
6704 Property floater		
6705 Other insurance		
Allow		140,000
6800 General expense		
6801 Telephone and telegraph		
6803 Xerox and mimeograph		
6804 City license		
6805 Sales tax		

	Detail		Account	Total
6807	Facility sales tax			
6809	Code seal	Allow	60,000	
6812	Office supplies			
6813	Accounting fee			
6885	Other costs			
6895	Studio charges			
	Office rentals wks. @			
	wks. @			
	wks. @			
				60,000
6900	Retroactive salaries			
6901	Salary adjustments			
	Total below-the-line			4,613,763

Sample Budget for
a Low-budget Feature

Budget Recap

Title _____ Production company _____

Above-the-line

	100 Screenplay	$ 16,000	
	200 Producer	17,000	
	300 Director	12,500	
	400 Cast	55,000	$100,500

Below-the-line
Production

	500 Production staff	20,700	
	600 Extras	6,000	
	700 Set operations	34,800	
	800 Sets	17,000	
	900 Props	10,600	
	1000 Costumes	6,900	
	1100 Makeup and hairdressing	7,000	
	1200 Production equipment	21,000	
	1300 Locations/studio	12,800	
	1400 Laboratory and film	39,000	
	1500 Tests	500	
	1600 Production miscellaneous	16,500	192,800

Postproduction

	1700 Editing	46,000	
	1800 Sound	14,500	
	1900 Music	26,000	
	2000 Titles and opticals	5,000	
	2100 Laboratory	12,800	
	2200 Sound mix	11,800	116,100

Other costs

	2300 Insurance	20,000	
	2400 Miscellaneous	25,100	45,100
		Total	454,500
		10% Contingency	45,500
		Grand total	$500,000

Budget Detail

100 Screenplay

	101 Story rights	$ —	
	102 Writer, screenplay	15,500	
	103 Research and travel	—	
	104 Mimeograph	140	
	105 WGA registration	10	
	106 Script timing	350	$16,000

200 Producer

	201 Executive producer	—	
	202 Producer	15,000	
	203 Associate producer	—	
	204 Secretary	2,000	
	205 Assistants	—	17,000

300 Director

	301 Director	12,500	
	302 Dance director	—	
	303 Secretary	—	12,500

400 Cast

	401 Lead players	35,000	
	402 Supporting players	15,000	
	403 Stuntpersons	3,000	
	404 Looping allowance	2,000	55,000

500 Production staff

	501 Production manager	8,500	
	502 First assistant director	4,000	
	503 Second assistant director	2,000	
	504 Script supervisor	2,800	
	505 Technical advisors	—	
	506 Production assistants	1,200	
	507 Secretary	2,000	20,700

600 Extras

	601 Extras	5,000	
	602 Stand-ins	—	
	603 Stuntpersons	1,000	6,000

700 Set operations
       701 Director of photography   4,800
       702 Camera operator   —
       703 First camera assistant   3,000
       704 Second camera assistant   2,000
       705 Sound mixer   4,000
       706 Boom operator   3,000
       707 Gaffer   3,000
       708 Best boy   2,000
       709 Generator operator   —
       710 Electrician   2,000
       711 Key grip   3,000
       712 Set grips   6,000
       713 Dolly grip   —
       714 Wranglers   —
       715 Still photographer   1,000
       716 Special effects person   1,000
       717 Welfare worker   —
       718 Guards   —   34,800

800 Sets
       801 Art director   4,000
       802 Construction crew   8,000
       803 Construction costs   5,000   17,000

900 Props
       901 Property master   2,500
       902 Assistant   1,600
       903 Props purchase   2,000
       904 Props rental   3,000
       905 Prop truck   1,500   10,600

1000 Costumes
       1001 Wardrobe supervisor   2,500
       1002 Assistant   1,600
       1003 Wardrobe purchase   1,500
       1004 Wardrobe rental   500
       1005 Cleaning   700
       1006 Miscellaneous supplies   100   6,900

1100 Makeup and hairdressing
       1101 Makeup person   4,000
       1102 Hair stylist   3,000
       1103 Assistants   —
       1104 Body makeup   —
       1105 Supplies purchase   —
       1106 Supplies rental   —   7,000

1200 Production equipment
       1201 Camera package   11,000
       1202 Sound package   2,000

Production equipment (cont.)

	1203 Lighting package	3,000	
	1204 Grip package	3,000	
	1205 Generator	—	
	1206 Vehicles	2,000	
	1207 Miscellaneous	—	21,000
1300	Locations/studios		
	1301 Location manager	4,000	
	1302 Location rental	5,500	
	1303 Permits	600	
	1304 Police and firemen	200	
	1305 Studio rental	1,000	
	1306 Studio personnel	800	
	1307 Dressing rooms	—	
	1308 Portable rest rooms	1,000	12,800
1400	Laboratory and film		
	1401 Negative film stock	15,000	
	1402 Developing negative	8,000	
	1403 Daily printing	15,000	
	1404 Still film and printing	1,000	39,000
1500	Tests		
	1501 Makeup tests	500	
	1502 Screen tests	—	500
1600	Production miscellaneous		
	1601 Animals	—	
	1602 Telephone	2,000	
	1603 Catering	7,000	
	1604 Mileage	6,000	
	1605 Shipping	1,500	16,500
1700	Editing		
	1701 Editor	18,000	
	1702 Assistant editor	9,000	
	1703 Apprentice editor	4,000	
	1704 Editing facility rental	7,000	
	1705 Editing equipment rental	4,000	
	1706 Supplies purchase	800	
	1707 Coding	3,000	
	1708 Preview screenings	200	46,000
1800	Postproduction Sound		
	1801 Sound transfer	4,000	
	1802 Dialogue editing	3,000	
	1803 Looping costs	2,000	
	1804 Sound effects editor	3,000	
	1805 Sound effects costs	2,000	
	1806 Foley recording	500	14,500

1900 Music
	1901 Composer	10,000	
	1902 Conductor	—	
	1903 Musicians and singers	10,500	
	1904 Arranger	—	
	1905 Copyist	1,000	
	1906 Recording facility	2,500	
	1907 Instrument rental and cartage	500	
	1908 Miscellaneous supplies	500	
	1909 Music rights	—	
	1910 Music editor	1,000	26,000

2000 Titles and opticals
	2001 Main and end titles	4,000	
	2002 Optical effects	1,000	5,000

2100 Laboratory
	2101 Black and white dupes	1,000	
	2102 Reprints	—	
	2103 Stock footage	—	
	2104 Optical sound track developed	300	
	2105 Answer print	8,000	
	2106 CRI	—	
	2107 Answer Print from CRI	—	
	2108 Miscellaneous laboratory costs	1,000	
	2109 Negative cutting	2,500	12,800

2200 Sound mix
	2201 Mixing facility	10,000	
	2202 3-stripe magnetic stock	800	
	2203 Optical transfer	500	
	2204 ¼" protection copy	200	
	2205 Special equipment rental	300	11,800

2300 Insurance
	2301 Negative insurance	—	
	2302 Errors and omissions	—	
	2303 Workman's compensation	—	
	2304 Cast insurance	—	allow
	2305 Other	—	20,000

2400 Miscellaneous
	2401 Business license	600
	2402 Accounting	3,000
	2403 Legal	10,000
	2404 Miscellaneous supplies	2,500

Miscellaneous (cont.)

2405	Office and phone	6,000	
2406	Postage	500	
2407	Promo	2,500	25,100
	Subtotal		454,500
	10% Contingency		45,500
	Grand total		$500,000

APPENDIX D

National Directory
of Motion Picture Equipment
Rental Houses

CALIFORNIA

Adolph Gasser
168 Second St.
San Francisco, Ca. 94105
(415) 495–3852
full facility

Alan Gordon Enterprises
1430 N. Cahuenga Blvd.
Hollywood, Ca. 90028
(213) 466–3561
full facility

Audio Services Company
4713 Lankershim Blvd.
N. Hollywood, Ca. 91602
(213) 766–5255
specializes in location recording
equipment

Birns and Sawyer
1026 No. Highland Ave.
Hollywood, Ca. 90038
(213) 466–8211
full facility

Christy's Editorial Film Supply
135 No. Victory Blvd.
Burbank, Ca. 91502
(213) 845–1755
Specializes in postproduction equipment

Cinemobile Systems
11166 Gault St.
No. Hollywood, Ca. 91605
(213) 764–9900; (800) 423–2457
full facility

Cine-Pro
1037 No. Sycamore Ave.
Hollywood, Ca. 90038
(213) 461–4794
full facility

Cine Rent West
991 Tennessee St.
San Francisco, Ca. 94107
(415) 864–4644
full facility

Cine Video
958 No. Cahuenga Blvd.
Hollywood, Ca. 90038
(213) 464–6200
full facility

Continental Camera Rentals
7240 Valjean Ave.
Van Nuys, Ca. 91406
(213) 989–5222
specializes in helicopter mounts, jet photography, helmet cameras, tabletop and miniature photography, handheld stabilization systems, and underwater photography

Ferco
750 Bryant St.
San Francisco, Ca. 94107
(415) 957–1787
full facility

Filmart
353 So. LaBrea
Los Angeles, Ca. 90036
(213) 933–8296
full facility

Gunner Lighting
1125 No. Lodi Place
Hollywood, Ca. 90038
(213) 467–9802
specializes in lighting and grip equipment

Hill Production Service
1139 No. Highland Ave.
Hollywood, Ca. 90038
(213) 463–1182
full facility

Horizontal Editing Studios
2625 Olive Ave.
Burbank, Ca. 91505
(213) 461–4643
specializes in postproduction equipment

Lee Motion Picture
1016 No. Sycamore Ave.
Hollywood, Ca. 90038
(213) 876–1100
full facility

Leonetti Cine Rentals
5609 Sunset Blvd.
Hollywood, Ca. 90028
(213) 469–2987
Full facility

Lloyd's Camera Exchange
1612 No. Cahuenga Blvd.
Hollywood, Ca. 90028
(213) 467–7189 or 467–7156
specializes in antique motion picture equipment

Los Angeles Stage Lighting Co.
1451 Venice Blvd.
Los Angeles, Ca. 90006
(213) 384–1241
specializes in lighting equipment

Miller Professional Equipment
10816 Burbank Blvd.
No. Hollywood, Ca. 91601
(213) 766–9451
specializes in fluid tripod heads

Otto Nemenz International
7531 Sunset Blvd.
Hollywood, Ca. 90046
(213) 874–0811
full facility

Pro 16 Rentals
6561 Santa Monica Blvd.
Hollywood, Ca. 90038
(213) 462–2524
full facility; cameras are exclusively 16mm.

Production Systems
1123 No. Lillian Way
Hollywood, Ca. 90038
(213) 469–2704 or 461–8271
full facility

Sawyer Camera Rentals
6820 Santa Monica Blvd.
Hollywood, Ca. 90038
(213) 466–6111
full facility

Tech Camera Rentals
6370 Santa Monica Blvd.
Hollywood, Ca. 90038
(213) 466–5391
full facility

Tyler Camera Systems
14218 Aetna St.
Van Nuys, Ca. 91401
(213) 989–4420
specializes in vibrationless camera
mounts for helicopters, airplanes,
boats, and cranes.

COLORADO

Cinema Sales
338 Pearl St.
Denver, Colorado 80209
(303) 777–7699
full facility

FLORIDA

Image Devices
1825 N.E. 149th St.
No. Miami, Florida 33181
(305) 945–1111
full facility

N.C.E. of Florida
1994 N.E. 149th St.
No. Miami, Florida 33181
(305) 949–9084 or 949–9085
full facility

GEORGIA

Atlanta Film Equipment Rentals
1848 Briarwood Rd. N.E.
Atlanta, Georgia 30329
(404) 325–3676
full facility

Image Devices
P.O. Box 490250
Atlanta, Georgia 30349
(800) 327–5181
full facility

Production Services Atlanta
Atlanta Lakewood Studios,
Building 4
Atlanta, Georgia 30315
(404) 622–1311
full facility

ILLINOIS

Behrend's
225 W. Ohio
Chicago, Il. 60610
(312) 527–3060
full facility

Fanfilm Services
Division of Fred A. Niles
Communications Centers
1058 W. Washington Blvd.
Chicago, Il. 60607
(312) 738–4181
full facility

Victor Duncan
200 E. Ontario
Chicago, Il. 60611
(312) 321–9406
full facility

MAINE

Capron Lighting and Sound
278 West St.
Needham, Maine 02194
(617) 444–8850
specializes in lighting and sound
equipment

New England Production
Services
14 Edgewood Ave.
Natick, Maine 01760
(617) 444–8858 day; (617) 655–1180
night
specializes in lighting, grip, and portable communication equipment

Talama Company
10 Mount Auburn St.
Watertown, Maine 02172
(617) 923–0166
specializes in sound equipment

MICHIGAN

Victor Duncan
32380 Howard
Madison Heights, Mich. 48071
(313) 589–1900
full facility

MINNESOTA

Cinequipt
2434 University Ave.
St. Paul, Minnesota 55114
(612) 646–1780
full facility

MISSOURI

Midwest Cine Services
626 East 75th St.
Kansas City, Missouri 64131
(816) 333–0022
specializes in lighting, grip, and camera mounting equipment

NEW YORK

Audio Services Company
565 Fifth Ave.
New York, N.Y. 10017
(212) 972–0825
specializes in sound equipment

Bob Carmichail-Moore
P.O. Box 5
New York, N.Y. 10014
(212) 255–0465
leases motor homes and crew vans for use on location

The Camera Mart
456 West 55th St.
New York, N.Y. 10019
(212) 757–6977
full facility

Camera Service Center
625 West 54th St.
New York, N.Y. 10019
(212) 757–0906
full facility

Charles Ross
333 West 52nd St.
New York, N.Y. 10019
(212) 246–5470
specializes in lighting and grip equipment

Cine 60
630 Ninth Ave.
New York, N.Y. 10036
(212) 586–8782
specializes in camera, sound, and grip equipment

Cine Cam
1619 Broadway
Room 717
New York, N.Y. 10019
(212) 489–9777
full facility

Cinemobile Systems
601 West 29th St.
New York, N.Y. 10001
(212) 695–7585 or (800) 223–0844
full facility

Cinergy Communications Corp.
33 West 94th St.
New York, N.Y. 10025
(212) 222–2644
deals exclusively in Steenbeck editing machines

Ferco
797 Eleventh Ave.
New York, N.Y. 10019
(212) 245–4800
full facility

Front Projection Company
49 East 1st St.
New York, N.Y. 10003
(212) 673–7290
rents front projection equipment for
photographic backgrounds

General Camera Corporation
471 Eleventh Ave.
New York, N.Y. 10018
(212) 594–8700

General Camera Studio Complex
512 West 19th St.
New York, N.Y.
full facility; panavision and Chapman representative

Lee Lighting America
534/548 West 25th St.
New York, N.Y. 10011
(212) 730–0172
specializes in lighting equipment

Laumic Company
306 East 39th St.
New York, N.Y. 10016
(212) 889–3300
specializes in postproduction equipment; exclusive dealership for Magnasync/Moviola

MPCS Video Industries
MPCS Video Center Building
514 West 57th St.
New York, N.Y. 10019
(212) 586–3690
full facility

Robert Van Dyke
542 LaGuardia Place
New York, N.Y. 10012
(212) 982–8868
specializes in sound and postproduction equipment

Ross-Gaffney
21 West 46th St.
New York, N.Y. 10036
(212) 582–3744
full facility

TEXAS

Victor Duncan
2659 Fondren Dr.
Dallas, Texas 75206
(214) 369–1165
full facility

UTAH

Brickyard Limited
Motion Picture Arts Division
P.O. Box 1752
Salt Lake City, Utah 84110
(801) 363–3757
full facility

APPENDIX E

References and Sources
for Additional Information

Academy Players Directory, available from the Academy of Motion Picture Arts and Sciences, 8949 Wilshire Blvd., Beverly Hills, Ca. 90211. Complete photographic listing of actors and actresses including their guild affiliation and agency representation.

American Cinematographer's Manual, available from the American Society of Cinematographers, P.O. Box 2230, Hollywood, Ca. 90028. A comprehensive text dealing with all aspects of professional cinematography.

Audio Cyclopedia by Howard M. Tremaine, published by Howard W. Sams, New York. Complete encyclopedia of audio information.

Brook's Standard Rate Book, available at Larry Edmunds Bookshop, 6658 Hollywood Blvd., Hollywood, Ca. 90028. Contains rates and rules for motion picture unions and guilds.

Counseling Clients in the Entertainment Industry, available from the Practicing Law Institute, 810 Seventh Ave., New York, N.Y. 10019. Deals with motion picture legal problems including contract negotiations, personal management, and television and film packaging.

Current Developments in Copyright Law, available from the Practicing Law Institute, 810 Seventh Ave., New York, N.Y. 10019.

Directors Guild of America Directory, available through the Directors Guild of America, 7950 W. Sunset Blvd., Los Angeles, Ca. 90046. Complete listing of DGA members.

Enterprise Printers and Stationers, 7401 W. Sunset Blvd., Los Angeles, Ca. 90046. Complete supply of motion picture production forms, including budget sheets, breakdown sheets, and industry contracts.

Evaluating Tax Shelter Offerings, Available from the Practicing Law Institute, 810 Seventh Ave., New York, N.Y. 10019. Examines the valuation and depreciation of motion pictures in a tax shelter situation.

Guide to Location Information, available through the Association of Motion Picture and Television Producers, 8480 Beverly Blvd., Los Angeles, Ca. 90048. Complete Listing of locations and contacts throughout the United States, revised annually.

Gadney's Guide to 1800 International Contests, Festivals and Grants in Film & Video, Photography, T.V.-Radio Broadcasting, Writing, Poetry, Playwriting & Journalism, by Alan E. Gadney, available from Festival Publications, P.O. Box 10180, Glendale, Ca. 91209.

The Hollywood Production Manual, available from *The Hollywood Production Manual,* 1322 No. Cole Ave, Hollywood, Ca. 90028, (213) 552–0021. This publication is an invaluable aid to motion picture production and budgeting. It contains rules, rates, and regulations for motion picture guilds and unions, lists motion picture facilities and services including equipment houses, laboratories, sound facilities, agencies, and videotape facilities along with many of their prices. It also contains information regarding locations, government agencies, and military bases. Currently most of the information is applicable only to the Los Angeles area but the manual is in the process of expanding to include the rest of the United States, Canada, and Mexico. The manual is continually revised to keep up with changes in information. The cost of the manual is $79 plus tax. There is an annual fee of $39 for persons wishing to receive regular updates.

Larry Edmunds Bookshop, 6658 Hollywood Blvd., Hollywood, Ca. 90028, (213) 463–3273. A unique bookstore that carries books related to cinema exclusively.

Legal and Business Problems of Financing Motion Pictures, available from the Practicing Law Institute, 810 Seventh Ave., New York, N.Y. 10019. Covers traditional and nontraditional methods of financing as well as tax and accounting problems of motion pictures.

Pacific Coast Studio Directory, available at Larry Edmunds Bookshop, 6658 Hollywood Blvd., Hollywood, Ca. 90028. Directory and wall chart of motion picture production services, equipment, facilities, organizations, associations, and personnel.

The Technique of Special Effects Cinematography, by Raymond Fielding, published by Hastings House, New York. A comprehensive text on the making of optical and special photographic effects.

Writers Guild Directory, available through the Writers Guild of America West, 8955 Beverly Blvd., Los Angeles, Ca. 90048. Complete listing of WGA members, including their agency representation and many of their credits.

INDEX

About the Author

GREGORY GOODELL is an independent writer-producer-director with sixteen years of experience in the film industry. He has lectured and taught over the past several years for the American Film Institute and other organizations. Mr. Goodell lives in Los Angeles, California.